THE
ESSENTIAL
EDGAR CAYCE

❖

THE ESSENTIAL EDGAR CAYCE

EDITED AND INTRODUCED BY

Mark Thurston, Ph.D.

JEREMY P. TARCHER / PENGUIN
A MEMBER OF PENGUIN GROUP (USA) INC.
NEW YORK

Most Tarcher/Penguin books are available at special quantity discounts for bulk purchase for sales promotions, premiums, fundraising, and educational needs. Special books or book excerpts also can be created to fit specific needs. For details, write Penguin Group (USA) Inc. Special Markets, 375 Hudson Street, New York, NY 10014.

Jeremy P. Tarcher/Penguin
a member of
Penguin Group (USA) Inc.
375 Hudson Street
New York, NY 10014
www.penguin.com

Library of Congress Cataloging-in-Publication Data

Cayce, Edgar, 1877–1945.
[Selections. 2004]
The essential Edgar Cayce / edited and introduced by Mark Thurston.
p.   cm.
Includes bibliographical references and index.
ISBN 1-58542-315-7
1. Parapsychology.   2. Occultism.   I. Thurston, Mark A.   II. Title.
BF1027.C3A25   2004   2004044007
133.8'092—dc22

Printed in the United States of America
15   17   19   20   18   16   14

BOOK DESIGN BY DEBORAH KERNER/
DANCING BEARS DESIGN

This book is dedicated to Hugh Lynn Cayce,
eldest son of Edgar and Gertrude Cayce.

From 1968 until his passing in 1982, Hugh Lynn
was a treasured teacher, mentor, friend,
and professional colleague who was
the most valuable person in my
life for understanding the
principles in his father's
remarkable teachings.

CONTENTS

ACKNOWLEDGMENTS

I wish to thank several individuals who have been instrumental in helping to shape the ideas in this book. In addition to Hugh Lynn Cayce, I am grateful to Gladys Davis Turner, Edgar Evans Cayce, Mae St. Clair, Mary Elizabeth Lynch, Harmon Bro, Herbert Puryear, Richard Drummond, Richard Otto, Linda Quest, Scott Sparrow, Henry Reed, Christopher Fazel, Charles Thomas Cayce, Paul Johnson, Kevin Todeschi, and Stuart Dean.

My thanks also go to Mitch Horowitz, executive editor at Tarcher/Penguin, for his support, enthusiasm, creative insight, and professionalism in helping bring this project to fruition; thanks also to Tarcher/Penguin publisher Joel Fotinos for his support of the project; and to Tony Davis for his excellent copyediting.

THE
ESSENTIAL
EDGAR CAYCE

INTRODUCTION

THE LIFE AND THOUGHT OF EDGAR CAYCE

❖

Edgar Cayce was one of the most remarkable and mysterious men of the twentieth century. Sometimes called "the Sleeping Prophet" or "the Miracle Man of Virginia Beach," he was stuck with taglines that more often than not reflected the sensationalistic side of his work rather than its real depth and meaning. At the core, Cayce was a Christian mystic philosopher and an intuitive healer. For the forty-three years of his adult life, he taught by delivering discourses, or by giving "readings" while in a prayer-induced trance, which were transcribed by a secretary or family member because he could recall nothing once the twenty- to forty-five-minute sessions were over.

The sheer volume of Edgar Cayce's output is immense. There are some 14,306 transcripts in existence today, both in print and, since the early 1990s, electronic format. Two-thirds of his readings offer holistic recommendations for treating specific physical ailments and diseases, due to the fact that he began his career as a medical intuitive and throughout his life most of those who sought him out requested readings of a medical nature; all of his biographers, in fact, provide fascinating anecdotal evidence of the success of these prescriptive readings (see appendix 4, "Recommended Resources," page 276). The remaining third of Cayce's work focused on spiritual growth, dream interpretation, ancient civilizations, reincarnation, life purpose, and the many pragmatic issues of trying to integrate body, mind, and spirit into daily life, including such everyday issues as parenting and even business practices.

Although *The Essential Edgar Cayce* is fundamentally about his teachings and philosophy, it is important to know something about the man as well. Cayce's ideas were often shaped by his personal beliefs and by the difficult times in which he lived, including the Great Depression and two world wars. As editor and commentator for this book, I should begin by noting that I never met Edgar Cayce; he died in 1945, five years before I was born. But for more than thirty years I have worked professionally for the two organizations he cofounded, and I have spent countless hours with dozens of individuals who knew him and worked with him directly, including his two sons, Hugh Lynn and Edgar Evans, and his secretary, Gladys Davis Turner. Thanks to their memories of him, I feel I have garnered at least my own personal understanding of what this man was like and the bedrock from which his extraordinary teachings sprang. I personally have applied many of the readings to my everyday life, including his recommendations for maintaining health through nutrition, massage, and various home remedies. I have also been helped greatly by Cayce's suggestions for practical spiritual disciplines—meditation, dream interpretation, developing intuition, to name just a few.

Before looking into the details of Edgar Cayce's life, let's consider briefly how the man and his work are viewed in the early twenty-first century, which differs according to the audience. Here are three groups that have been intrigued by his work.

For those interested in *holistic health,* Cayce is generally revered as a pioneer of the body-mind-spirit approach to healing. Yet many people today view his understanding of the human body and his recommendations as antiquated. He was doing the best with what he had, they might argue, but surely we know so much more now that it hardly seems worthwhile studying him closely. Others see things differently; they assert that we are only just beginning to understand Cayce and his natural approach to healing.

Another audience is in the field of *parapsychology*—the scientific study of psychic ability. They have long been puzzled about what to do with Cayce, even while he was still alive. While the anecdotal evidence for his gift was almost overwhelming, there were no carefully controlled double-blind experiments conducted to test his skills. And so he remains an awkward figure for parapsychologists, someone who has caused millions to look at the possibilities of the psychic yet who has no scientifically proven ability.

A still larger audience is made up of those in the so-called *New Age* movement. They are seeking meaning, purpose, and direction in life in ways that have taken them outside of mainstream religion. How is Cayce seen and understood by these nontraditional seekers? Unfortunately, many have an image of him as prognosticator. Their seeking is largely a matter of trying to find out what will make them feel safer in this troubled world. And so what catches their eye is the ubiquitous newsstand tabloid with Cayce's picture on the front announcing some heretofore unknown prophecy about the year ahead. For them, he is another Nostradamus. Unseen by them are his teachings about health, spirituality, and responsible living.

But there is another audience of seekers who have seen past this superficial take on Edgar Cayce. For them, his teachings become a stimulus to look at their lives in a whole new way, to see their own religious traditions in a new light, to recognize new pathways to spirituality open to them, to generally rethink what life is all about. It's a worldview that recognizes the capacity of each individual to make an intuitive connection with the spiritual world, even exploring such concepts as reincarnation. In fact, Cayce was a significant pioneer in the many disciplines that have gained widespread acceptance in the decades since his death. Among these approaches:

- The value of *dreams* as a tool for self-understanding and guidance. Cayce foresaw dreams as a safe and reliable way to explore one's own soul and to gain insight about practical life decisions. What's more, he was among the first to advocate dream interpretation as best done by the dreamer himself.

- The importance of *meditation* as a spiritual discipline. Although meditation is an ancient practice best known to Eastern religions, Cayce evolved an approach that was easy to learn and easy to apply to the Judeo-Christian world in which he lived.

- A perspective on *reincarnation, karma,* and *grace* that is potentially acceptable to the Judeo-Christian world. Cayce presents reincarnation as an inescapable reality of how the universe operates; but, according to his theories, the harsh, retributive flavor of karma is softened by insistence that the healing and reconciling influences of grace are also available to every soul.

- An approach to *astrology* that recognizes past lives and the influence of the planets, especially with regard to helping people find a sense of purpose in life. Cayce's approach to astrology was not the familiar, benign sun signs of today, nor the deterministic brand that believes that the stars control our fate. Instead, he used the influence of the planets as a way of describing innate temperament and its impact upon the personality and aptitude.

The many ways in which Edgar Cayce is viewed today is testimony to the breadth of his work. People are able to relate to him in different ways not only because of their own "filters" but also because of the scope of the material itself. It is very easy to get lost, in fact, in its sheer variety, and very hard to grasp all that he has to offer.

And it is just this problem that this book addresses. What is the "essence" of Cayce's material? What are the most basic theories, principles, and teachings illuminated in the thousands of discourses he presented between 1901 and 1944?

There are no simple answers. But if we're willing to put aside preconceived notions about clairvoyantly derived knowledge or Cayce's qualifications as a spiritual philosopher (or lack thereof), then we really can find the heart of his material. Indeed, there really is an "essential" Edgar Cayce, and it may reveal some real surprises.

THE LIFE OF AN INTUITIVE HEALER

• •

One of the most significant books written in recent years about Edgar Cayce is K. Paul Johnson's 1998 *Edgar Cayce in Context*. Johnson's theme is that Cayce can be understood only by viewing the man in the context of his own life story, and, more important, in the context of his own time. Adhering to this premise, let's consider the prominent events of Cayce's life, as well as some of the social and cultural factors that went into shaping it and his teachings.

Born in 1877, in rural Kentucky, Edgar Cayce was largely the product of a conservative Southern Protestant upbringing. It was just a dozen years since the end of the Civil War, and even though his home state had not joined the Confederacy—Kentucky was one of the so-called border states—it was surely a place where the tensions between North and South were still acutely felt.

The farm Cayce grew up on was in the southwestern part of the state, just outside the small town of Hopkinsville; the nearest big city was Nashville, Tennessee, nearly two hundred miles to the southeast. Hopkinsville is right in the heart of Christian County, and in Cayce's youth it was a God-fearing agricultural community with tobacco as its primary crop.

Like all of us, Cayce's developing personality was profoundly influenced by his parents. His mother, Carrie, was, by all accounts, a powerful influence. Warm and nurturing, she was a deeply religious woman, and surely a major factor in fostering the young Edgar's profound dedication to the Bible and religious life. While still a boy, he made a deep commitment to read the Bible daily. Photographs of Carrie show a pleasant-looking, rather round-faced woman with kind eyes.

But the young Cayce's relationship with the men in the family was seemingly more complex. By some accounts, his paternal grandfather, Thomas Cayce, was a strong influence on him, better modeling the masculine aspects of strength and accomplishment coupled with sensitivity than did Edgar's own father, Leslie. Sadly, however, Thomas drowned when the horse he was riding threw him into a lake, which the four-year-old witnessed and no doubt was traumatized by. Years later, as an adult, Edgar wrote of this trying experience in his diary, which was not published until 1997 in *Edgar Cayce: My Life as a Seer,* edited by A. Robert Smith. About the death of his grandfather Cayce wrote, "I often wonder just what effect these associations of thought have had on my mental being or my activities in this life."

Thomas Cayce, a rather handsome man with a full beard but no mustache, was considered a clairvoyant in his own right, although he was confused about his gift and therefore cautious about it. Edgar recalled riding with Thomas and being able to hear disembodied voices speaking to him. "I also saw him move tables and other articles, apparently without any contact with these objects themselves." But when the younger Cayce asked about these strange phenomena, the elder Cayce said, simply, "I don't know what the power is, but don't fool with it." Although Edgar was so young when Thomas died, modern psychology has it that his childhood experiences shaped his adult personality profoundly, and from his grandfather Edgar learned that psychic ability was a real force deserving of his greatest respect.

Edgar Cayce's relationship with his father is glossed over by many biographers. Often referred to affectionately as "the Squire," Leslie in photographs is dashingly good-looking, sporting a prominent handlebar mustache. But he was not a particularly successful man, moving from one job to another and never really settling into a career. And although pretty much a family secret, some report that he had a problem with alcohol for much of his adult life. When Edgar began to demonstrate clairvoyance as a young man, it was Leslie who was eager to explore this mental power, including its commercial potential. Since exploitation dogged Cayce for most of his adult life, it is difficult to say whether he considered his father's involvement as a supportive, protective influence, or as a potentially threatening one.

Family stories about Edgar Cayce's early years reveal that from a very early age he possessed uncanny powers that would surface spontaneously. At the age of six or seven, he told his parents he sometimes saw visions, and even occasionally spoke with relatives who had recently died. His parents, for the most part, attributed these experiences to an overactive imagination and paid them little attention.

Perhaps the most celebrated psychic experience of Edgar's childhood happened when he was thirteen years old, an event his first biographer, Thomas Sugrue, made the centerpiece of his highly influential *There Is a River* of 1943. Edgar had become an avid

Bible reader when he was ten, no doubt inspired by his mother and her attendance at Christian revival meetings so very popular in America during the Reconstruction era. He had vowed to read the Bible in its entirety every year for the rest of his life, a promise he apparently kept—an expression of true dedication and a remarkable achievement in its own right. One day, he had a vision, which he describes in his own memoirs:

One evening I had my first vision. I had read through the Book [i.e., the Bible] several times by then. I had been reading the vision of Manoah, for I loved the story of Samson. I prayed very earnestly that afternoon as I sat in the woods by my favorite tree that had so often seemed to speak to me. . . .

[That night] I was not yet asleep when the vision first began, but I felt as if I were being lifted up. A glorious light as of the rising morning sun seemed to fill the whole room, and a figure appeared at the foot of my bed. I was sure it was my mother, and I called to her, but she didn't answer. For the moment I was frightened, climbed out of bed, and went to my mother's room. No, she hadn't called. Almost immediately after I returned to my couch, the figure came again. Then it seemed all gloriously bright—an angel, or what, I knew not; but gently, patiently, it said, "Thy prayers are heard. You will have your wish. Remain faithful. Be true to yourself. Help the sick, the afflicted."

The very next evening, the remarkable capacity of his mind began to show itself. Heretofore, Cayce had not been a particularly good student, sometimes even being punished for forgetting his lessons. But that night, as Leslie grilled Edgar on his lessons, Edgar intuitively felt the need to take a short nap. Falling asleep after having just studied, intuition seemed to tell him, would make a big difference in his ability to retain knowledge. And, in fact, it

did. He began to demonstrate a kind of "photographic memory"—
ironic, perhaps, given his later career as a portrait photographer.
As he wrote in his memoirs, "From that day on, I had little trouble in school, for I would read my lesson, sleep on it a few sec-
onds, and then be able to repeat every word of it." Cayce had begun
a journey of self-discovery that would link falling asleep to tapping
in to his mind's potential. At this stage, it merely facilitated re-
connecting with what he had studied already. But in his early adult
years, he would find that he could connect to deeper, more mysterious wisdom within his reach.

A hint of this talent came at age fifteen when Cayce was playing baseball with other boys and he was hit accidentally by a
thrown ball at the base of the spine. In the hours immediately after, he exhibited erratic behavior—giggling, laughing, making faces,
even standing in the middle of the road stopping buggies with his
upraised hands. Just as Edgar was about to fall asleep that night,
he announced that a poultice of cornmeal, onions, and some
herbs should be administered to the back of his skull to counter-
act the shock sustained from the injury. His parents followed his
instructions—virtually, his first medical reading—and following a
night's sleep he was normal once again. Little did anyone realize
then how this medical clairvoyance would foreshadow the work
he would pursue later as an adult.

In 1901, when he was twenty-four years old, Edgar happened
serendipitously upon his talent for tapping in to the wisdom of the
unconscious mind. It was at this time that he met and fell in love
with Gertrude Evans, his future wife and mother of their three
sons (one of whom died as an infant), and an ardent supporter of
his life's work. But in this first year of the new century, he was
stricken with an ailment that threatened to undermine his current
career as a traveling salesman—and, even more alarmingly, his
long-term hopes of becoming a minister in the church someday.

A severe case of laryngitis plagued Cayce for months and baffled doctors. In the end, it proved responsive only to hypnosis. When hypnotized, Edgar could not only talk again but was able to diagnose the cause and prescribe a treatment to effect a lasting cure.

Some months later, Cayce tried out his diagnostic and prescriptive skills on other people to remarkable effect. And so began his work—albeit, for many years only occasional—as an intuitive healer.

Edgar Cayce quickly found that a hypnotist wasn't needed to access his unconscious wisdom. Following an interlude of prayer, he could move into this state on his own. It was a fragile, vulnerable condition because his unconscious was wide open, he said; hence, his insistence that a family member be present to direct the experience, to act as what came to be called *the conductor* of the reading, because on more than one occasion people tried to take advantage of his gift. Usually, Gertrude or his elder son, Hugh Lynn, served in this role.

Typically, when giving a reading, Cayce first lead the others with him—the conductor, the stenographer, and sometimes the person(s) for whom the reading was being given—in prayer. Then he would lie down on a couch on his back, close his eyes, and place his hands on his forehead. The conductor would then read aloud a hypnotic-like suggestion tailored to the type of reading desired. For example, for a physical health reading the suggestions might be: "You will go over this body carefully, examine it thoroughly, and tell me the conditions you find at the present time; giving the cause of the existing conditions, also suggestions for help and relief of this body; answering the questions, as I ask them." On the other hand, for a reading addressing reincarnation and the purposes of life currently, the suggestion might be:

"You will give the relation of this entity and the universe, and the universal forces; giving the conditions which are as personali-

ties, latent and exhibited in the present life; also the former appearances in the earth plane, giving time, place and the name,
and that in each life which built or retarded the development for
the entity; giving the abilities of the entity in the present, that to
which it may attain, and how. You will answer the questions, as I
ask them."

Listening to the suggestion, Cayce would allow himself to
move into a trancelike, meditative state, and he would move his
hands down from his forehead to cover his solar plexus. To observers in the room, it appeared that he had fallen asleep. But he
was not asleep, and he would begin to address the request posed
in the suggestion. After an opening discourse that may or may not
be brief—sometimes only a minute in length, other times as long
as twenty minutes or more—Edgar then would invite questions
for further elaboration. The reading would end when he would
announce "We are through for the present," at which point the
conductor read aloud a suggestion that Cayce regain normal consciousness and he would slowly awake, much like a person awakening from a nap.

Because Cayce was unable to remember what he had said, the
stenographer would transcribe every word recorded so that Cayce
could review the reading for himself. Then a transcript would be
forwarded to the subject of the reading. Sometimes Cayce maintained a correspondence with the individual in which he added
his own conscious interpretive comments or advice. On occasion,
the stenographer was not sure about a word uttered by Cayce, and
therefore she inserted a bracketed reference to an alternative
word—for example, in reading 281-13 found in chapter 3: ". . . that
which shadows [shatters?] much in the experiences of others."

The source of the information that came through Edgar Cayce's
readings is an important issue. Although Cayce sometimes has
been labeled a *medium,* or a *channeler* of psychic information, he

insisted that it was almost never some external source speaking or channeling through him; in other words, it was not some deceased soul or some enlightened master broadcasting from beyond in the spiritual world. Instead, the origin of the information—what Cayce called *the source*—was his own superconscious, or universal, mind, a level of awareness from which all experience up to that time is accessible and from which the solution to any problem is available. In fact, Cayce often stated that all of us potentially have access to this superconsciousness if we can only learn how to access it.

It should be noted that there were some dozen rare occasions on which a voice spoke through Cayce that identified itself as something other than Cayce's superconsciousness. Most were in the 1930s, and it was frequently the Archangel Michael claiming to speak through Cayce, usually admonishing Cayce and his followers to practice in their own lives the very teachings promoted by Cayce. And in 1934, yet another being spoke through Cayce, offering to become the source of the readings thereafter. After careful consideration, however, Cayce decided that he was not interested in such an offer.

As curious as this *methodology* surely was—although today, in the early twenty-first century, an era of psychics on every corner, it doesn't sound quite so strange—it was the *content* of what he said in his readings that is most important. Holistic, natural approaches to healing were advocated, and any illness was essentially a body, mind, spirit phenomenon and healing must happen in all three areas. Over the many years in which Edgar Cayce gave medical readings, he finally received the credit due him in an article published in 1979 in *The Journal of the American Medical Association:* "The roots of present-day holism probably go back 100 years to the birth of Edgar Cayce in Hopkinsville, Kentucky."

Nineteen twenty-three, when Edgar was forty-six years old,

was an important turning point in his life. During this new phase
of his work, he discovered that he was capable of clairvoyant discourses on a whole range of nonmedical topics as well. It was in
September of that year that Gladys Davis, all of eighteen years of
age, came into Cayce's life and served as his secretary/stenogra-
pher for the rest of his life.

Edgar Cayce was befriended at this time by several wealthy
individuals who supported his move to Virginia Beach, Virginia,
in 1925, where his full-time pursuit of his spiritual gifts began in
earnest. Edgar's own life readings indicated that Virginia Beach
would be ideal for him; it was near a large body of water, in close
proximity to the nation's capital, and he predicted tremendous
growth in the decades to come. What's more, he had had a significant past-life experience there several centuries earlier and it
would feel like home to him.

But the next twenty years were difficult times for the Cayce
family. Not only was it no easy task trying to be a full-time clairvoyant healer and spiritual philosopher seventy years ago, but the
Great Depression and World War II tended to direct national attention toward priorities other than exploring the extrasensory. Nevertheless, Cayce and his supporters made several attempts to establish
institutions and a school that embodied the readings.

In that regard, the Cayce Hospital of Research and Enlightenment was founded in Virginia Beach in 1928. Here was a courageous pioneering effort to launch a body-mind-spirit healing facility.
But after only two years, it collapsed financially. The same fate
befell an advanced educational program Cayce cofounded called
Atlantic University. It, too, shut its doors after only two years (only
to open again in 1985, exactly forty years after Cayce's death).

The remaining years of Edgar Cayce's life were similarly difficult,
with the family usually teetering on the brink of poverty. With the
close of Atlantic University and the demise of both the Cayce hos-

pital and the Association of National Investigators—the organization that had supervised the hospital's development—a few core supporters remained to gather around Cayce. In 1931, they created a new organization, the Association for Research and Enlightenment, which made Cayce's clairvoyant services available to members for a fee of twenty dollars. It was no small sum in the Depression era, and it was the principal means by which Cayce supported himself and his family. Yet many of the readings during this time were free of charge because people just didn't have the money.

In 1932, some of Cayce's most ardent followers worked with him to found a study group program. Over the next eleven years, the group received 130 readings on character development and spiritual growth topics. These readings were summarized in essays written by group members and published in a two-volume set titled *A Search for God*. Topics included "Know Thyself," "Faith," "Patience," and "Wisdom." In the decades following Edgar Cayce's death, this program has grown into one of the most important aspects of his legacy, with hundreds of ongoing groups in the United States and in more than thirty countries worldwide.

The 1930s were complicated for Cayce not only because of depressed economic conditions but also because of difficulties finding recognition for his work. Parapsychology was a budding science, with pioneers such as J. B. Rhine, who had been trained as a botanist but conducted groundbreaking research in psychic ability through the department of psychology at Duke University. There was some passing interest in Cayce's gifts expressed by a handful of scientists, but these gifts were in turn expressed in probably too anecdotal and uncontrolled a fashion for them. They were much more interested in proving the veracity of ESP under laboratory conditions.

And so Edgar Cayce had to look to less scientific pathways to gain acceptance. His son Hugh Lynn moved to New York City in

1938 to help produce a regular radio series titled *Mysteries of the Mind,* to help generate interest in psychic ability generally and in his father's work particularly. Broadcast on WOR, the programs dealt with various psychic experiences in a dramatized form, but they met with only marginal success.

It wasn't until the early 1940s that the mainstream press became aware of Cayce's gifts. Marguerite Bro, a renowned theologian and author, came to Virginia Beach to personally investigate what she had heard about Cayce's intuitive healing powers and came away so impressed that she published an article about him in 1942 in *Coronet* magazine, one of the most widely read periodicals of the time. Letters of inquiry and requests for readings began to pour in.

But an even more significant publishing event gave Cayce's work something that had been long sought. In 1943, the lengthy and beautifully written biography of Cayce, *There Is a River,* was published by Henry Holt. Penned by newspaper reporter and family friend Thomas Sugrue, the book marked a watershed in the public's appreciation of Cayce's achievements. Widely praised, it resulted in an even greater influx of requests for readings—a demand beyond anything Cayce himself could keep up with.

Sadly, Edgar Cayce was not able to enjoy these publishing milestones for very long. With both of his sons serving overseas as soldiers in World War II, he and his small circle of supporters did the best they could to deal with the newfound deluge of interest. But, now in his mid-sixties, Edgar's health was not robust, and with his fervent efforts to keep abreast of the new demands in his work—sometimes involving giving more than ten readings in a single day—it began to deteriorate. There were warning signs as to how detrimental this output could really be to his health, but the warning signs were largely ignored.

Nineteen forty-four was a catastrophic year for Cayce's

health. Early in the year, he contracted pneumonia. Later, he suffered a series of strokes that left him partially paralyzed. After one especially debilitating episode, he spent three months at a recuperative facility in Roanoke, Virginia, but there was little improvement and he was brought back home to Virginia Beach in December 1944. There, he was diagnosed with pulmonary edema, which led to his death on January 3, 1945.

AFTER EDGAR CAYCE'S DEATH

• •

In spite of the many frustrations and challenges of his life, Edgar Cayce left an extraordinary legacy in the thousands of discourses. Indeed, he became far better known to the public *after* his death than when he was alive and doing his work. A considerable amount of attention was focused on just several dozen readings—a number significantly less than *one percent* of the total number of readings—because they dealt with prophecies for the years 1958 through 1998, and, to a lesser extent, prophecies for the twenty-first century and beyond.

Many of the prophecies sounded a dire note, warning of rather catastrophic geological events and severe changes in the earth that never came to pass. These images of the world in turmoil became the centerpiece of a landmark best-seller about Edgar Cayce published in 1967, *The Sleeping Prophet,* in which author and newspaper reporter Jess Stearn captured the imagination of hundreds of thousands of readers. In the years following Cayce's death until the book's publication, the organization he founded in 1931, the Association for Research and Enlightenment (ARE), had grown very slowly but steadily under the tireless leadership of Hugh Lynn Cayce. But with the publication of Stearn's book, interest swelled, not unlike what happened in 1943 with the publication of *There Is a River,* and membership in ARE increased dramatically, the number of active study groups increased four-fold in three years, and an entire series of books about the readings were published by mainstream publishers both in the United States and abroad.

Even though it was Cayce's prophecies that initially captured the public's attention, other readings began attracting growing interest. The physical health readings—some nine thousand of them—were by far the largest category. In between were the "life readings," dream interpretation readings, and readings offering spiritual advice and even business advice—each numbering in the hundreds, or, in the case of the life readings, nearly two thousand. The life readings were in-depth character analyses addressed to specific individuals to help them see the purpose of their lives; they also included Cayce's views on the mission of the soul in this life as well as the next, and his views on reincarnation.

From early on in Edgar Cayce's career as a clairvoyant, it was clear that his discourses should be recorded in writing. At first, notes were taken in a rather haphazard manner; later, a steno-graphic transcript was compiled, the vast majority of which was accomplished by longtime secretary Gladys Davis. Years later, the readings were numbered, both to protect the privacy of the recipient and to facilitate research and publication. The name of the individual (or, in some instances, the group) was assigned a *case number;* and because many people received multiple readings, a second number was assigned to indicate a given reading's place in sequence. For example, Cayce's own son Hugh Lynn, who received dozens of readings over the years, was assigned case number "341," so the thirty-first reading he received was numbered "341-31." (It is included here in chapter 3, "Healthy Living." The numbering system is employed throughout this book.)

Many people find the discourses somewhat difficult to read,

especially at first. They often seem rather stilted, and they are full of references to the King James Bible. The sentences are frequently long, complex, and discursive in nature, and much reads like poetic advice-giving. Those new to Cayce may find reading appendix 1, "How to Read and Study a Cayce Reading," page 263, helpful *before* starting the text.

Given the wide range of topics that Edgar Cayce addressed over the years, what was it that finally allowed his work to make a significant impression both here and overseas? Beginning in the 1960s, the increased appreciation of Cayce ultimately came not from sensationalistic earth-change prophecies or even clairvoyant diagnoses; it came from his holistic philosophy of life, his skillful blending of Eastern and Western traditions to heal the body *and* feed the soul. What's more, Cayce himself is an exemplar of Americana: raised in a lower-middle-class, rural environment, with only an eighth-grade education, he "made good" somehow. But his achievements weren't typically American entrepreneurial; they were life-enhancing, and they were for the common good. In many ways, he was ahead of his time, and truly appreciated only after all these decades following his death.

THE ESSENCE OF THE CAYCE PHILOSOPHY

• •

Before exploring theories and models of human experience proposed by Edgar Cayce, let's identify the key themes that run throughout his work. Here are twelve points that speak to the heart of his philosophy—the "Cayce dozen," as it were, of the essential principles of life. Some, such as the purposefulness of life and the reality of evil, are explored in much more detail in later chapters.

1. *Everything is connected—all is one.*

The oneness of all life is the foundation on which the teachings of Edgar Cayce rest. He even said on one occasion that those interested in studying spiritual law should first study the principles of oneness for six months before moving on. Clearly, oneness means more than just some platitude we toss about—"All is one"—and then keep living our lives based on superficial *distinctions* rather than the deeper reality of *unity.*

To call Cayce a *mystic* means to see his work in terms of oneness, for surely the essence of mysticism is a belief in the underlying unity of all things that otherwise appear to be distinct. Mysticism means going beyond differentiating such qualities as inner and outer, light and dark, good and bad, and bringing together the extremes. As Cayce often put it, "Only in the Christ Consciousness do the extremes meet." His point here was *not* to rank one religion over another but to champion a state of consciousness that lives *as potential* within all of us.

But Cayce's mystical approach takes things a step further. Once we perceive that unity links the apparent differences in life, then it's our challenge to return to the world of distinctions and apply what we have learned as *practical* mystics. We can bring this sense of oneness to everything we do, which leads to the second essential principle.

2. *Life is purposeful.*

Edgar Cayce's readings remind us that life has a central purpose. We are born to bring the creative, spiritual world *into* the daily material world—"making the infinite finite." What's more, each of us is born with a personal mission, a "soul-purpose," which we will examine in more detail in chapter 5, "The Soul's Journey." Essentially, Cayce suggests that each of us is created with certain talents, skills, and aptitudes that equip us for a unique "way of being" in the world. That way of being promotes our own spiritual awakening; and, equally important, that way of being promotes the well-being of others. There is an aspect of service to soul-purpose, a sense of making a contribution to the world. Cayce often helped people see the soul-purpose in their lives by articulating individual personal mission statements for those receiving life readings.

3. *Approach life as an adventure.*

Life is meant to be a playful search for the truth. It is *research* in the broadest sense of the word. Edgar Cayce named his holistic facility the Cayce Hospital of Research and Enlightenment. And when it failed financially, he and his supporters launched a new venture: the Association for Research and Enlightenment. Its very name speaks of its commitment to explore the experimental side of Cayce's concepts.

Edgar Cayce repeatedly taught that we learn only by testing ideas in our own lives. He often emphasized, in fact, that people should take from his teachings only what worked for them personally, which can be determined only through personal research and application. To those who wanted to jump straight to wisdom or enlightenment without the hard work of testing, he might comment:

Let there be outlined each phase that is to be studied, each phase that is to be a research. It's often stated that the work IS a research and enlightenment program; but how much research have you done? Isn't it presented rather as enlightenment with-

out much research? Then, don't get the cart before the horse! It
doesn't work so well!   254-81

4. Be noncompetitive; show compassion.

Nothing takes us away quicker from the sense of oneness, and
therefore away from our own soul-purpose, than the drive for com-
petitiveness. Here, competition is not so much about playing sports
in which one team tries to outscore the other but about compar-
ing ourselves to others and making a bid for superiority—competition that paralyzes the growth of the soul. It is the opposite of
compassion.

Compassion is the capacity to be present for another person
and experience how we are all really the same. It is a matter of
feeling with another person, not taking responsibility *for* that person but being responsible (and responsive) *to* that person. And
compassion is a matter of serving others, not just feeling a connection to them but helping them in a way that demonstrates that
oneness. As Cayce sometimes put it:

For, to obtain the consciousness and awareness of coming into
His presence, or as one would call to heaven, it will be as if it
were leaning on the arm of someone ye have tried to help. For
as ye do it unto thy brother, ye do it unto thy Maker. Know they
are immutable laws. God is, and ye as a daughter, as a servant of
the most high God, are His handmaid. Then act like it!

                                                           5177-1

5. Take responsibility for yourself.

No one else can fix things for you. Yes, help is available, but ultimately each soul is accountable for itself and each of us must

use our free will to promote purposeful, healthy living. This principle of self-responsibility is a cornerstone of Edgar Cayce's holistic
health recommendations, and it's core to his approach to spiritual
development as well.

People usually don't take this personal responsibility message
seriously. It's far easier to blame others for our problems; in fact,
it takes considerable maturity to see how we create our own difficulties. The question Cayce would ask us all to ponder is: What
am I going to do with the challenges, limitations, and obstacles
that I face in my life right now? Too readily, we can end up wast-
ing time and energy by trying to pin blame on someone else—our
parents, other family members, the government. Take responsibility for your own life and find the resources, both inside and
outside yourself, that can lead to a resolution.

Edgar Cayce was especially adept at articulating this responsibility issue for those suffering from health problems. And yet,
rather than embracing self-responsibility and self-care, it seems
so much easier to let someone else take care of us, especially doctors and other health care professionals. Cayce was quick to af-
firm that prescriptive medicines and surgery have their place, but
real healing—in body, mind, and spirit—is going to happen only if
we take hold of the situation and do our own part fully.

6. Look ahead rather than back.

Edgar Cayce had a strong sense of history, especially history as
presented in the Old Testament. For him, the present and the future cannot be understood outside the context of the past. Yet as
rooted as Cayce was in this worldview, it came as a shock to him
when his readings spontaneously began to address reincarnation—
in his case, reincarnation as previous *human* lives and not other

life-forms. The idea that each of us has had previous lives was totally alien to his conservative Christian belief system, and it took
years for him to become comfortable with the concept personally.

This reincarnation aspect of Cayce's spiritual philosophy is
still a major obstacle for many. Although the percentage of people
in the Western world who accept (or at least entertain) the idea of
reincarnation has grown in recent decades, it is still a minority point
of view, and it is generally viewed as coming from Eastern religious thought. One argument against reincarnation is that it becomes counterproductive as a belief system, easily leading people
into a preoccupation with the past, and an easy excuse to put off
today the work of spiritual development.

In chapter 5, we will look more closely at Edgar Cayce's concept of reincarnation and karma (that is, the law of cause and
effect that governs reincarnation). Since a majority of his nonmedical discourses include extensive material about reincarnation, we can hardly expect to grasp the "essential" Edgar Cayce
without addressing this controversial topic. But, surprisingly, *Cayce's
emphasis was on the future.* Reincarnation and past lives are only
meant to help the individual understand the present and how it
and the past play a powerful role in shaping the future. Rather
than have the individual obsess on who or where he was hundreds
of years ago, Cayce helps him understand how it all leads to the
future.

Although Edgar Cayce never used the term, it was almost as if
he was more interested in *preincarnation* than reincarnation. In
essence, he was saying to always look ahead and never back. Realize that you have been here before. But, more interesting, realize you're going to be here *again.* So make choices in this lifetime
that will help create the best possible results in the next lifetime.

This line of reasoning, of course, can be taken too far, and you can lose touch with today because of preoccupation with tomorrow. But Cayce's readings always seem to steer a pragmatic course through such pitfalls. Live today, he taught, but know you have a stake in tomorrow, and not just because it's the world your children will inherit but because *you* may be part of it, too.

7. Changing anything starts with an ideal.

Motives, purposes, and ideals are at the center of Edgar Cayce's psychology. We shape our own material life with our own attitudes and emotions. "Mind is the builder," as he often put it. But behind any attitude or emotion is always a motive. If you want to change anything in life, you need to start at the motivational level. Then you need to decide what is the purpose—what Cayce called the *ideal*—for making the change. Once you've settled on your purpose/ideal, something almost magically seems to shift inside. It's a shift in intentionality that allows you to start seeing and responding to life in a whole new way. As your motives clarify, in turn, your *attention* focuses. You begin to see things about yourself and other people that escaped your notice before. And with a new orientation toward your purpose in life, you begin to see opportunities for creative expression where before you saw only obstacles.

Of course there are many ideals that can promote soul growth and health: love, joyfulness, freedom, truth. Echoing the first of our twelve principles (Everything is connected—all is one), an ideal that Cayce encouraged people to adopt was *oneness,* a motivation to relate to the world around them in terms of their *connectedness* with it rather than their differences from it. And with oneness comes the intentionality to act in a way that benefits not just the self but everyone involved. The desire to use one's talents to serve others becomes a natural impulse.

Psychologically, the essence of a health reading was to challenge the recipient to find a higher motivation for getting well other than to just be free of discomfort. If getting well is just a matter of going back to what you were doing before, then it's very likely you would get sick all over again. To change anything, including your health, in a truly lasting way requires a fundamental shift in life orientation. It's a matter of finding a new vision of the purpose of your life and setting a new ideal.

8. All time is one time.

Common sense tells us that the past is unchangeable and the future unknowable. But sometimes something else stirs inside us to suggest otherwise. Sometimes, often in subtle ways, we get hints about the deeper mysteries of time—a precognitive dream, perhaps, or a déjà vu experience. If we pay as close attention to our inner lives as our outer lives, we find clues that time is more complex than we thought.

"All time is one time—see?" Cayce recorded. "That is a fact ..." (294-45). A radically new idea of time is required if we hope to understand how the universe is structured and how we can meet the practical challenges of spirituality. But what are the chances of actually understanding how time works? Modern physics presents a dizzying analysis of time that allows for time frames of a relativistic nature that move at different speeds and, more mystifying yet, might even move backward. Could this be part of what Cayce meant by "All time is one time"?

Or consider the human wish to experience *eternity*. What does eternity really mean? Is it the desire to live for a long, long time—maybe forever? A different understanding emerges once we release the simplistic idea that time is only a line that stretches back into the distant past and forward into the endless future. Eternity has much more to do with the quality of how we experience the present moment. It is this *experience of the infinite* that cuts through every moment in time. Just imagine how life would change if we redirected energy devoted to worrying about the future into trying to awaken to the eternity of right now.

9. Success cannot be measured by material standards.

Measuring success, especially in terms of one's soul, is elusive. We can't use the same standards for measuring our outer life as we use for measuring our internal life. As Edgar Cayce put it, we should not "attempt to measure spiritual things by material standards, nor MATERIAL things by SPIRITUAL standards" (254-60). In other words, while the conditions of one's life may seem a dismal failure outwardly, inwardly there may be authentic spiritual progress being made.

While this way of looking at the relative nature of success seems to fly in the face of the West's preoccupation with achieving, even the business world today has started to seize on certain spiritual and holistic disciplines because they, too, promise certain outward results—whether it's using meditation to manage stress and promote greater employee productivity, or employing dream guidance to make better decisions about the stock market. Yet outward success does not necessarily translate into concurrent spiritual growth.

To push this line of reasoning a little further, sometimes it is our failures in the practical, material world that stimulate us to look more deeply into the invisible world of our spiritual life. This anomaly applies to Cayce's own story. How often he seemed to fail at what he tried to do. His story is full of disappointments, even catastrophes (his photographic studio burned down twice), and yet when we read his biography with an eye toward spiritual success we see that sometimes his failures outwardly pushed him deeper inwardly into his spiritual gifts. He often made this point to people in the midst of apparent failure. And he often perceived clairvoyantly that inner success was possible even if the outer world was in disarray.

10. Courage is essential to any spiritual growth.

As important as high aspirations and ideals are, we have to do something with them, and that takes courage. "He without an ideal is sorry indeed; he with an ideal and lacking courage to live it is sorrier still. Know that" (1402-1).

The spiritual quality of courage is indeed a crucial yet often misunderstood key to the growth of the soul. We are presented with superficial, sensationalistic images of courage by the media. It's depicted as a kind of daredevil recklessness. But true courage is something different. The Latin root word for *courage* is *cor,* which means "heart." Courage awakens in us not in the absence of fear but in the face of it. Courage is the decision that there is something more important than the fear we feel.

11. Evil is real and comes in many forms.

Edgar Cayce treats evil as very real, and two points from his philosophy are worth considering in that regard. First, evil has many "faces," many ways it presents itself in daily life. Unless we are prepared to deal with its multifaceted ways, we surely will be confused and overwhelmed by it as it swirls around us.

Second, we recognize and deal with evil in the outer world only to the extent that we undertake the distasteful yet courageous work of meeting it within ourselves. Cayce sometimes made this point with the following aphorism: "There is so much good in the worst of us, and so much bad in the best of us, that it hardly behooves any of us to talk about the rest of us." And so even though our self-justifying minds are quick to point out that we don't do those atrocious, abusive things we see on the nightly news, there *are* nevertheless ways in which each of us—albeit on a smaller scale—acts out some of the same themes in our own lives.

In order to see our personal role in evil, it's useful to return to the first point that there are many faces of evil and that some of these faces are more alive in us personally than others. According to Cayce, there are at least five *angles* from which we can understand and relate to evil (or *bad,* as he sometimes referred to it):

A lack of awareness. Sometimes evil can be understood as a deficit in conscious awareness, a state of being "asleep" spiritually. Evil constantly tugs at us to become less and less conscious, more and more distracted. Temptation surrounds us daily.

Extremism. As noted earlier, Cayce sometimes liked to remind seekers that Christ Consciousness is the meeting point between two extremes—that is, the middle path. Therefore, one face of evil involves embracing an extreme point of view, even denying the validity of any counterbalancing view, and surely our world is full of such extremists right now. What's a little harder to see is our *own* tendency to go to extremes. For example, we may be tempted to embrace *other-worldliness* in the extreme in an attempt to have a more spiritual life and in the process lose connection with and appreciation of the practical aspects of material life. But just as likely, we might be tempted to go the other way and become so pragmatically down-to-earth that we ignore the invisible side of life. Either approach is a kind of evil. Christ Consciousness creates a meeting ground for the two extremes, creating a life that integrates the mystical with the mundane.

Aggression and invasion. We think of these terms in connection with warfare, but all human relations have the potential for these forms of evil. We try to subvert the free will of others by overpowering them with our own will. One gift of authentic practical spirituality is the capacity to stand up for oneself (and one's ideals) with integrity but without becoming aggressive and invasive in the process.

Transformation. Here is a particularly hopeful way of viewing evil. Evil is something that just falls short of the mark, just misses it. "How far, then, is ungodliness from godliness? Just under, that's all!" (254-68). That doesn't mean ignore the fact that evil falls short; it means stay engaged with anything ungodly and keep working to transform it. Sometimes, only a mere readjustment is required.

For example, an individual might have a destructive tendency to manipulate others, but that trait may be just short of something that is constructive and healthy. While he may have a talent for motivating people, that talent has become distorted or is being misused in such a way that it qualifies as manipulation. Instead of rejecting that manipulative trait, he can uplift and transform it into its full potential. If he only tries to suppress the fault, he will miss out on a valuable side of himself.

Rebellion and willfulness. This is Edgar Cayce's most fundamental idea about evil. We are given the choice daily between good and evil. Perhaps what tips the scale toward evil is *rebellious willfulness,* as Gerald May refers to it in his 1987 book *Will and Spirit*. "Evil seeks to mislead or fool one into substituting willfulness for willingness, mastery for surrender."

And so the choices are always ours in the big and little decisions we make each day in response to evil. As concerned as we must be about evil on the national and international scale, an essential principle Cayce challenges us to look at is our own relationship to these very themes.

12. Learn to stand up for yourself; learn to say no when it's needed.

Life-affirmation is great, but sometimes we must learn to say no before we can say yes. Hearing this may give us pause, fearing that we're about to go down a path to negativity. Do we really want to honor *negation* in this way? But, in fact, a higher degree of mental health is required to set boundaries and define ourselves with a no.

Consider Cayce's bold advice: "So live each and every day that you may look any man in the face and tell him to go to hell!" (1739-6). People usually laugh nervously when they first hear this passage. Surely this is not Edgar Cayce, the life-affirming spiritual counselor, saying something like this! Perhaps it's just another example of his wry humor. But Cayce was dead serious about the need for us to define and defend our boundaries vigorously, and sometimes that means telling someone to go to hell. More often, it's enough to just firmly say no, letting it be known who you are and how you need to be treated.

It's all a matter of affirming one's personhood. Beneath the negation there is actually a more significant *affirmation* of something. The point is this: *There is no love and no intimacy with others unless we can first define our own boundaries.* Saying no is a matter of the most basic practical spirituality. Then, from that position of relative strength, we can enter into relationship with another individual. As strange as it may sound, loving someone may start by stepping back, saying no, defining oneself, and *then* reaching out and building an authentic bridge to that person.

This sounds a lot like *self-assertion,* as popularized in modern psychological practice and as Edgar Cayce himself sometimes advocated. One good example was advice given to a thirty-four-year-old machinist foreman who suffered from the social illness of letting other people take advantage of him. Cayce's blunt advice: "The entity because of his indecisions at times allows others to take advantage of him. The entity must learn to be self-assertive; not egotistical but self-assertive—from a knowledge of the relationship of self with the material world" (3018-1).

Another example is Cayce's repeated admonition of just how important it is to be able to get angry. Anger is an emotion directly related to saying no. Of course, he isn't saying we need to run around blowing our stacks every day, but he *did* emphasize the need to express anger in the *right* way. "Be angry but sin not. For he that never is angry is worth little" (1156-1). But then Cayce adds how important it is to have a *container* for that anger. "But he that is angry and controlleth it not is worthless." Note here that control does not mean "suppression" but "proper direction." It's a crucial distinction.

THE MODELS AND STRUCTURES
OF THE CAYCE PHILOSOPHY

• •

With the twelve essential themes of Edgar Cayce's philosophy in mind, we're still left wondering how it all fits together. What are the structures and universal laws of life that integrate these dozen principles? Over the years, Cayce proposed several different *formulas* and *models* in his readings. Taken together, they create a comprehensive *map* of how life works for a *spiritual* being who is experiencing *materiality.*

1. Links among body, mind, and spirit.

The holistic philosophy presented by Edgar Cayce emphasized the interconnections of the physical, the mental, and the spiritual. Often he offered a formula showing the sequence of how material reality (including physical health or the lack of it) comes into being: "The spirit is the life, mind is the builder, and the physical is the result."

The spirit is the life means that there is just one fundamental energy of the universe. It is the life-force, and it is fundamentally a spiritual, nonmaterial vitality. It can, however, manifest itself in the material world.

Mind is the builder means that with the mind each of us is able to give that one spiritual life-force a *vibration* or a pattern. We create with the mind. Thoughts are things, so to speak, although the reality of a *thought-form,* as Cayce sometimes called it, is not immediately apparent to our physical senses.

The physical is the result means that all we perceive as material reality is an expression in the physical world of what was previously mental. Our life circumstances, and even the condition of our physical bodies, are shaped by our attitudes and emotions.

One analogy that Cayce proposes is that of a movie projector. The projector's lightbulb is like the spiritual life-force; the images on the film are like the mental creations of our thoughts and feelings; and the image projected upon the screen is analogous to what we experience as our physical reality.

All of this emphasizes the *creative* element within us. We create our own reality in the world; we create our own future. The arts—painting, music, dance, etc.—are profound ways to bridge the apparent gap between the spiritual and the material. So emphatic was Cayce about the significance of this creative principle that a frequent synonym he invoked for God was *the Creative Forces*.

2. Links among ideals, free will, and soul growth.

A second formula from Edgar Cayce's philosophy is not stated explicitly in the readings but can be gleaned form the spiritual advice he gave to hundreds of people. There are three factors involved in this formula, and they flow out of the relationship among the three: ideals, free will, and the development of our potential as souls. In the formula, they are presented in sequence: "Envision an ideal, awaken and apply the will, and soul growth will be the result."

We noted earlier that one essential theme in Cayce's philosophy is that "changing anything starts with an ideal." And here that theme is expanded upon and linked to other essential principles. One explication has the ideal as something we *envision* rather than figure out logically—"it comes and find us," so to speak. Our task is to be open and attentive, ready to notice and reaffirm what arises spontaneously from the soul. In fact, if one's ideal is merely something that has been figured out logically, then probably its potency and impact is limited to the material world of cause and effect where logic reigns supreme. An ideal that is truly life-transforming must come from a deeper place within ourselves. It is something we intuit as it reveals itself to us. Envisioning an ideal is the *recognition and affirmation of something that calls to us from our own depths*.

Once the ideal has been discovered, we have to do something with it. That requires the use of the free will, which is the hallmark of our individuality. But the free will tends to be asleep inside us; we cruise through life on automatic pilot just reacting to things that trigger us. For the ideal to make a difference in our lives, the free will has to be awakened and then applied.

Applying the ideal is at the heart of what Cayce calls *soul-growth*. No authentic transformation of the soul can take place unless guided by the ideal. And, just as important, the essence of developing the soul is allowing for the free will to emerge.

3. Three levels of the mind.

One way to understand the human mind is to see it as three levels, or layers, that interact and influence one another. Edgar Cayce calls these layers the *conscious mind,* the *subconscious mind,* and the *superconscious mind.* Because the subconscious and the superconscious tend to be outside our immediate awareness, together, they make up what is widely termed *the unconscious*.

While Cayce was not alone in proposing this three-layer scheme, or the first to employ these terms, his image of the relationship between the layers is special. Many schools of psychology suggest that the higher mind (or superconscious) is like the attic of a house, the lower mind (subconscious), as the storehouse of all memory, is like the basement, and the mind of everyday awareness (conscious) is in between, the main floor of the house. Cayce felt such a scheme was misleading. Relative to the conscious mind, the subconscious and superconscious are not in different directions, so to speak; rather, we must pass through our subconscious memories in order to make a connection with the unlimited potential of our superconscious.

The three-layer model shown in Figure 1 on page 36, therefore, is different than a three-story house. It's based on a dream that Cayce had in 1932: "There was a center or spot from which, on going into the state, I would radiate upward. It began as a spiral, except there were rings all round—commencing very small, and as they went on up they got bigger and bigger." He offered an interpretation of his dream in a reading (294-131), indicating how, when giving a reading, he was able to elevate his consciousness (which he likened to a *dot* or *tiny speck*), through the subconscious, and on into the superconscious (or what he termed *the heavens*). As he put it, "[A] tiny speck, as it were, a mere grain of sand; yet when raised in the atmosphere or realm of the spiritual forces it becomes all inclusive, as is seen by the size of the funnel—which reaches not downward, nor outward, nor over, but direct to that which is felt by the experience of man as into the heavens itself." Herbert Puryear, a clinical psychologist, drew the V-shaped diagram shown in Figure 1 to illustrate Cayce's interpretation of his own dream.

Cayce's model has significant implications for how we understand our spiritual quest. As we strive to make a connection with the higher self—or *the divine*—then we should expect to encounter our own subconscious "stuff"—our unconscious desires, fears, resentments. Quite simply, it means that our quest to connect with the superconscious very likely will involve a profound encounter with ourselves, including those aspects we are ashamed or afraid of—our *shadow*, to use a term from Jungian psychology. And although Edgar Cayce was not conversant in the ideas of

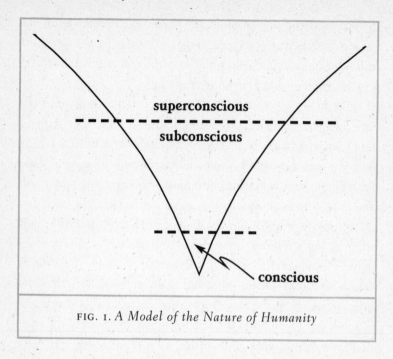

FIG. 1. *A Model of the Nature of Humanity*

Carl Jung, his picture of the human mind bears a strong resem-
blance.

Cayce's model of the mind, furthermore, is insightful regarding
the *source* of his information in a given reading. He claimed it came
from his own superconscious, that he acted as an *open channel* so
that it could reveal its wisdom through him. But it's not what is
called *psychic channeling* of other noncorporeal beings, as with a
medium. Cayce affirmed the validity of mediumship—at least as
demonstrated by a gifted few—but he denied that he was one.
Only with a few rare readings (perhaps a dozen total) did his subconscious mind serve as a mouthpiece for another being, such as
an angel or a disembodied soul. In more than ninety-nine percent
of Cayce's readings he claimed that his source was the knowledge
within himself—or, for that matter, within any of us if we are only
willing to learn how to tap into it.

4. *The seven spiritual centers.*

Edgar Cayce echoed the wisdom of the East in proposing that human experience can be understood largely in terms of seven spiritual centers of the body. Theology, philosophy, and psychology traditionally have been concerned about the connection between the finite and the infinite. If there is such a thing as a soul, with its infinite nature, how is it able to affect the finite physical human being? One ancient answer was to codify the spiritual centers of the body, what are known as the *chakras* (Sanskrit for "wheel," referring to the wheels, or vortices, of energy that clairvoyants claim to perceive in the body).

Spiritual centers can be found primarily in man's higher-energy body—the *subtle body,* as it is sometimes called, although Cayce preferred the term *finer physical body,* emphasizing the strong connection to the physical even though the spiritual activity of these centers is difficult if not impossible to measure with scientific instrumentation. Cayce also emphasized that each of the seven centers has its own representation in the flesh, in the endocrine glands, organs that secrete chemical hormones directly into the bloodstream and thereby influence every cell of the body. From the first spiritual center up to the seventh, he named the respective glands as follows: the *gonads* (the testes in the male, the ovaries in the female), the *cells of Leydig,* the *adrenals,* the *thymus,* the *thyroid,* the *pineal,* and the *pituitary.*

According to Edgar Cayce's model for health, the activity of the endocrine centers represents in the flesh what is happening in the mind and spirit. The term to describe the function of these centers is *transducer,* which is defined as a device activated by one form of power from one system and supplying another form of power to a second system. With the spiritual centers, the two systems are: the soul (with its access to an infinite supply of energy), and the energy system we perceive as the physical human being. Although not an exact analogy, the centers function somewhat like valves in regulating the flow of the creative life-force into the physical body. What's more, they are a storehouse of patterns of consciousness in the soul, and our thoughts, feelings, and memories (even past-life memories, Cayce would argue) find expression in the body largely through the spiritual centers and the endocrine glands linked to them.

5. Four phases of self-care for health.

Edgar Cayce emphasized learning how to care for one's own health. In the 1930s and 1940s, he sent many people to the New York City clinic of Dr. Harold J. Reilly, who became an insightful interpreter of Cayce's healing and health maintenance recommendations. Reilly identified four aspects of Cayce's formula for physical well-being, a model that has become the foundation from which many health care professionals have attempted to research and apply what Cayce had to offer. They spell out the anagram CARE:

Circulation. Paying attention to the body's need for both blood and lymph circulation. Poor circulation can result in a host of ailments.

Assimilation. Eating nutritionally and breathing properly. Also, creating the right conditions in the body so that nutrients can be absorbed and used by the body.

Relaxation. Practicing stress-releasing techniques. Our bodies can quickly become out of balance and toxic, and illness is sure to follow.

Elimination. Just as important as assimilating nutrients in the body is eliminating waste products from the body. Many of Cayce's remedies involved not so much putting something in the body as stimulating the body's nature wisdom to get rid of what is no longer needed.

EDGAR CAYCE AS CREATOR OF
A NEW CULTURAL MYTH

• •

Some of the most fascinating material presented by Edgar Cayce involves stories that seem to fly in the face of modern historical scholarship. Tales of Atlantis. Tales of ancient Egypt and the building of its great monuments, but with a timeline that violates the timelines of virtually all mainstream Egyptologists. Tales of elaborate ancient civilizations in the Gobi Desert and in Persia completely unknown to historians. What are we to make of these remarkable pronouncements?

In short, Cayce proposed that Atlantis is not a whimsical legend or metaphoric myth but rather a long-standing culture that actually existed. He dated its final destruction to 10,500 B.C., and he proposed that remnants of the lost continent and its artifacts can be found under the waters of the Caribbean. While intriguing anomalies and seductive hints suggest that there is more to ancient history than we ever realized, clearly there is *no definitive proof* that Atlantis existed. For many people, Atlantis remains a provocative yet unsupportable part of Cayce's overall philosophy.

Egypt is another matter, perhaps, since the monuments and artifacts *do* exist and are sometimes subject to debate. Cayce's perspective on Egypt is quite controversial. He suggests that the Great Pyramid and the Sphinx were not built around 2600 to 2500 B.C., the traditional dating, but some eight thousand years earlier. And the pyramid was built as a kind of temple of initiation and not as a tomb for a pharaoh. Cayce claims that records of prehistoric civilization, including Atlantis, are buried in a chamber hidden in the sands not far from the Sphinx, a chamber as yet not uncovered in spite of diligent efforts over the past twenty-five years.

Edgar Cayce's theory of ancient Egypt is not without its contemporary supporters. His timeline, for instance, coincides with that of Egyptologists John Anthony West and Robert M. Schoch, who maintain that water erosion on the Sphinx suggests that its oldest portion was built thousands of years before the widely accepted date of 2500 B.C. In his book *Voyages of the Pyramid Builders*, Schoch dates it between 7000 and 5000 B.C.—not quite as old as Cayce suggested but close nonetheless.

In spite of the intriguing evidence, many experts would argue that all of this material on Atlantis is not history at all but a precognitive vision of what lies ahead for humanity. Others would say that Cayce's account of Atlantis as well as Egypt are best understood as myth in the most positive sense of the word, that myth is a story that explains the *meaning* behind things. It's unfortunate that, in our time, myth has become virtually synonymous with erroneous thinking. Myth attempts to speak the unspeakable, and, in trying to explain the extraordinary in ordinary terms, myth must use metaphors, analogies, and symbols. Edgar Cayce's stories of Atlantis and Egypt at the very least can be taken as powerful and valuable stories that account for how we shape our own reality, how we must choose oneness over divisiveness, and how the purification of the body is needed to achieve our spiritual potential. All these stories point out how we face those same challenges in the modern world.

It might be said that Edgar Cayce's Atlantis and Egypt are the foundation of a new cultural myth. Without falling into the convoluted, unresolvable arguments about what can and cannot be supported historically in his work, we can appreciate it for the rich symbolism and profound teachings about the human condition. The historical validity of his accounts may be beyond our ability to ever judge definitively. But the "moral of the story," as we sometimes refer to it, is solid. Only when humanity embraces the principle of oneness to guide society do we have any chance of building a sustainable future together.

EDGAR CAYCE AS AN AGENT OF PERSONAL CHANGE

• •

Edgar Cayce's philosophy and recommendations always had a palliative quality. People came to him with all kinds of pain—physical, mental, spiritual—and an essential part of his work was to help alleviate that pain. But short-term "Band-Aid" help is one thing; truly helping an individual change is another. And Cayce intentionally provoked people to change, usually in a gentle, prodding way. But change they must if healing was to be successful.

Some who came to Cayce were prepared to make only superficial changes; others were ready to tackle the more daunting task of changing at the soul level. When we consider what personal change means, it's important to distinguish between *improvement* and *transformation,* terms often misleadingly linked as synonyms; both involve change, but transformation is more radical and, ultimately, much more significant.

Improvement—self-improvement—means making a better version of essentially the same person. In the language of the readings, it would be a matter of *polishing up* or *adjusting* the personality, the familiar person we know we are and show the world. Transformation, on the other hand, is a quantum leap in our sense of self; it's the awakening of our individuality, the essence of who we are. While improvement is a worthy, even necessary endeavor, we shouldn't kid ourselves into thinking it alone brings about genuine spiritual awakening. "PERSONALITY is certainly something NOT to be paraded or boasted of!" Cayce pronounced. "Well to have, and necessary! if used properly! WITHOUT INDIVIDU-ALITY, you are nothing!" (257-79). Transformation is more challenging because the personality doesn't easily surrender its claim on the whole of who we are. But without transformation, the soul remains restless and unfulfilled.

The following wonderful passage from Cayce defines transformation succinctly:

Q Explain what is meant by the transformation taking place or to take place in connection with the work of Edgar Cayce?

A In an explanation, let's all understand in their own speech. To some, an awakening to the greater channels of power; to others, more spirituality THAN materiality. To others, the karmic influences have reached THEIR changing point, that the vibrations may be brought one to another. In transformation comes a light for those that LOOK for same. **262-7**

What a truly remarkable statement; in essence, it's the heart of the Cayce legacy. Notice the final sentence: it's a summary of what the previous sentences are trying to capture. Transformation brings *light* into our lives, but we have to be *looking* for it. Light, or *illumination,* as soul awakening is sometimes called, brings a new capacity to see what's going on inside and outside of ourselves. It also brings vibrancy and vitality, sure signs that a transformation is taking place.

Returning to Cayce's answer, he points out early on that transformation may mean different things to different people. There are three ways we can experience transformation:

"Awakening to greater channels of power." When we make the quantum leap of transforming the soul, we gain access to *a new kind of power* in our lives. But with that power comes greater responsibility.

"More spirituality than materiality." Spirituality emphasizes oneness, whereas materiality emphasizes distinctions, competition. With authentic transformation, we begin to respond to life in terms of oneness.

"Karmic influences reach their changing point." Here, it sounds like Edgar Cayce may be referring simply to *grace*, the law that complements karma. Karma means we are constantly contending with situations of our own making. Grace does not eradicate karma; it introduces an additional element to it that can turn "stumbling blocks into stepping-stones," as Cayce often stated. Transformation comes when we are open to grace, that seemingly magical force of love that heals our most vexing problems. Grace lets us know we are undergoing transformation and not just improvement.

EDGAR CAYCE'S WORK FOR THE TWENTY-FIRST CENTURY

• •

E dgar Cayce cofounded three organizations, two of them still active today.

In 1925, Cayce joined forces with supporters to create the Association of National Investigators. It provided a legal framework for conducting Cayce's work in general and a framework for parapsychological investigation in particular, especially with regard to medical clairvoyance. The ANI, as it was known, raised money to build and run the Cayce Hospital of Research and Enlightenment for two years starting in 1928. But when the hospital failed due to lack of funds and discord among its directors, ANI also collapsed.

Concurrently, Cayce and several colleagues founded a small institution of higher learning, Atlantic University, in Virginia Beach, which opened its doors in the autumn of 1929. While there were great plans to expand the school's scope, enrollment, and influence, less than two years later it, too, ran into severe financial difficulty and had to close its doors.

But while ANI folded along with the hospital, Atlantic University was kept alive as a legal entity chartered in the state of Virginia, and some forty years after Edgar Cayce's death, in the mid-1980s, it was reactivated as a small graduate school entitled by Virginia's Council of Higher Education to grant master's degrees. The program, referred to as *Transpersonal Studies,* is interdisciplinary, including courses in psychology, parapsychology, philosophy, religious studies, health sciences, and the arts. Although it offers an on-site resident program at its Virginia Beach campus, the majority of its students participate off-site by utilizing computer-based learning, which effectively makes its offerings available worldwide.

Atlantic University offers in-depth study not only of the teachings of Edgar Cayce but also of a wide range of body-mind-spirit practitioners. The university also maintains an extensive Web site at *www.atlanticuniv.edu,* and is accredited through the Distance Education and Training Council, an organization authorized by the U.S. Department of Education to monitor schools' delivery of curricula to students off-site.

The third organization cofounded by Edgar Cayce is also still active today, and it is by far the largest of the three endeavors. Soon after the demise of ANI, several of Cayce's most ardent supporters helped him start a new nonprofit organization to continue his work, even though the treasured hospital project had been abandoned. The Association for Research and Enlightenment (ARE), created in 1931, has for more than seventy years served to make Cayce's work known to a wide array of audiences through publishing, membership, small group study, and conferences. As of the early twenty-first century, more than thirty thousand people are dues-paying members of ARE worldwide, but there are also literally hundreds of thousands of others who are students of Cayce's work and access the various resources of ARE, especially its online materials at www.edgarcayce.org.

One prominent branch of ARE is publishing. Not only has ARE Press issued a CD-ROM edition of all the Cayce readings and supporting documents, each year it also publishes several new books about how the principles detailed in the readings can be applied to daily life.

Since 1931, ARE also has maintained a small group study program under the aegis of "A Search for God," initially a single group in which Edgar Cayce himself was involved, eventually expanding over the decades to thousands of groups around the world. Cayce's teachings have found a welcome audience in dozens of countries, many with their own organizations and translations of his teachings.

Edgar Cayce had some very specific intentions for ARE, which he articulated in a lecture he delivered on June 27, 1935, to the fourth annual gathering of members of ARE. Most pointedly, he said:

Do not get the idea that the Association is trying to revolutionize the world; or that it is entirely different from or better than that which anyone else has. As I understand the purpose of the Association, it is like this: If ONE individual during the past year has been aided in finding his relationship to God, then indeed the Association has been a marvelous success. On the other hand, if this has not been done, then, it has been a failure—no matter how many members it may have or how great an outward show it may make.

REPORT ATTACHED TO 254-87

And so it is the actual transformation of individual lives that Cayce himself set as a benchmark against which to evaluate the effectiveness of his teachings. The individual reader needs to decide for himself what in the teachings seems ripe for study and application and see if he feels his life is being changed for the better because of it. In this book, we will explore the "essential" Edgar Cayce, in eight chapters organized by theme, by examining the readings at the heart of his philosophy.

CHAPTER ONE

THE NATURE OF REALITY

❖

Although the vast majority of Edgar Cayce's readings were for ordinary people and dealt with everyday issues, there was a foundation underlying his pragmatic advice, a metaphysical system defining the orderliness of the universe.

In this opening chapter, we explore three readings that present the essence of Cayce's view of reality and our place in it. While the first of these readings was for a middle-aged woman who was ardently seeking her own spiritual answers, it has a profound message for *all* seekers. The second reading was Cayce's attempt to depict reality in the broader sense, to paint the big picture, which was intended to be part of the 1943 biography *There Is a River*. Indeed reading 5749-14 is the pivotal reading given to Thomas Sugrue dealing with the overall philosophy governing the readings. The third reading addresses the problem of good and evil, and it was presented originally to a small group of Cayce's followers who were preparing study materials for dissemination worldwide.

In exploring these three readings, notice how often Cayce attempts to weave together the theoretical and the personal—the head and the heart—and how often he satisfied (or at least intrigues) the mind while speaking to the heart and its need for values, ideals, and inspiration.

THE LAWS OF LIVING

• •

A t the heart of Edgar Cayce's view of reality is this essential teaching: The universe is a lawful, orderly place, and there is a rhyme and reason to the events that unfold there, that life is built on dependable rules. Reading 1567-2 spells out this philosophy in its most direct and succinct expression. It was given to a fifty-two-year-old woman who was deeply involved in "New Thought," spiritual teachings originating in the late nineteenth century that contain many principles that overlap Cayce's own, including the importance of self-discipline, meditation, and prayer. No doubt this background made her a particularly good candidate to receive his message.

In many ways, here is Edgar Cayce the metaphysician at his best. Metaphysics largely deals with two issues: the nature of existence or being (*ontology*), and the orderly systems of the universe (*cosmology*). Cayce deals eloquently with both issues in the reading: he addresses who we are really and how we came into being; he addresses the question of God's most basic nature; and he addresses the laws that govern our experience—for example, the roles of mind and free will in shaping our experience, or the deeper meaning of astrology. The following four points stand out as centerpieces of Cayce's metaphysical system:

All life is an expression of the one God, who truly exists. God is not a figment of our imagination, something that humans dreamed up long ago because they feared death. God is the foundation of all that is. Furthermore, the life that comes from God is continuous, eternal, and therefore our own lives as spiritual beings are continuous, eternal, and go beyond the grave.

Life is purposeful. God started with a plan for us as souls. And even though each one of us chose to drift away—we made an "error of individual activity," as Cayce puts it—that plan is still available to us. The good new is that the plan is all-inclusive, including all aspects of ourselves: physical, mental, and spiritual. That means that in discovering and fulfilling God's plan for us, we are not required to deny any aspect of our human experience.

The outer universe is represented in our own inner universe. The macrocosm reflects the microcosm, and vice versa. An event that happens on the broader scale of the universe also happens on the narrower scale of ourselves. One illustration of this principle is found in astrology (see appendix 2, "Edgar Cayce and Astrology," page 267, for more detail).

Each of us has a free will and the power to create. Mind and free will are the two attributes through which each soul can express spiritual energy. The mind exists with one foot in the material world, the other in the spiritual world. While the mind has the potential to be creative in either world, it's the free will—the "ability to choose for self"—that determines which one will dominate the other. Those choices of the will shape the very essence of one's character and individuality.

As valuable as these four principles are, we nevertheless need to look for an even broader message in reading 1567-2. Edgar Cayce is more than a teacher of metaphysics, and this reading clearly

THE ESSENTIAL EDGAR CAYCE

shows he goes beyond how and why things are the way they are and ventures into the dimension of purposes, moral values, and ethics. It's that extra dimension that lends his philosophy its depth.

We miss the point of Cayce's life and work if we reduce his philosophy to the metaphysical exclusively. It's easy to fall into this trap because he does such a good job answering tough metaphysical questions. For instance, reading 1567-2 is full of fascinating clues about the many riddles of our existence. But in our delight in finding such a treasure chest of explanations, we need to notice some of the quieter, less sensationalistic truths about our purposes and ideals, about our values and ethics. Two such truths stand out especially in this reading.

There is meaning in suffering. Suffering is not simply punishment for things we've done wrong in the past. Suffering is unavoidable; each of us experiences frustrations, disappointments, and pain. That's just the character of physical life, as the Buddha said. Or, as Edgar Cayce said, we've entered into a realm of "trials of body and of mind" that tend to cloud the glories we might see. The good news is that even suffering can serve a higher purpose: It's where we are tested so that we may be open to receive the reassuring, healing grace of the Divine. And what does suffering teach us about values and ideals? It shows us a new way of seeing and understanding our own pain, that guilt and shame aren't appropriate, that it is at these very times that quiet encounters with the spirit are most likely to occur.

We are responsible to each other. The essential issue of life is how we treat our fellow human beings. We aren't so much responsible *for* each other as we have obligations *to* each other. In fact, it's in this social realm that we have the best chance to fulfill the purpose that our soul enters into the material realm in the first place. We're here to become aware of our relationship to God, and that awareness comes primarily in the ways we think about, talk to, and interact with other human beings.

Taken together, these two truths of Edgar Cayce's philosophy give us the big picture of his thinking: insightful, metaphysical laws that teach us why things are the way they are alongside the quieter, more modest reminders of what we need to value most in who we are. When we understand and apply what the readings have to offer from *both* these points of view, then we become students of Edgar Cayce in the deepest sense. The following life reading was given in 1938, and although intended for a specific individual, it is a beautiful illustration of what Cayce had in mind for all of us.

THE READING

❖

THIS PSYCHIC READING, 1567-2,
WAS GIVEN BY EDGAR CAYCE ON MAY 26, 1938.
The conductor was Gertrude Cayce.

EC: Yes, we have the records here of that entity now known as or called Miss [1567].

These as we find may be said to be very beautiful records, yet in ways such that it may be questioned by some as to why one who has been so far advanced in some experiences has been so little in the limelight or in the position of prominence through the same ways in the present.

If the varied experiences are studied with an eye single to service, these may possibly be understood or comprehended.

For remember that God looketh on the heart and not, as man, upon the outward appearances.

Hence there are lessons to be gained by the entity from even those feelings, those innate urges that cry for expression. For in their very expression, not finding outlet they turn as it were upon those influences from within.

But we find that if these are used, the entity may yet find a peace, a manner or way of expression that will bring joy into the experience in this sojourn.

In giving the interpretations, know that these are chosen with the purpose that they are to become helpful experiences.

An experience, then, is not only a happening, but what is the reaction in your own mind? What does it do to you to make your life, your habits, your relationships to others of a more helpful nature, with a more hopeful attitude?

These are the criterions for every individual's experience— sincerity of purpose, of desire; putting the whole law into effect in the activities—which is to love the Lord thy God with all thy heart, thy mind, thy body, and thy neighbor as thyself.

This is the whole law. All the other things given or written are only the interpreting of same.

Then what does such a proclaiming preclude? From what basis is the reasoning drawn? What is the purpose of an individual experience of an entity or soul into the earth at any given period?

These answered then give a background for the interpreting of *why*.

There are urges latent and manifested in the experience of each soul, each entity, each body.

First we begin with the fact that God *is;* and that the heavens and the earth, and all nature, declare this. Just as there is the longing within *every* heart for the continuity of life.

What then is life? As it has been given, in Him we live and

move and have our being. Then He, God, *is!* Or life in all of its phases, its expressions, is a manifestation of that force or power we call God, or that is called God.

Then life is continuous. For that force, that power which has brought the earth, the universe and all the influences in same into being, is a continuous thing—is a first premise.

All glory, all honor then, is *due* that creative force that may be manifested in our experiences as individuals through the manner in which we deal with our fellow man!

Then we say, when our loved ones, our heart's desires are taken from us, in what are we to believe?

This we find is only answered in that which has been given as His promise, that God hath not willed that any soul should perish but hath with every temptation, every trial, every disappointment made a way of escape or for correcting same. It is not a way of justification only, as by faith, but a way to know, to realize that in these disappointments, separations, there comes the assurance that He cares!

For to be absent from the body is to be present with that consciousness that we, as an individual, have worshiped as our God! For as we do it unto the least of our brethren, our associates, our acquaintance, our servants day by day, so we do unto our Maker!

What is the purpose then, we ask, for our entering into this vale, or experience, or awareness, where disappointments, fears, trials of body and of mind appear to mount above all of the glories that we may see?

In the beginning, when there was the creating, or the calling of individual entities into being, we were made to be the companions with the Father-God.

Now flesh and blood may not inherit eternal life; only the spirit, only the purpose, only the desire may inherit same.

Then that error in individual activity—not of another but of ourselves, individually—separated us from that awareness.

Hence God prepared the way through flesh whereby all phases of spirit, mind and body might express.

The earth then is a three-dimensional, a three-phase or three-manner expression. Just as the Father, the Son, the Holy Spirit are one. So are our body, mind and soul one—in Him.

Now we have seen, we have heard, we know that the Son represents or signifies the Mind.

He, the Son, was in the earth-earthy even as we—and yet is of the Godhead.

Hence the Mind is both material and spiritual, and taketh hold on that which is its environ, its want, in our experiences.

Then Mind, as He, was the Word—and dwelt among men; and we beheld Him as the face of the Father.

So is our mind made, so does our mind conceive—even as He; and *is* the builder.

Then that our mind dwells upon, that our mind feeds upon, that do we supply to our body—yes, to our soul!

Hence we find all of these are the background, as it were, for the interpreting of our experience, of our sojourns in the earth.

For the astrological or the relative position of the earth (our immediate home) is not the center of the universe, is not the center of our thought; but the kingdom of the Father or the kingdom of Heaven is within! Why? Because our mind, the Son, is within us.

Then with that consciousness of His awareness, we may know even as He has given, "Ye abide in me, as I in the Father—I will come and abide with thee."

In that consciousness, then, the purposes for which each soul enters materiality are that it may become aware of its relationships to the Creative Forces or God; by the material manifestation of the things thought, said, *done,* in relation to its fellow man!

As the earth then occupies its three-dimensional phase of experience in our own solar system, and as each of those companions that are about the solar system represents as it were one of the phases of our conscience—the elements of our understanding—or our senses; then they each in their place, in their plane, bear a relationship to us, even as our desires for physical sustenance; that is: foods for the body; with all of the attributes, all of the abilities to take that we feed upon and turn it into elements for our body.

All of the elements are gathered from that upon which we have fed to build blood, bone, hair, nails; the sight, the hearing, the touching, the feelings, the expressions.

Why? Because these are *quickened* by the presence of the spirit of the Creative Force (within).

So our mind, with its attributes, gathers from that upon which we feed in our mental self; forming our concepts of our relationship with those things that are contrariwise to His biddings or in line with that law which is all-inclusive; that is, the love of the Father, with our mind, our body, our soul, and our neighbor as self.

Then all of these influences astrological (as known or called) from without, bear witness—or *are* as innate influences upon our activity, our sojourn through any given experience. Not because we were born with the sun in this sign or that, nor because Jupiter or Mercury or Saturn or Uranus or Mars was rising or setting, but rather:

Because we were made for the purpose of being companions with Him, a little lower than the angels who behold His face ever yet as heirs, as joint heirs with Him who *is* the Savior, the Way, then we have brought these about *because* of our activities through our *experiences* in those realms! Hence they bear witness by being *in* certain positions—because of our activity, our sojourn in those environs, in relationships to the universal forces of activity.

Hence they bear witness of certain urges in us, not beyond our will but controlled by our will!

For as was given of old, there is each day set before us life and death, good and evil. We choose because of our natures. If our will were broken, if we were commanded to do this or that, or to become as an automaton, our individuality then would be lost and we would only be as in Him without conscience—*conscience*—(consciousness) of being one with Him; with the abilities to choose for self!

For we *can*, as God, say yea to this, nay to that; we *can* order this or the other in our experience, by the very gifts that have been given or appointed unto our keeping. For we are indeed as laborers, co-laborers in the vineyard of the Lord—or of they that are fearful of His coming.

And we choose each day *whom* we will serve! And by the records in time and space, as we have moved through the realms of His kingdom, we have left our mark upon same.

Then they influence us, either directly or indirectly, in the manner as we have declared ourselves in favor of this or that influence in our material experience. And by the casting of our lot in this or that direction, we bring into our experience the influence in that manner.

❖

PHILOSOPHY

• •

E dgar Cayce's philosophy of life is not summarized easily, but that was just exactly what Thomas Sugrue did in the concluding chapter of his authorized biography of Cayce, *There Is a River.* To help Sugrue, Cayce gave a reading to answer a series of problematic questions that Sugrue had identified; reading 5749-14 is arguably one of *the* most significant readings ever given by Cayce. Since 1943, Sugrue's remarkable book has introduced the work of Edgar Cayce to hundreds of thousands of people, and the philosophy chapter is a foundation for beginning to work with the ideas presented in the readings. Sugrue probably would not have been able to write it without this reading.

Once you've studied 5749-14 carefully, read the philosophy chapter. Sugrue tells the story of the creation of souls and how souls came to be trapped in materiality. His narrative creates the context for understanding Cayce's *Christology* and his approach to such topics as meditation, dreams, and reincarnation. Any reader of the chapter will no doubt recognize points that are clearly articulated in the reading. But in other passages from the chapter, Sugrue interpreted what he understood from the reading and then added to it. It's an especially fine illustration of the author extrapolating the essence of Cayce and presenting it in an understandable way to general readers.

To prepare for the reading, Sugrue clearly had done his homework. He studied the readings carefully, along with biblical and other philosophical sources. For most of the eleven "problem" issues Sugrue hoped Cayce would clarify, he already had tried to formulate his own best thinking on the matter, offering Cayce a possible solution and requesting comment. This sound strategy is consistent with the approach often encouraged by the readings for consulting psychic sources.

Although there are many subtleties and interesting nuances found in the reading, at least five major themes are addressed:

- Creation and the purpose of life.
- The importance of free will.
- A cosmic view of the soul's journey.
- The process of incarnation and influences that shape a lifetime.
- The mysteries of Jesus, the Christ.

There are, of course, other readings on creation, and Thomas Sugrue was able to draw upon them as well. But in this reading, we find an especially straightforward description of the fall of humanity. Edgar Cayce takes evil seriously. But to answer the ancient problem of its origins, he focuses on the misuse of free will by souls. To decipher essential points in this portion of the reading, it may be helpful to notice that the term *soul* is used for the spiritual component of our nature, whereas *man* refers to the physical creation that happened much later.

Were souls meant to come to earth? Here, the answer is a little more cryptic ("The earth [was] . . . *not necessarily* as a place of tenancy for the souls of men" [emphasis added]). Apparently, it became a place for meaningful experience after souls had fallen through their own misuse of free will.

The issue of free will is so prominent throughout this discourse, in fact, that reading 5749-14 might well be considered Cayce's most important statement on the subject. Free will, one of the three attributes of the soul along with mind and spirit, is described in a variety of ways:

- The cause of the Fall.
- The greatest factor (surpassing both heredity and environment) in helping or hurting the soul's growth.
- The agent by which the soul makes use of opportunities due to the circumstances of birth.
- The awakener of the Christ Consciousness resident in the unconscious mind of every soul.

Another particularly significant portion of this reading concerns the distinction between *Jesus* and *the Christ*—a topic explored in more depth in chapter 7, "Esoteric Christianity." In other readings, we find not only the idea that "Jesus is the pattern" but that the "power is in the Christ." That is to say, Jesus was a man who was one incarnation of a soul that had many lifetimes, whereas Christ is a consciousness to which a soul can attain. In this reading, the mission of the soul we know as Jesus is clarified.

However, Edgar Cayce's answer regarding Jesus's past lives leaves us bewildered. Thomas Sugrue complicates matters by putting the question of Jesus's past lives and the Christ's past lives in a single question. Cayce responds that the Christ had incarnations as Enoch and Melchizedek, but then he describes another sequence of lifetimes belonging to a soul that became Jesus, including Joseph, Joshua, and Jeshua. Does this latter sequence denote a new phase of the same soul's development? We can't be sure—it's open to interpretation.

The final question-and-answer exchange may seem like a request for *personal* advice on Sugrue's part. Up to this point, Cayce has presented a thoughtful dissertation on metaphysics, a clairvoyant view of the structure of the universe and human history. Now comes the twist: Cayce adds a moral dimension. Don't try to "go around the Cross," he states. There is no real understanding of all these matters—creation, the past lives of Jesus, or anything else—unless one also embraces the meaning of self-sacrifice.

The passage reminds us of Gandhi's famous warning: "Be on guard against science without humanity, politics without principle, knowledge without character, wealth without work, commerce without morality, pleasure without consciousness, and work without sacrifice." Edgar Cayce seems to be speaking in the same spirit: Don't collect knowledge of higher matters unless you also have the idealism and the will to put them into practice. Don't explore the mysteries of philosophy and psychology unless you're willing to surrender your own personal agenda and sacrifice your own limited goals in living. That willingness is the most telling aspect of Cayce's or any authentic spiritual philosophy.

THE READING

❖

THIS PSYCHIC READING, 5749-14,
WAS GIVEN ON MAY 14, 1941,
AT THE REQUEST OF THOMAS SUGRUE.
The conductor was Hugh Lynn Cayce.

HLC: You will have before you the inquiring mind of the entity, Thomas Sugrue, present in this room, and certain of the problems which confront him in composing the manuscript of *There Is a River.*

The entity is now ready to describe the philosophical concepts which have been given through this source, and wishes to parallel and align them with known religious tenets, especially those of Christian theology. The entity does not wish to set forth a system of thought, nor imply that all questions of a philosophical nature can be answered through this source—the limitations of the finite mind prevent this.

But the entity wishes to answer those questions which will naturally arise in the mind of the reader, and many of the questions which are being asked by all people in the world today. Therefore the entity presents certain problems and questions, which you will answer as befits the entity's understanding and the task of interpretation before him.

EC: Yes, we have the inquiring mind, Thomas Sugrue, and those problems, those questions that arise in the mind of the entity at this period. Ready for questions.

Q The first problem concerns the reason for creation. Should this be given as God's desire to experience Himself, God's desire for companionship, God's desire for expression, or in some other way?

A God's desire for companionship and expression.

Q The second problem concerns that which is variously called evil, darkness, negation, sin. Should it be said that this condition existed as a necessary element of creation, and the soul, given free will, found itself with the power to indulge in it, or lose itself in it? Or should it be said that this is a condition created by the activity of the soul itself? Should it be described, in either case, as a state of consciousness, a gradual lack of awareness of self and self's relation to God?

A It is the free will and its losing itself in its relationship to God.

Q The third problem has to do with the fall of man. Should this be described as something which was inevitable in the destiny of souls, or something which God did not desire, but which He did not prevent once He had given free will? The problem here is to reconcile the omniscience of God and His knowledge of all things with the free will of the soul and the soul's fall from grace.

𝒜 He did not prevent, once having given free will. For, He made the individual entities or souls in the beginning. For, the beginnings of sin, of course, were in seeking expression of themselves outside of the plan or the way in which God had expressed same. Thus it was the individual, see?

Having given free will, then—though having the foreknowledge, though being omnipotent and omnipresent—it is only when the soul that is a portion of God *chooses* that God knows the end thereof.

𝒬 The fourth problem concerns man's tenancy on earth. Was it originally intended that souls remain out of earthly forms, and were the races originated as a necessity resulting from error?

𝒜 The earth and its manifestations were only the expression of God and not necessarily as a place of tenancy for the souls of men, until man was created—to meet the needs of existing conditions.

𝒬 The fifth problem concerns an explanation of the life readings. From a study of these it seems that there is a trend downward, from early incarnations, toward greater earthliness and less mentality. Then there is a swing upward, accompanied by suffering, patience, and understanding. Is this the normal pattern, which results in virtue and oneness with God obtained by free will and mind?

𝒜 This is correct. It is the pattern as it is set in Him.

𝒬 The sixth problem concerns interplanetary and inter-system dwelling, between earthly lives. It was given through this source that the entity Edgar Cayce, after the experience as Uhjltd, went to the system of Arcturus, and then returned to earth. Does this indicate a usual or an unusual step in soul evolution?

A As indicated, or as has been indicated in other sources besides this as respecting this very problem—Arcturus is that which may be called the center of this universe, through which individuals pass and at which period there comes the choice of the individual as to whether it is to return to complete there—that is, in this planetary system, our sun, the earth sun and its planetary system—or to pass on to others. This was an unusual step, and yet a usual one.

Q The seventh problem concerns implications from the sixth problem. Is it necessary to finish the solar system cycle before going to other systems?

A Necessary to finish the solar cycle.

Q Can oneness be attained—or the finish of evolution reached—on any system, or must it be in a particular one?

A Depending upon what system the entity has entered, to be sure. It may be completed in any of the many systems.

Q Must the solar cycle be finished on earth, or can it be completed on another planet, or does each planet have a cycle of its own which must be finished?

A If it is begun on the earth it must be finished on the earth. The solar system of which the earth is a part is only a portion of the whole. For, as indicated in the number of planets about the earth, they are of one and the same—and they are relative one to another. It is the cycle of the whole system that is finished, see?

Q The eighth problem concerns the pattern made by parents at conception. Should it be said that this pattern attracts a certain soul because it approximates conditions which that soul wishes to work with?

THE ESSENTIAL EDGAR CAYCE

A It approximates conditions. It does not set. For, the individ-ual entity or soul, given the opportunity, has its own free will to work in or out of those problems as presented by that very union. Yet the very union, of course, attracts or brings a channel or an opportunity for the expression of an individual entity.

Q Does the incoming soul take on of necessity some of the parents' karma?

A Because of its relative relationship to same, yes. Otherwise, no.

Q Does the soul itself have an earthly pattern which fits back into the one created by the parents?

A Just as indicated, it is relative—as one related to another; and because of the union of activities they are brought in the pattern. For in such there is the explanation of universal or divine laws, which are ever one and the same; as indicated in the expression that God moved within Himself and then He didn't change, though did bring to Himself that of His own being made crucified even in the flesh.

Q Are there several patterns which a soul might take on, de-pending on what phase of development it wished to work upon—i.e., could a soul choose to be one of several person-alities, any of which would fit its individuality?

A Correct.

Q Is the average fulfillment of the soul's expectation more or less than fifty percent?

A It's a continuous advancement, so it is more than fifty percent.

Q Are hereditary, environment, and will equal factors in aiding or retarding the entity's development?

A Will is the greater factor, for it may overcome any or all of the others; provided that will is made one with the pattern, see? For, no influence of heredity, environment or whatnot, sur-

64

passes the will; else why would there have been that pattern shown in which the individual soul, no matter how far astray it may have gone, may enter with Him into the holy of holies?

Q The ninth problem concerns the proper symbols, or similes, for the Master, the Christ. Should Jesus be described as the soul who first went through the cycle of earthly lives to attain perfection, including perfection in the planetary lives also?

A He should be. This is as the man, see?

Q Should this be described as a voluntary mission, One Who was already perfected and returned to God, having accomplished His Oneness in other planes and systems?

A Correct.

Q Should the Christ Consciousness be described as the awareness within each soul, imprinted in pattern on the mind and waiting to be awakened by the will, of the soul's oneness with God?

A Correct. That's the idea exactly!

Q Please list the names of the incarnations of the Christ, and of Jesus, indicating where the development of the man Jesus began.

A First, in the beginning, of course; and then as Enoch, Melchizedek, in the perfection. Then in the earth of Joseph, Joshua, Jeshua, Jesus.

Q The tenth problem concerns the factors of soul evolution. Should mind, the builder, be described as the last development because it should not unfold until it has a firm foundation of emotional virtues?

A This might be answered Yes and No, both. But if it is presented in that there is kept, willfully, see, that desire to be in the at-onement, then it is necessary for that attainment before it recognizes mind as the way.

Q The eleventh problem concerns a parallel with Christianity. Is Gnosticism the closest type of Christianity to that which is given through this source?

A This is a parallel, and was the commonly accepted one until there began to be set rules in which there were the attempts to take shortcuts. And there are none in Christianity!

Q What action of the early church, or council, can be mentioned as that which ruled reincarnation from Christian theology?

A Just as indicated—the attempts of individuals to accept or take advantage of, because of this knowledge, see?

Q Do souls become entangled in other systems as they did in this system?

A In other systems that represent the same as the earth does in this system, yes.

Q Is there any other advice which may be given to this entity at this time in the preparation of these chapters?

A Hold fast to that ideal, and using Him ever as the Ideal. And hold up that *necessity* for each to meet the same problems. And *do not* attempt to shed or to surpass or go around the Cross. *This* is that upon which each and every soul *must* look and know it is to be borne in self *with* Him.

We are through for the present.

✤

THE PROBLEM OF GOOD AND EVIL

• •

Edgar Cayce suggested repeatedly that in a given lifetime a soul could either progress or regress. Evil essentially promotes *soul retrogression*—a moving away from our spiritual destiny of oneness. And so what are we to make of selfish ambition, greed, and violence, some of the so-called faces of evil? How does the individual who is trying to see the world from a spiritual point of view understand this blatant abuse of power and its harm to others?

Some of the most insightful comments on this problem are found in this reading, originally presented to the first "A Search for God" group, which received some 130 readings from Cayce on two dozen principles for spirituality and growth of the soul. Reading 262-52 was delivered when the group was studying "Opportunity," part of the second dozen lessons (we will examine the first dozen in chapter 6, "Soul Development and Spiritual Growth"). The essential opportunity we face in the material world is choosing either to serve life-promoting values *or* be a slave to selfish, destructive values. As we find near the end of 262-52: "Will is given to man . . . for the choice."

The primary intent of the reading was to systematically codify principles of *oneness* that could be presented to students. No doubt several group members recalled that four years earlier an accomplished scholar of the Cayce readings, Morton Blumenthal, had wanted to create a curriculum for students. At that time, the advice given to him was: "The first lesson for *six months* should be *One—One—One;* Oneness of God, oneness of man's relation, oneness of force, oneness of time, oneness of purpose, *oneness* in every effort—oneness—oneness!" (900-429).

Although what makes reading 262-52 especially noteworthy is the question-and-answer exchange on evil, Cayce's story of creation and the law of oneness sets an invaluable context for appreciating his approach to good and evil generally.

God is the first cause, the one source. And in the great, creative act that gave birth to the universe, God *moved*. Polar opposites were the result: positive and negative, attraction and repulsion. There were now choices to be made between options. That dynamic tension was the key to what lay ahead.

Where does the human soul fit into this story? Each of us was created with a potentiality for what we could become. With the gift of free will, each of us could choose to follow God's plan for our development *or* rebel against it. In the plan for spiritual evolution, the infinite spirit penetrates matter—that is, the universal spirit comes to know itself in individual human form. We have an opportunity, therefore, to "be aware of that first cause moving within his realm of consciousness."

So how had humanity gone wrong, how has evil entered into the equation? We are tempted by two fundamental forms of evil, alluded to by Edgar Cayce and described more explicitly by such spiritual philosophers as Martin Buber and Rudolf Steiner. Both forms are a type of rebellion, as Cayce describes it. Both mean going against the impulse to bring the spirit into the material world.

One type of evil tempts us to believe there is no such thing as spiritual reality. It denies the oneness of God—or even the existence of a higher force. It leads us to resist the *inter-penetrating* spirit and to focus on physical reality exclusively. The result can be blind materialism, coldhearted, self-interested thinking, and a fear of death.

The other type of evil is harder to recognize. It claims more for ourselves than we're entitled to. Despite our delusions, we really aren't the *source* of the one, creative energy; we are merely able to *reflect* and *direct* it. Cayce asks us to think about a mirror, which doesn't emit its own light but simply reflects light and redirects its path. Rather than saying, in effect, "I am God," we need to be saying "I serve the one God who lives in me."

Is there a particular *being*, a personal devil, that leads us astray? Reading 262-52 speaks of one, but that is *not* the same as saying evil is personified any more than a "personal God" means God is literally a person. Instead, Cayce reminds us that each of us has a personal capacity for evil, a capacity to rebel that leads us away from the true purpose of life.

Evil is not the idle talk of theologians and philosophers; it hits right at the heart of our modern culture and the mess we've gotten ourselves into. In groping for the values that will revitalize and heal our society, we first need to recognize the underlying oneness of God. Then we need to recognize that some choices really are life-promoting and others are not, and that the influence of evil on these choices is a very real thing. Evil is not separate from God; instead, it's a negative way of using that one source. Ultimately, confronting the problem of good and evil isn't so much a matter of unraveling a philosophical knot as it is the willingness to take responsibility for our choices.

THE READING

✧

THIS PSYCHIC READING, 262-52,
WAS GIVEN BY EDGAR CAYCE ON AUGUST 25, 1933.
The conductor was Gertrude Cayce.

GC: You will give at this time a discourse which will sum up and correlate the data already given through this channel on the fundamental truths regarding the Oneness of all Force, and will furnish us with some basic, logical, systematically arranged statements which can be given out as fundamental truths to students of this work. You will answer the questions on this subject which will be asked.

EC: Yes. In giving that which may be given out as basic truth, and correlating the statements that have been made from time to time, it would have been better to have gathered from that given the basis for expansion through these channels.

Yet, we may give that which may be the basis or the foundation of truth that may be gathered here and there.

As to the correlation and the setting out of paragraphs, at least you should do something!

The basis, then: "Know, O Israel, (Know, O People) the Lord Thy God is One!"

From this premise we would reason, that: In the manifestation of all power, force, motion, vibration, that which impels, that which detracts, is in its essence of one force, one source, in its elemental form. As to what has been done or accomplished by or through the activity of entities that have been delegated powers in activity is another story.

As to the one source or one force, then, are the questions presented in the present.

God, the first cause, the first principle, the first movement, *is!* That's the beginning! That is, that was, that ever shall be!

The following of those sources, forces, activities that are in accord with the Creative Force or first cause—its laws, then—is to be one with the source, or equal with yet separate from that first cause.

When, then, may man—as an element, an entity, a separate being manifested in material life and form—be aware or conscious of the moving of that first cause within his own environ?

Or, taking man in his present position or consciousness, how or when may he be aware of that first cause moving within his realm of consciousness?

In the beginning there was the force of attraction and the force that repelled. Hence, in man's consciousness he becomes aware of what is known as the atomic or cellular form of movement about which there becomes nebulous activity. And this is the lowest form (as man would designate) that's in active forces in his experience. Yet this very movement that separates the forces in atomic influence is the first cause, or the manifestation of that called God in the material plane!

Then, as it gathers of positive-negative forces in their activity, whether it be of one element or realm or another, it becomes magnified in its force or sources through the universe.

Hence we find worlds, suns, stars, nebulae, and whole solar systems *moving* from a first cause.

When this first cause comes into man's experience in the present realm he becomes confused, in that he appears to have an influence upon this force or power in directing same. Certainly! Much, though, in the manner as the reflection of light in a mirror. For, it is only reflected force that man may have upon those forces that show themselves in the activities, in whatever realm into which man may be delving in the moment—whether of the nebulae, the gaseous, or the elements that have gathered together in their activity throughout that man has chosen to call time or space. And becomes, in its very movement, of that of which the first cause takes thought *in* a finite existence or consciousness.

Hence, as man applies himself—or uses that of which he becomes conscious in the realm of activity, and gives or places the credit (as would be called) in man's consciousness in the correct sphere or realm he becomes conscious of that union of force with the infinite with the finite force.

Hence, in the fruits of that—as is given oft, as the fruits of the spirit—does man become aware of the infinite penetrating, or inter-penetrating the activities of all forces of matter, or that which is a manifestation of the realm of the infinite into the finite—and the finite becomes conscious of same.

As to the application of these as truths, then:

It may be said that, as the man makes in self—through the ability given for man in his activity in a material plane—the will one with the laws of creative influence, we begin with:

"Like begets like—As he sows, so shall he reap—As the man thinketh in the heart, so is he."

These are all but trite sayings to most of us, even the thinking man; but should the mind of an individual (the finite mind) turn within his own being for the law pertaining to these trite sayings, until the understanding arises, then there is the consciousness in the finite of the infinite moving upon and in the inner self.

So does life in all its force begin in the earth. The moving of the infinite upon the negative force of the finite in the material, or to become a manifested force.

Ready for questions.

Q Explain how so-called good and evil forces are one.

A This has just been explained. When there is delegated power to a body that has separated itself from the spirit (or coming from the unseen into the seen, or from the unconscious into the physical consciousness, or from God's other door—or opening from the infinite to the finite), then the activity is life; with the will of the source of that which has come into being. As to what it does with or about its associations of itself to the source of its activity, as to how far it may go afield, depends upon how high it has attained in its ability to throw off both negative and positive forces.

Hence we say, "The higher he flies the harder the fall." It's true!

Then, that which has been separated into the influence to become a body, whether celestial, terrestrial, or plain clay manifested into activity as man, becomes good or bad. The results to the body so acting are dependent and independent [interdependent?] (inter-between, see) upon what he does with the knowledge of—or that source of—activity.

Q In relation to the Oneness of all force, explain the popular concept of the Devil, seemingly substantiated in the Bible by many passages of scripture.

A In the beginning, celestial beings. We have first the Son, then the other sons or celestial beings that are given their force and power.

Hence that force which rebelled in the unseen forces (or in spirit) that came into activity, was that influence which has been called Satan, the Devil, the Serpent; they are One. That of *rebellion!*

Hence, when man in any activity rebels against the influences of good he harkens to the influence of evil rather than the influence of good.

Hence, will is given to man as he comes into this manifested form that we see in material forces, for the choice. As given, "There is set before thee (man) good and evil."

Evil is rebellion. Good is the Son of Life, of Light, of Truth; and the Son of Light, of Life, of Truth, came into physical being to demonstrate and show and lead the way for man's ascent to the power of good over evil in a material world.

As there is, then, a personal savior, there is the personal devil.

We are through.

❖

SUMMARY
of Edgar Cayce on the
Nature of Reality

• •

We live in an orderly universe that is governed by universal laws. Humanity has a purposeful place in this universe, and there is a plan for us as souls: to bring the qualities of spiritual life into the material world consciously. That plan requires that we make proper use of two great gifts that God has given each of us: a *creative mind* and a *free will.* Such freedom makes it possible for us to go astray—that is, to rebel, or to fall under the influence of evil. The task of helping the soul grow is to align our free will with the higher will of God, the Creator. In so doing, we awaken to the unity underlying all existence.

CHAPTER TWO

THE PSYCHOLOGY
OF THE SOUL AND SPIRIT

❖

EDGAR CAYCE WAS AMONG THE PIONEERS OF SPIRITUAL PSY-
chology, or *transpersonal psychology,* an approach to the
human mind that shows how integrating the body and spirit is
possible. Of course, Cayce never would have thought of himself
as a psychologist due to a lack of formal training. What's more,
the psychology of his era (with a possible few exceptions he probably knew little about) had scant appreciation for any links among
body, mind, and spirit.

Nevertheless, in reviewing the thousands of readings Cayce
gave we can see that often he acted as a therapeutic counselor
and spiritual psychologist. Some of the themes he addressed are
dealt with in later chapters, but here we examine four principal
ones at the heart of his innovative psychology:

- The distinction between *personality* and *individuality.*
- The importance of core values, or what Cayce called *ideals.*

- The transformative power of *meditation*.
- The insights and guidance that can come from *dreams*.

While the concept of *ideals* has been addressed already in the introduction, it is so central to Cayce's work that it warrants more attention here. Single readings beautifully capture the essence of his teachings on the first three themes, while in the case of dream psychology the essential points are best illustrated by brief excerpts from many readings that demonstrate the breadth of his dream interpretation strategy.

PERSONALITY AND INDIVIDUALITY

A s Edgar Cayce moved into the final years of his career, we see his spiritual psychology at its most mature. Many of the readings given at this time were relatively short, in some cases due to the sheer load of work he had undertaken. But brevity is often the hallmark of wisdom, and some of these shorter readings are among his most important.

The following reading, given only nine months before a serious health crisis forced Cayce to discontinue his work, is perhaps his most eloquent discourse about *personality* and *individuality*. The terms are key to the spiritual psychology that runs throughout the readings. Don't expect to hear about this distinction in a college psychology course, particularly from a professor with a traditional point of view. Even some seventy years later, such a perspective is far from mainstream despite the pioneering work of Cayce, Carl Jung, Viktor Frankl, and many others.

The reading is based on an assumption of *lawfulness*. The universe follows certain laws, just as we are created according to certain laws. Halfway through the reading, Cayce offers a helpful analogy about society's laws, then refers to how Jesus the Christ is an example for us of the right relationship between personality and individuality. But what do these two terms mean?

Personality is the self that we present to the outside world. It resembles what Jungian psychology calls *the persona*, the mask that each of us wears and that we hide behind when interacting with people and situations in daily life. It is the familiar self-identity that we know. In an external way, it's the self we see in the mirror or a videotape of ourselves. But personality *also* is made up of elements of our inner lives. For example, it can be observed in the familiar, routine ways we silently talk to ourselves, those little voices with which we second-guess or criticize ourselves. They are based on habitual patterns we've learned along the way.

More often than not, the personality is preoccupied with the self and its own sense of importance, what's referred to in this reading as the desire to have other people "recognize your personal superiority." And so we might think of the personality as starting from a certain *willfulness* to put oneself at the center of things, which in turn builds habits of thinking, feeling, and acting that begin to take on an automatic life of their own.

The personality can operate either consciously *or* unconsciously. Unfortunately, it's unconscious most of the time. We tend to be on automatic pilot, with strong habit patterns driving us. The personality is the conditioned, or ingrained, element of our being, and it can be a formidable obstacle to our growth, especially when it tries to supplant individuality.

Individuality is our more authentic being. It's the self that has continuity from one lifetime to the next. It's the *higher self,* a term Edgar Cayce used infrequently, preferring the term *individuality* instead. Perhaps he shied away from using higher self because he did *not* want us to think of this deep, most authentic self as already perfect; the individuality still needs to grow and develop.

What makes it so special is its *capacity* for growth, its strong *impetus* in that direction. The personality, on the other hand, is often quite content with the status quo, including when it involves some degree of discomfort or even pain.

Individuality is the identity that one awakens in meditation. One of Cayce's best definitions of this vital spiritual discipline, in fact, is an activity that partakes not of the personality but of the individuality instead. If you meditate, you probably recall times when you felt yourself make a shift: suddenly, the habitual thinking and emotional patterns quieted down, and, as they did, you remembered clearly another side of yourself, that freshly awakened part in touch with *universal consciousness.* Connecting with your individuality probably made you feel safe and secure, and that made it easy to offer prayers for others at the end of the meditation session.

At the most basic level, what makes personality and individuality so different? How is personality not like individuality, the more genuine way of knowing ourselves? The essential distinction is perspective and worldview, as beautifully illustrated in this reading's example of "Jim, John, and Susan." Our personality selves think, say, and do things with a very specific motive: *our own needs.* On the other hand, our individuality selves can look at the same situation with a different motive: a concern for the *greater good* and the ability to honor the *needs of others.* Essentially, this is the golden rule Edgar Cayce refers to indirectly in the reading.

Admittedly, personality sounds pretty bad and individuality sounds pretty good. In other readings about the subject, however, Cayce reminds us that the personality is necessary in order to live in the material world. To a certain extent, we even need to look out for ourselves and develop some habits and routines. (Can you imagine driving a car and constantly having to be attentive to every little thing you do? Here, the personality serves a very useful purpose indeed.) The problem is when we lose touch with individuality and believe that personality is all there is.

THE READING

+

THIS PSYCHIC READING, 3590-2,
WAS GIVEN BY EDGAR CAYCE ON JANUARY 26, 1944.
The conductor was Gertrude Cayce.

GC: You will give a mental and spiritual reading for this entity, with information, advice and guidance that will be helpful at this time; answering the questions, that may be asked:

EC: Yes, we have the body, the inquiring mind, [3590].

In giving that which may be helpful for this entity, as we find, many of the conditions that are as personalities and individualities are to be considered.

Here, for the entity, personality and individuality should have some analysis, so as to give the entity a concept of what we mean by personality and individuality:

Personality is that which the entity, consciously or unconsciously, spreads out before others to be seen of others. As to whether you will say Good Morning to Jim or John, and ignore Susan or not—these are parts of the personality, because of some difference or because of some desire to be used or needed by *that* others would have to give.

While individuality in that same circumstance would be: I wish to do this or that for Susan or Jim or John, because I would like for Jim or John or Susan to do this if conditions were reversed.

One is for the universal consciousness that is part of the soul-entity's activity. The other is the personal, or the desire for recognition, or the desire for the other individual to recognize your personal superiority.

These are variations to this individual entity.

Then, in analyzing the mental and spiritual influences as may be applicable in the experience, the entity finds itself—if it will stop to analyze—a body, a mind, with the hope for a soul eternal, that will constantly, eternally have recognition of those relationships to the universal consciousness or God.

Then, as the entity in this material plane has found, it is necessary physically to conform to certain moral and penal laws of society, of the state, of the nation, even to be termed a good citizen. Thus if there is to be preparation for the entity as the soul-entity, as a citizen of the heavenly kingdom, isn't it just as necessary that there be conforming to the laws pertaining to that spiritual kingdom of which the entity is a part? And there has been an ensample, a citizen of that kingdom, the Son Himself, has given the example to the entity as well as to others. Isn't it well, then, that the entity study to show self approved unto that kingdom, rightly putting the proper emphasis upon all phases of His admonitions, His judgments, His commandments, and thus become such a one as to be a good citizen of that individual kingdom?

These are just reasons within self, if there is the time taken to interpret what ye believe and what ye hope for.

Do not do it just mentally. Do it mentally and materially. Set it down in three distinct columns: The physical—what are the attributes of the physical body? Eyes, ears, nose, mouth—these are means or manners through which the awarenesses of the physical body may become known to others, by sight, by hearing, by speaking, by feeling, by smelling. These are consciousnesses. Then there are the emotions of the body. These come under the mental heading, yes—but there are also those phases where the mental and emotional body is born, or under the control of the physical and sometimes under the control wholly of the mental. What are the mental attributes, then? The ability to think, the ability to act upon thought. From whence do these arise? Do you use the faculties of the physical being for such? You do in many instances, yet you can think by sitting still—you can think yourself wherever your consciousness has made an impression upon the physical being of what exists. For you can sit in your office and see yourself at home, and know exactly what your bed looks like and what you left set under it when you left this morning! These are physical, not material at all; yet you judge them by paralleling with that knowledge, that understanding.

The spiritual self is life, the activity of the mental and of the physical is of the soul—and thus a soul-body.

Set down the attributes of each, and as to when and how you use them, and how you change them. What is the ideal of each? Of your mental, your physical and your spiritual or soul body? And as you grow in grace, we will find that the individuality will change—until you become one, as the Father and the Son and the Holy Spirit are one.

This is the manner in which you grow.

Then study to show thyself approved unto God, a workman not ashamed, rightly dividing the words of truth, keeping self unspotted from the world; not condemning, even as ye would not be condemned. For as ye pray, as He taught, "Forgive me as I forgive others." So in thy condemning, so in thy passing judgment, let it be only as ye would be judged by thy Maker.

We are through for the present.

✠

THE PSYCHOLOGY OF IDEALS
AND CORE VALUES

• •

By knowing what we believe in and what we hold true as core values, we have a simple, direct way of calling individuality back to awareness. The key to walking a spiritual path is found in those little choices—potentially, dozens a day—to resist the habitual tug of personality and listen to the wisdom of individuality.

All who study the Edgar Cayce readings know how important ideals are, if for no other reason than how often they are mentioned. The approach to meditation advocated in the readings, for example, is ideals-centered. Furthermore, one of Cayce's most innovative dream interpretation strategies is to measure what's happening in your dream against the ideals you hold dear. Another example: His philosophy of healing rests upon having an ideal and a purpose for wanting to get well.

The most quoted Cayce passage about ideals comes from this reading (357-13) for a forty-year-old woman working as a clerk during World War II. "Then, the more important, the most important experience of this or any individual entity is to first know what *is* the ideal—spiritually." But far more than this claim makes reading 357-13 special; in fact, the entire reading is valuable because it points to how ideals work in our lives, and outlines the spiritual ideal that Cayce's source held in the highest esteem: *the universal Christ*.

As you study the reading, first notice how Edgar Cayce describes in the second and third paragraphs the essential human dilemma: Our minds, with extraordinary creative potential, are pulled in two directions. On the one hand is the attraction of an ideal, a positive, creative image of what is possible. On the other hand is the pull of the material world. Unfortunately, it's the limiting, destructive material influences that frequently gain the upper hand.

How do desires focused on the material garner our attention? Usually, it's either by crisis, or good rationalization. Think about your own life: What interrupts or diverts you? What interferes with your pursuit of your ideals? For some, it's the endless demands of material life that seem too important to ignore; for others, it's the confusion created by such emotions as worry, anger, resentment, and fear. In these stressful times, almost everyone has days that seem to be ruled either by crisis or emotion.

A second diverter of attention is the impulse to say or do something that seems justifiable at the time. Because we can rationalize it, we can justify settling for something less than best.

See if you can recall examples personally from the past twenty-four hours, instances that took you away from your ideal. This exercise isn't meant to make you feel guilty; it's to see just how commonplace crisis and rationalization are.

Merely recognizing this aspect of the psychology of ideals, of course, still leaves one vital question unanswered: What is the best ideal for us to hold? Clearly, Edgar Cayce had a specific spiritual ideal in mind: the universal Christ, as lived by Jesus. Just as significant, it's a seed for each one of us. In the reading, Cayce eloquently describes this universal Christ pattern, beginning with "a teacher who was bold." (In chapter 7, "Esoteric Christianity," we explore his Christology more closely.)

What happens when we commit to that pattern as our own? Or, for that matter, what happens when we invest in *any* ideal? Setting an ideal engages the unconscious mind in ways that can alter our lives dramatically. That's why Cayce called it the most important experience that a soul can have.

But what does it mean to *set a spiritual ideal*? Is it just a matter of telling someone else what you've done, or writing it down on a sheet of paper? Reading 357-13 alludes to two crucial elements that are central to the psychology of ideals. Both play a role in stirring to life the forces of the soul, lying dormant in the unconscious. Both involve an act of free will and the engagement of the creative mind.

Aspiration is the first ingredient. To hold the universal Christ Consciousness as an ideal means to aspire to its qualities. (Much of reading 357-13 is just such a message of inspiration.) Maybe those qualities seem out of reach, but we can feel ourselves *inwardly stretching and reaching* for all that Christ Consciousness promises us. The same would hold true for any other spiritual ideal chosen. Striving involves both the free will and the creative side of the mind: We have to make a choice, *and* we have to use our imaginations to relate the ideal to ourselves.

It probably comes as no surprise that aspiration is one of the ingredients. Just think about how people use the term *ideal* in everyday language. Usually, it has the flavor of aspiration; for example, the ideal home is something we can imagine as the best possible way of getting along with family members. The ideal job imagines a workplace where all our talents are utilized. Aspiration means something more than *desire;* there is an element of intuition to the process. We long for, or aspire to, something because in part we sense that it is really possible.

Trust is the second ingredient in Edgar Cayce's psychology of ideals. A more subtle factor than aspiration, think about how you might aspire to something but not trust that it's really alive in you, not trust that it's possible for you. Without trust, you haven't yet set a spiritual ideal.

Trust is not easy to swallow because most of us find trust very difficult. It requires a more challenging use of free will than does aspiration alone. Trust means a willingness to let go of fears and doubts. It means believing ultimately in forces beyond our conscious selves. You can't set the universal Christ—or anything else—as your spiritual ideal until you let go and put your trust in it.

Here's another, somewhat superficial example: When you turn on a light, you trust that electricity will be there to light up the room. When you turn on a faucet, you trust water will start flowing. In other words, you worry little about the availability of electricity and water. Now, a critic could say that you're mindlessly taking it all for granted, that many people in the world don't have such immediate access to these resources. But the point isn't how fortunate we are; the point is to teach us about trust.

An authentic ideal is one you don't have to think about or question. It has become so much a part of life that it's a given. When you come up against a challenge, you know you can count on the ideal just as surely as you can count on electricity or water when you need them. *Some days, your genuine ideal is almost invisible because it's so much a part of how you view the world.*

We live in an era vitally needing a renewed vision of the power of ideals. Not pie-in-the-sky idealism, which all too often fails to connect with real life. Today's world needs respect—even reverence—for "setting an ideal for one's own individual life." Edgar Cayce offers a very effective way to hone in on how to do it and make it work. Aspiration is one key; courage to trust is the other.

THE READING

✤

THIS PSYCHIC READING, 357-13,
WAS GIVEN BY EDGAR CAYCE ON JUNE 11, 1942.
The conductor was Gertrude Cayce.

GC: You will have before you the body and inquiring mind of [357], at . . . Jewelry Co., . . . , Va., in regard to her health, her home life, her work, and her general welfare. You will give a mental and spiritual reading, with information, advice and guidance that will be helpful; answering the questions she has submitted, as I ask them:

EC: In giving an interpretation of the physical, mental and spiritual well-being of a body, in terms of a mental and spiritual reading—as we have so oft indicated, Mind is the Builder.

The mind uses its spiritual ideals to build upon. And the mind also uses the material desires as the destructive channels, or it is the interference by the material desires that prevents a body and a mind from keeping in perfect accord with its ideal.

Thus, these continue ever in the material plane to be as warriors one with another. Physical emergencies or physical conditions may oft be used as excuses, or as justifications for the body choosing to do this or that.

Ought these things so to be, according to thy ideal?

Then, the more important, the most important experience of this or any individual entity is to first know what *is* the ideal—spiritually.

Who and what is thy pattern?

Throughout the experience of man in the material world, at

various seasons and periods, teachers or "would be" teachers have come; setting up certain forms or certain theories as to manners in which an individual shall control the appetites of the body or of the mind, so as to attain to some particular phase of development.

There has also come a teacher who was bold enough to declare himself as the son of the living God. He set no rules of appetite. He set no rules of ethics, other than "As ye would that men should do to you, do ye even so to them," and to know "Inasmuch as ye do it unto the least of these, thy brethren, ye do it unto thy Maker." He declared that the kingdom of heaven is within each individual entity's consciousness, to be attained, to be aware of—through meditating upon the fact that God is the Father of every soul.

Jesus, the Christ, is the mediator. And in Him, and in the study of His examples in the earth, is *life*—and that ye may have it more abundantly. He came to demonstrate, to manifest, to give life and light to all.

Here, then, ye find a friend, a brother, a companion. As He gave, "I call ye not servants, but brethren." For, as many as believe, to them He gives power to become the children of God, the Father; joint heirs with this Jesus, the Christ, in the knowledge and in the awareness of this presence abiding ever with those who set this ideal before them.

What, then, is this as an ideal?

As concerning thy fellow man, He gave, "As ye would that others do to you, do ye even so to them," take no thought, worry not, be not overanxious about the body. For He knoweth what ye have need of. In the place thou art, in the consciousness in which ye find yourself, is that which is *today, now,* needed for thy greater, thy better, thy more wonderful unfoldment.

But today *hear* His voice, "Come unto me, all that are weak or that are heavy-laden, and I will give you rest from those worries, peace from those anxieties." For the Lord loveth those who put their trust *wholly* in Him.

This, then, is that attitude of mind that puts away hates, malice, anxiety, jealousy. And it creates in their stead, in that Mind is the Builder, the fruits of the spirit—love, patience, mercy, long-suffering, kindness, gentleness. And these—against such there is no law. They break down barriers, they bring peace and harmony, they bring the outlook upon life of not finding fault because someone "forgot," someone's judgment was bad, someone was selfish today. These ye can overlook, for so did He.

In His own experience with those that He had chosen out of the world, if He had held disappointment in their leaving Him to the mercies of an indignant high priest, a determined lawyer and an unjust steward, what would have been *thy* hope, thy promise today?

For He, though with the ability to destroy, thought not of such but rather gave Himself; that the Creative Forces, God, might be reconciled to that pronouncement, that judgment. And thus mercy, through the shedding of blood, came into man's experience.

❖

THE TRANSFORMATIVE POWER
OF MEDITATION

· ·

Edgar Cayce provided specific recommendations and guidance about meditation to hundred of individuals in readings. But he also gave several readings about meditation exclusively that were meant for everyone. Reading 281-13 is widely recognized as the most practical, poetic, and inspirational of his discourses on the subject. There are three central themes:

- Definitions that allow us to distinguish prayer from meditation.
- The importance of cleansing.
- Techniques for engaging the imagination as a kind of transformed thinking.

Several definitions of meditation are offered in the reading, including one near the end that has been quoted frequently: "[E]mptying self of all that hinders the creative forces from rising." But perhaps the most useful definition is found early in the reading and could be overlooked easily because it's not announced as a definition: "[Meditation] partakes of the individuality, not the personality."

As noted previously, personality is our normal physical consciousness—our likes and dislikes, our habits, our agendas for getting things done. It's the familiar sense of identity that each of us holds—or, we might say, that holds us. In this regard, prayer largely is an activity of the personality; it's a special effort made by the personality, the "pouring out of the personality," so that we may be filled. "Prayer is the concerted effort of the physical consciousness . . ."

Meditation, on the other hand, requires that the personality become still. Meditation is an emptying; it is the cessation of thinking—even the high-minded kind—as we experience it typically. It involves awakening and engaging the other side of our being—individuality—which is connected more immediately to the spiritual world.

What is the *language* of individuality? How does it operate in meditation? In this reading, Edgar Cayce suggests that the key is in the imaginative forces. We are transformed in meditation by holding in our attention and raising up a certain image within ourselves. Actual *creation* takes place in meditation; or we might say that we are being *re-created* in meditation. In the final paragraphs of the reading, there is a very clear image: the Christ, although it is evident that what is intended here is universal Christ Consciousness, since it's equated with "love of the God consciousness." Cayce's approach to meditation, however, can be practiced by people of any faith, even though devout Christians received this particular reading and the language is decidedly Christian in nature.

One secret to effective meditation is the ability to stop normal thinking processes and to imaginatively focus on a very high ideal. In many of Cayce's readings on meditation, he suggests using an *affirmation*, what is called a *mantra* in many Eastern religions. The affirmation, or mantra, contains a short statement of one's ideal. The point in meditation is not to think about the affirmation in the ordinary way but *to allow oneself to feel the meaning behind the words and to hold that feeling in silent attention*. It is a creative use of the imaginative forces but directed very purposefully. It's not daydreaming; it's perceiving the reality of that ideal with one's feelings and intuition. As Edgar Cayce put it, our sense of self moves "deeper—deeper—to the seeing, feeling, experiencing of that image in the creative forces of love." *The imaginative forces allow us to experience and feel the meaning*.

Another key to effective meditation is obviously *cleansing*, and almost half the reading deals with cleansing in one way or another. Why is the purification of our bodies and our minds so significant? One reason goes back to the beginning of the reading. The subject of the reading was looking for advice on how to meditate "without the effort disturbing the mental or physical body." One way is to cleanse before meditating.

But another need for cleansing is also proposed. Consider what happens as we hold our ideal in silent attention. The influence, or vibration, of that image rises up within the body through the spiritual centers, or chakras. Edgar Cayce linked the traditional seven chakras of the higher energy body to seven of the endocrine glands in the physical body. What's more, he alludes to the theory that in meditation creative energy moves from the first two chakras (which he linked to the reproductive glands and the cells of Leydig) all the way up to the two highest chakras (the pineal and pituitary glands in the brain).

But what can keep that image from connecting with the highest spiritual centers? The reading identifies two factors: If we have been mentally self-abusive (with doubt, self-condemnation, fear, etc.) and can imagine only a very limited ideal, then the movement of that image is greatly restricted; it won't resonate at the higher level or even reach that far. The other limitation, however, can easily be present even if we've honed in on the Christ ideal. Impurities in our physical and mental selves have to be worked against so that the image can disseminate itself to "these centers, stations or places along the body." The impurities become resistive hindrances.

Of course, this is not an all-or-nothing proposition. If we waited until we were totally purified before trying to meditate, we might never get around to it. Effective cleansing, like effective meditation, has levels; the point simply is to do whatever we can before we start to meditate in order to minimize any hindrances.

Reading 281-13 also raises the issue of sexuality. Edgar Cayce associates the first spiritual center with the reproductive glands (the ovaries in the female, the testes in the male). He states that the creative forces find their origin and impetus in the reproductive center: "The reproductive forces themselves, which are the very essence of Life itself within an individual . . ."

What was Cayce's stand on sexuality? He recognized that this is a very important subject to us: "For there is no soul but what the sex life becomes the greater influence in life. Not as always in gratification in the physical act, but rather that that finds expression in the creative forces and creative abilities of the body itself" (911-2).

In fact, there was not any strict moral code that Cayce tried to push on people as he gave them advice in his readings. Instead, he asked that we consider the ways in which sexual activity is an expression of the creative forces, but he always came back to the principle of a personal ideal. In deciding what is personally right or wrong in terms of sex, each individual must decide how an activity relates to the ideal that he or she has chosen in life. As Cayce told one woman whose husband was impotent and who was considering a discreet affair to meet her sexual needs, "Such questions as these can only be answered in what is thy ideal. Do not have an ideal and not attempt to reach same. There is no condemnation in those who DO such for helpful forces, but if for personal, selfish gratification, it is sin" (2329-1). For more about Cayce on sexuality, see appendix 3, page 270.

In summary, reading 281-13 is a remarkable discourse about the creative life-force generally and about meditation specifically. Valuable to anyone who wants to meditate daily, the beginner will discover a straightforward approach here, the experienced practitioner will no doubt find this reading worth studying again. It captures the essential themes of this vital spiritual discipline.

THE READING

THIS PSYCHIC READING, 281-13,
WAS GIVEN BY EDGAR CAYCE ON NOVEMBER 19, 1932.
The conductor was Gertrude Cayce.

GC: You will have before you the psychic work of Edgar Cayce, present in this room, the information that has been and is being given from time to time, especially that regarding meditation and prayer. You will give, in a clear, concise, understandable manner just how an individual may meditate, or pray, without the effort disturbing the mental or physical body. If this can be given in a general manner, outline it for us. If it is necessary to be outlined for specific individuals, you will tell us how individuals may attain to the understanding necessary for such experiences not to be detrimental to them.

EC: Yes, we have the work, the information that has been and that maybe given from time to time; especially that in reference to meditation and prayer.

First, in considering such, it would be well to analyze that difference (that is not always understood) between meditation and prayer.

As it has been defined or given in an illustrated manner by the Great Teacher, prayer is the *making* of one's conscious self more in attune with the spiritual forces that may manifest in a material world, and is *ordinarily* given as a *cooperative* experience of *many* individuals when all are asked to come in one accord and one mind; or, as was illustrated by:

Be not as the Pharisees, who love to be seen of men, who make long dissertation or prayer to be heard of men. They *immediately* have their reward in the physical-mental mind.

Be rather as he that entered the temple and not so much as lifting his eyes, smote his breast and said, "God, be merciful to me a sinner!"

Which man was justified, this man or he that stood to be seen of men and thanked God he was not as other men, that he paid his tithes, that he did the services required in the temple, that he stood in awe of no one, he was not even as this heathen who in an uncouth manner, not with washed hands, not with shaven face attempted to reach the throne of grace?

Here we have drawn for us a comparison in prayer: That

which may be the pouring out of the personality of the individual, or a group who enter in for the purpose of either outward show to be seen of men; or that enter in even as in the closet of one's inner self and pours out self that the inner man may be filled with the Spirit of the Father in His merciful kindness to men.

Now draw the comparisons for meditation: Meditation, then, is prayer, but is prayer from *within* the *inner* self, and partakes not only of the physical inner man but the soul that is aroused by the spirit of man from within.

Well, that we consider this from *individual* interpretation, as well as from group interpretation; or individual meditation and group meditation.

As has been given, there are *definite* conditions that arise from within the inner man when an individual enters into true or deep meditation. A physical condition happens, a physical activity takes place! Acting through what? Through that man has chosen to call the imaginative or the impulsive, and the sources of impulse are aroused by the shutting out of thought pertaining to activities or attributes of the carnal forces of man. That is true whether we are considering it from the group standpoint or the individual. Then, changes naturally take place when there is the arousing of that stimuli *within* the individual that has within it the seat of the soul's dwelling, within the individual body of the entity or man, and then this partakes of the individuality rather than the personality.

If there has been set the mark (mark meaning here the image that is raised by the individual in its imaginative and impulse force) such that it takes the form of the ideal the individual is holding as its standard to be raised to, within the individual as well as to all forces and powers that are magnified or to be magnified in the world from without, *then* the individual (or the image) bears the mark of the Lamb, or the Christ, or the Holy One, or the Son, or any of the names we may have given to that which *enables* the individual to enter *through it* into the very presence of that which is the creative force from within itself—see?

Some have so overshadowed themselves by abuses of the mental attributes of the body as to make scars, rather than the mark, so that only an imperfect image may be raised within themselves that may rise no higher than the arousing of the carnal desires within the individual body. We are speaking individually, of course; we haven't raised it to where it may be disseminated, for remember it rises from the glands known in the body as the lyden, or to the lyden [Leydig] and through the reproductive forces themselves, which are the very essence of Life itself within an individual—see? for these functionings never reach that position or place that they do not continue to secrete that which makes for virility to an individual physical body. Now we are speaking of conditions from without and from within!

The spirit and the soul is within its encasement, or its temple within the body of the individual—see? With the arousing then of this image, it rises along that which is known as the Appian Way, or the pineal center, to the base of the *brain*, that it may be disseminated to those centers that give activity to the whole of the mental and physical being. It rises then to the hidden eye in the center of the brain system, or is felt in the forefront of the head, or in the place just above the real face—or bridge of nose, see?

Do not be confused by the terms that we are necessarily using to give the exact location of the activities of these conditions within the individuals, that we may make this clarified for individuals.

When an individual then enters into deep meditation:

It has been found throughout the ages (*individuals* have found) that self-preparation (to *them*) is necessary. To some it is necessary that the body be cleansed with pure water, that certain types of breathing are taken, that there may be an even balance in the whole of the respiratory system, that the circulation becomes normal in its flow through the body, that certain or definite odors produce those conditions (or are conducive to producing of conditions) that allay or stimulate the activity of portions of the system, that the more carnal or more material sources are laid aside, or the whole of the body is *purified* so that the purity of thought as it rises has less to work against in its dissemination of that it brings to the whole of the system, in its rising through the whole of these centers, stations or places along the body. To be sure, these are conducive; as are also certain incantations, as a drone of certain sounds, as the tolling of certain tones, bells, cymbals, drums, or various kinds of skins. Though we may as higher thought individuals find some fault with those called savages, they produce or arouse or bring within themselves—just as we have known, do know, that there may be raised through the battle-cry, there may be raised through the using of certain words or things, the passion or the thirst for destructive forces. Just the same may there be raised, not sedative to these but a *cleansing* of the body.

"Consecrate yourselves this day that ye may on the morrow present yourselves before the Lord that He may speak through *you!*" is not amiss. So, to *all* there may be given:

Find that which is to *yourself* the more certain way to your consciousness of *purifying* body and mind, before ye attempt to enter into the meditation as to raise the image of that through which ye are seeking to know the will or the activity of the Creative Forces; for ye are *raising* in meditation actual *creation* taking place within the inner self!

When one has found that which to self cleanses the body, whether from the keeping away from certain foods or from certain associations (either man or woman), or from those thoughts and activities that would hinder that which is to be raised from *finding* its full measure of expression in the *inner* man (*inner* man, or inner individual, man or woman, meaning in this sense those radial senses from which, or centers from which all the physical organs, the mental organs, receive their stimuli for activity), we readily see how, then, *in* meditation (when one has so purified self) that *healing* of *every* kind and nature may be disseminated on the wings of thought, that are so much a thing—and so little considered by the tongue that speaks without taking into consideration what may be the end thereof!

Now, when one has cleansed self, in whatever manner it may be, there may be no fear that it will become so overpowering that it will cause any physical or mental disorder. It is *without* the cleansing that entering any such finds *any* type or form of disaster, or of pain, or of any dis-ease of any nature. It is when the thoughts, then, or when the cleansings of *group* meditations are conflicting that such meditations call on the higher forces raised within self for manifestations and bring those conditions that either draw one closer to another or make for that which shadows [shatters?] much in the experiences of others; hence short group meditations with a *central* thought around some individual idea, or either in words, incantations, or by following the speech of one sincere in abilities, efforts or desires to raise a cooperative activity *in* the minds, would be the better.

Then, as one formula—not the only one, to be sure—for an individual that would enter into meditation for self, for others:

Cleanse the body with pure water. Sit or lie in an easy position, without binding garments about the body. Breathe in through the right nostril three times, and exhale through the mouth. Breathe in three times through the left nostril and exhale through the right. Then, either with the aid of a low music, or the incantation of that which carries self deeper—deeper—to the seeing, feeling, experiencing of that image in the creative forces of love, enter into the Holy of Holies. As self feels or experiences the raising of this, see it disseminated through the *inner* eye (not the carnal eye) to that which will bring the greater understanding in meeting every condition in the experience of the body. Then listen to the music that is made as each center of thine own body responds to that new creative force that little by little this entering in will enable self to renew all that is necessary—in Him.

First, *cleanse* the room; cleanse the body; cleanse the surroundings, in thought, in act! Approach not the inner man, or the inner self, with a grudge or an unkind thought held against *any* man! or do so to thine own undoing sooner or later!

Prayer and meditation:

Prayer is the concerted effort of the physical consciousness to become attuned to the consciousness of the Creator, either collectively or individually! *Meditation* is *emptying* self of all that hinders the creative forces from rising along the natural channels of the physical man to be disseminated through those centers and sources that create the activities of the physical, the mental, the spiritual man; properly done must make one *stronger* mentally, physically, for has it not been given? He went in the strength of that meat received for many days? Was it not given by Him who has shown us the Way, "I have had meat that ye know not of"? As we give out, so does the *whole* of man—physically and mentally become depleted, yet in entering into the silence, entering into the silence in meditation, with a clean hand, a clean body, a clean mind, we may receive that strength and power that fits each individual, each soul, for a greater activity in this material world.

"Be not afraid, it is I." Be sure it is Him we worship that we raise in our inner selves for the dissemination; for, as He gave, "Ye must eat of my *body*; ye must drink of *my* blood." Raising then in the inner self that image of the Christ, love of the God Consciousness, is *making* the body so cleansed as to be barred against all powers that would in any manner hinder.

Be thou *clean*, in Him.

We are through for the present.

✤

THE PSYCHOLOGY OF DREAMS

• •

Edgar Cayce lived and worked in an era when dream psychology was just coming into its own. After centuries of disrepute and suppression, dreams were beginning to be seen as valuable windows into the human mind and soul.

Cayce interpreted over a thousand dreams for various individuals who requested it, and over the years it became one of the cornerstones of his methodology. He treated dreams as something very real—in a sense, more real than the experience of waking life because dreams provide an unadulterated, honest view of what is going on in one's interior life.

Dreams are an avenue to self-knowledge, but not every dream provides guidance about what we should do. Decisions are best made at the *conscious* level, but the information needed to make better decisions can be found in dreams. They reveal factors that influence us and that we can act upon. Cayce calls this *applica-*

tion the authentic *interpretation* of the dream. It's never enough just to *figure out* or *decipher* what a dream means; *the real interpretation is the new action the insight leads us to.*

As confusing as most dreams seem to be, Cayce claims they are a type of reasoning. Not deductive reasoning, which is the familiar way the conscious mind works, starting with an overall assumption and figuring out specific ways that assumption plays out. Instead, dreams are *inductive reasoning,* whereby the mind collects lots of scattered details and tries to reason back to an overall assumption linking them together. In a sense, at night your unconscious mind is picking through the scattered details of your life experiences and trying to *reason backward* to find the truth behind them.

Edgar Cayce, though, never settled for just one method for ferreting out the meaning of dreams. He instead employed a variety of strategies, among which he was able to determine intuitively which one was the most appropriate for a given dream. Recall that in Cayce's lifetime the Freudian model was paramount, with its emphasis on how conscious life tends to repress innate drives and desires, and how dreams are usually *wish fulfillment.* While Cayce's interpretations occasionally asserted that personal desire, whether conscious or unconscious, sometimes generated the dream, he also had at least five other approaches. With the excerpts that follow, each strategy is defined, described briefly, then applied by Cayce.

Interpretation Strategy 1.
Fitting the theme of the dream back in the dreamer's life.

A powerful first step is to identify the essence of the plot, or storyline, of the dream. It means finding the theme of the action, the *verbs* of the narrative, as you write the dream down. When using this approach, one initially pays no attention to the specific symbols of the dream, focusing instead on the action of the dream. Then one takes the plot and sees how it mirrors waking life.

Strategy 1 may not offer guidance about needed changes in the dreamer's life, but it calls attention to a *way of being* that needs more conscious awareness on the part of the dreamer.

Two examples follow. In the first, Cayce makes no effort to interpret the particular symbols in the dream, as tempting as it may be for us to assume that the "candy" mentioned surely has to do with the dreamer's diet or something else in her life that is superficial and not very nourishing.

Q "Went into store and asked for 10 cents worth of jelly beans and they handed me just 4 beans. 'Is that all I get for 10 cents?' I asked. They told me just 4. 'Well, then, how much are chocolates?' I asked, thinking to buy them instead of the beans. 'Three for $1.00,' came the reply. 'Just 3?' I asked. 'Three,' came the reply. 'Then you can keep your chocolates too,' I flatly stated and walked out."

A This shows to the entity the inconsistency at times in self, as regards the various conditions that arise in the daily life, if the entity would but take the time to consider same from every viewpoint. For, as inconsistent as the prices are asked of entity, as inconsistent do many actions of self appear to others.   **136-20**

The theme of the dream was essentially that things that are being demanded are inconsistent and unfair. (Remember, in 1925, when this dream occurred, ten cents was a lot of money and should have bought an entire bag of jelly beans!) And that theme, Cayce suggests, exactly applies to the way the dreamer has been *unfairly treating other people.*

Q A few nights ago. Saw my father, and it seemed he was oper-
ated on for appendicitis. I wanted to see the healed up
wound, but he was taking a bath. "Always take a warm bath
after an operation," he told me. When he got out of the tub I
was able to see and examine the scar left from the operation.

A ... These conditions represent, then, that in the emblematical way and manner of how the entity ... should act toward
each and every precept as is set down by the entity as regarding a given law or fact. That is, as it becomes necessary
from time to time, in the physical make-up of the body, that
portions that are not understood, and the activity of same not
understood, be removed ... It becomes necessary at times to
remove certain conditions, or certain ideas, or certain builded
forces in the mind.   900-296

The theme of this second dream is that someone is having
something removed. Cayce suggests that that theme fits the
dreamer because he must learn to "remove certain ideas" in his
waking life, to let go of old concepts.

Interpretation Strategy 2.
Compensatory dreams.

Balance is a key concept in Edgar Cayce's spiritual psychology.
Becoming mentally healthy is largely a matter of finding a point of
integration between polar extremes—the paradoxes and contra-
diction within us. Of course, this principle is at the heart of Carl
Jung's analytical psychology, but, again, it's not clear that Cayce
knew much about Jung or Jungian psychology, and the idea seems
to have sprung up in Cayce's teachings independently.

One way that Cayce refers to extremes is in terms of the universal Christ Consciousness, a topic explored in chapter 7. As de-

scribed earlier, Christ Consciousness is a state of awareness in which we perceive and relate to life in its *essential unity and interconnectedness*. Only in this special state of consciousness "do the extremes meet," as Cayce put it.

But what does all this talk about extremes have to do with dreams? Simply, they sometimes serve to re-create equilibrium when we go off on some extreme in daily life. The rebalancing function of the mind is something that Jung pointed to frequently, especially in the interpretation of dreams. Cayce, too, mentioned the principle of dream interpretations. The human mind operates by a *law of compensation*. Whenever we go to some extreme in waking life, the unconscious mind (the source of dreams) produces the opposite extreme to re-create equilibrium.

A good interpretation strategy, therefore, is to ask whether in a given dream there is something going on that is extreme, and, if so, what would be its *opposite* extreme in waking consciousness? A beautiful illustration of this approach is found in the following example in which a woman's dream of overindulging in sweets is a compensation for an opposite extreme of crash-dieting and eating no sweets at all. For her physical body, which was used to ingesting some sugar daily, the sudden change was experienced as an extreme, so her body produced an extreme dream. Note, too, Cayce's unusual advice to "Eat more sweets" as a call to practice moderation and find balance.

Q Wednesday morning, November 25, 1925, at home. "I was sitting at a table eating but more than eating—I was packing it in. There was chocolate cake and coconut cake and all kinds of sweets and goodies—I just had a great time eating it all up."
A In this there is presented to the entity, in this emblematical manner and way, the forces that are at work, as it were, in the physical being of the entity . . . For as is seen, the entity rec-

ognizes in this the opposite from that being enacted in the daily life, see? Yet the entity sees that in this constraining of self these detrimental conditions in a fashion, physically, mentally, truly, are being brought to the body those condition that bring detrimental effects. Then eat more sweets, see? Not in excess, in moderation, for with all things let them be done in moderation, in decency and in order . . . Then do it.

136-20

Another example is a dream interpretation Cayce offered to a broker from the New York Stock Exchange. In the dream, the broker acted silly and smart-alecky, which compensated for his lack of humor in dealing with colleagues in waking life. Again, the dream is a call for balance.

Q [I dreamed of] trouble on Exchange. I seemed unconsciously and unmeaningly to have been too gay with Max Bamberger and others. Herbert Son was pleading for me and felt badly and so did I. It seemed to be a case of my being too "Smart Aleckish."

A In this there is presented to the entity, in this emblematical manner, that of a condition which may be considered or treated as diagonal, or in the opposite from conditions. While the entity is considered above the average of men on the Exchange floor, yet there are times, especially with men of the character as are seen, that the entity is too staid, or oldish in manner toward.

137-76

Interpretation Strategy 3.
Fear-induced dreams.

Sigmund Freud pointed out how our unconscious drives can produce dreams. Edgar Cayce added fear to the list. Sometimes, when we are afraid that something might happen, we dream it. The meaning is not that it is a prediction that it is about to happen. Instead, it is an invitation to become more aware of patterns of fear and to recognize how fear is affecting us, directly and indirectly.

In the following examples, Cayce interprets the dreams of a husband and wife concerning having children and their marriage. The first dream, the wife's, happened before she got pregnant: She dreamed she learned she was unable to conceive a child. Cayce's interpretation is that the dream is merely the product of a conscious fear she harbors. In fact, she later did give birth to a son.

In the second example, with the wife now pregnant, the husband dreams of a miscarriage. Cayce's interpretation is that the husband's fear about the pregnancy has produced the dream.

Q-3 Dreamed that I could never have a child—that none would ever come to me—that I would never give birth.

A-3 This again is a mental condition that is being carried through the entity's forces, and presents only that of the mental . . . Hence the lesson that is necessary for the preparations for such a condition—motherhood, the highest service to the Maker . . . This will occur. Child will be born. Necessary that these [preparations] be carried out, however, as pertaining to the law concerning such . . .   136-16

Q-1 Morning of September 20, 1926. Saw [136] start to spot or menstruate—the first sign of a miscarriage. She was surprised and startled. Both of us were disappointed.

A-1 [There] has been some fear, some doubt, as to the full complete understanding. Then, put self in that attitude as is necessary to bring that force as gives the building of all creative energy in the right way and manner. Not an indication that this would happen. Rather the indication of the fear within the entity itself that it would happen, see?

900-269

In the third example, with the same couple, the wife reported: "Dreamed my husband . . . wasn't coming home any more and cried bitterly" (136-9). Is this predictive of the marriage breaking up, or at least of the relationship deteriorating? Quite the contrary: The dream means that the marriage has grown stronger! As the love between the two was deepening, the wife began to have fears (perhaps unconscious) that they might become separated, that greater closeness meant being more vulnerable to separation and therefore loneliness. Fear created the dream.

If the wife had not had Edgar Cayce interpret the dream, she might have asked herself, Does this dream give me an experience of something that I fear? With a minimum of self-analysis, she would have seen this was the case, and her next step would be to replace the fear (through meditation, prayer, counseling, talking with her husband, etc.) with trust and faith. If the dream continued to reoccur, she might more reasonably assume the dream is a warning of impending trouble in the marriage.

Interpretation Strategy 4.
Psychic dreams.

Edgar Cayce encourages us to look for extrasensory perception, or ESP, in our dreams. Sometimes, a predictive dream comes to warn us; other times, it's a telepathic dream meant to give us more information about another person, especially someone we are concerned about in waking life. According to Cayce's psychology, such warnings are commonplace, either in dreams or intuitively when we are awake.

Consider this businessman's pair of dreams (the husband, in fact, mentioned in strategy 3 above). His first dream, described below, is psychic in nature. The key person in the dream is his mother, and Cayce indicates that this reference is literal. The key image in the dream is money, and again Cayce suggests that it, too, is literal.

The businessman's second dream, again below, takes another angle. Here, the key person is the mother and again the reference is literal, but the other images in the dream (for example, snakes) are metaphorical references to things in the dreamer's life. In other words, the psychic quality of the dream while in part literal (the mother standing for herself), in part is also symbolic (the snakes stand for people who intend to take advantage of the businessman in his waking life). Cayce's interpretation is that the dream is a psychic warning *and* psychic advice: Follow the counsel of your mother and she will help you escape those who would take advantage of you.

Q Saturday morning, Jan. 29, or Sunday morning, Jan. 30, 1927. Dreamed I gave a check to my mother for $500, and dated it one day ahead, and some trouble came up about it.

A In this we find that the entity has the forewarning of troubles or conditions that may arise from some transactions as related between self and mother—or, as is seen, in notes, or in checks.

Then the entity should go over such papers in the mind and make the mind of the mother at ease as regarding same, that there be no indications of the entity not taking notice or allowing conditions to pass and not say something regarding same.

Well, too, were such conditions and relations entertained by the entity as respecting all associations with any individuals as regarding such—for, as is seen and indicated by such actions, misunderstandings arise, and conditions come about that bring trouble, worry, consternation, hard feelings, and conditions that are unsavory and not in keeping, or not being consistent. 900-298

Q "Saturday morning in bed at home . . . , Deal, N.J., [My wife], Ma and I were in the woods or field. [My wife] squatted on the ground, when suddenly an old man called to her. As we all looked his way, saw him grinning and pointing to an ugly snake, with outstretched head. Ma, [my wife] and I started to run madly, panic stricken. We leaped to other side of hill. I saw my mother zigzag, advising me to do the same. I started to and turned to also advise [my wife]. She was behind. It seemed we arrived safe."

A Again that injunction to follow in the advice as would be and is given through the mother. As is seen in emblematical condition of snake, those who would harm do so in the underhand manner, and the tact as is given through advice of mother shows the manner in which the subconscious forces gathers that higher condition of those who would protect under whatever condition that may arise. Then the advice and counsel as would be given in this: There has come the time when there should be the close counsel with the mother as regarding conditions that are to arise. 900-81

Interpretation Strategy 5.
Physical body dreams.

One major contribution to Edgar Cayce's dream psychology is somatic dreaming—that is, dreams about the physical body. In particular, he showed how we can receive warnings and advice about health issues from our own unconscious. The following pair of examples are good illustrations, the first a warning about how to avoid catching a cold, the second a warning that the dreamer should not try to get pregnant while her physical health is still so unstable or she risks having a miscarriage (symbolized by a "belly-whapper" dive that hurt). Archival records show that the woman did, in fact, get pregnant soon after that and suffered a miscarriage several months later.

Q I was in Newark as it was years ago when we used to live there, and was riding on a trolley car up close to Clinton Avenue, and lost my raincoat. The trolley car ran over it.

A In this we find that relating to the health of the individual, in an emblematical manner, that entity should use same, then, as a warning, keeping body dry, keeping feet dry, else the cold, the congestion, as comes from same, would prove the detrimental manner as is seen in dream—the loss of garments appears to the entity, see? 137-24

Q Sunday morning, November 29. "I was going into swim from a rickety platform—very unsubstantial in its structure. As I jumped in or tried to dive in, I made a belly whapper—i.e. landed on my stomach—it hurt."

A In this we find there is brought to the conscious mind in an emblematical manner and form, through physical conditions existent in the body, that which may be used as the lesson for the entity, see? For as the pain in the inmost portion of the torso gives rise to the emblematical condition presented, the entering the water, the desire to swim, to dive, the entering into those conditions as regard to motherhood—and as the body finds self in the attitude ready for that, the physical conditions or structure in which the body has kept self is not prepared in the manner as would bring the better conditions for the condition of that office at this time, see? and as this will soon occur, the body should take cognizance and be more sure of that position by and in self for this greatest of offices given to the sex—woman.   136-21

SUMMARY
of Edgar Cayce's Spiritual Psychology
* *

Some of Edgar Cayce's most essential teachings come from his role as a spiritual counselor and adviser. Although it might seem misleading to call him a psychologist because he lacked any professional training credentials, there nevertheless *is* a sophisticated model of the human mind and personality woven throughout his readings. Unlike some popular self-help psychologies that promise a quick fix, Cayce's approach to the soul and spirit demands that each individual take responsibility for his or her own life. Often, the circumstances in which we find ourselves are of our own making, sometimes even stretching back to previous lifetimes. Cayce's basic premise was that there are two sides to ourselves: personality (the familiar identity, our own sense of who we are) and individuality (the authentic self, the soul). Healthy living requires that we learn to forge a deeper connection to our individuality, and the process begins by paying attention to our purposes, intentions, and ideals. Two disciplines support his work: meditation, a process that according to Cayce is the complement of prayer, a receptive activity that is, in effect, "listening to the divine within"; and self-analysis through dream interpretation, which emphasizes that each one of us is our own best interpreter of our own dreams. Edgar Cayce's clairvoyant dream interpretations demonstrate specific techniques that any of us can learn to interpret dreams for a greater understanding of ourselves and how we can guide our soul's progress.

CHAPTER THREE

HEALTHY LIVING

❖

H EALTH IS A BROAD TOPIC; IT IS ABOUT FAR MORE THAN JUST a healthy body. Edgar Cayce's holistic philosophy always emphasizes *total health*—the well-being of our bodies, minds, souls, *and* our relationships with others.

In this chapter, we explore the essential principles of integrated, healthy living; issues related to healing and specific treatment remedies will be addressed in chapter 4, "Holistic Healing." Here, we start with the basics of a healthy lifestyle, and in that regard the first reading offers a succinct, powerful road map to balanced living, outlined in distinct steps, most of which are attitudinal in nature. By establishing the right mental orientation in life, we set the stage for healthy expression at every level of our experience.

Next, we examine how we stay physically fit. Cayce's discourses on healthy living offer a wide range of suggestions, and, in fact, his contributions about *staying healthy* may be more significant ultimately than his unorthodox natural healing methods. While virtually all of us can benefit from solid advice about maintaining health, most of us may find Cayce's readings about specific ailments interesting but irrelevant. The second reading, on fitness, originally for his son Hugh Lynn, is very relevant, and it contains wonderful advice for us all.

Finally, without addressing love relationships, we don't get a full picture of Cayce's essential principles for healthy living. A healthy body, mind, and soul make us better able to express love and creativity in our friendships, families, and work relationships. The third reading deals specifically with the elements that make for a healthy marriage. Although times have changed considerably in the decades since this discourse was given, the advice is valuable today.

A PATTERN FOR LIVING

A healthy life is not a random blessing but instead the result of living by certain universal principles. The first reading, 1747-5, given for a thirty-seven-year-old factory worker during World War II, beautifully describes a pattern for living that can help anyone meet the challenges of life. When there are disagreements, disappointments, or times of sickness, the real challenge is how we *respond*. If we meet these inevitable challenges in the right way, a healthy life is possible; otherwise, we fall into illness and *dis-ease*. The reading outlines the kind of response that fosters health and growth of the soul, and, ultimately, the resolutions of the problem.

Edgar Cayce's opening statements set the tone. An individual's beliefs and attitudes are the starting point for healthy living. It's counterproductive to focus on any problem prematurely—that is, without an accurate understanding of the big picture. To attain such a solid spiritual foundation, some *sorting out* is required. You must be able and willing to predict where various assumptions and beliefs can lead. One has to "determine or choose within self that as may be adhered to," as Cayce puts it here. One has to make decisions about core values and beliefs.

It's easy to imagine Edgar Cayce giving any one of us this reading. His words suggest a way to get at the big picture, the spiritual context of our lives here on earth. Then he goes into more specific detail about the optimal way to meet any challenge. There are five essential elements to this approach:

Set ideals. Very carefully select the values, priorities, and motives according to which you wish to chart your life's path. Cayce suggests starting with a spiritual ideal—that is, a core value that becomes the prime motivator in your life; examples include *love, joyful creativity,* and *oneness with God.* Then, to make that ideal more accessible, set some mental and physical ideals—something you can sink your teeth into and work with in a concrete way. Mental ideals are the optimal *attitudes* and *emotions* that help you express your spiritual ideal—for example, *optimism* or *forgiveness.* Physical ideals are the *actions* that are the manifestation of your spiritual ideal—for example, *twenty minutes of meditation daily* or *remember to smile more often.* (For more about ideals, see the seventh point in "Cayce's dozen" in the introduction.)

Apply what you believe. Act on your own values. Even though a solid mental and spiritual foundation is the basis of the pattern, it's not enough. If you stay in the mental realm exclusively, a given difficulty is not likely to be resolved. Admittedly, the mind is the creative faculty that instigates change, but unless you *do* what's required of you how can anything be healed? As Edgar Cayce says here, ". . . for the holding of a problem does not change it one whit—it is what one does about it that makes the change!" Furthermore, the very definition of *sin* points to an absence of action. This elusive, controversial term gets a new twist with Cayce: Ultimately, our spiritual progress is evaluated simply on how well we act on what we know.

Patience is the key. Patience is not only the keystone to Edgar Cayce's metaphysical description of life, it's also *the* essential characteristic that needs to be developed in all of us. In Cayce's scheme of an orderly universe, humans live in a three-dimensional state of consciousness: *Time* and *space,* two of the dimensions, are complemented by *patience,* allowing us to effectively meet the demands, paradoxes, and limitations imposed by time and space.

The trick is understanding what patience as a dimension of living really means. We come to the word *patience* with our own preconceptions and misunderstandings, but as this reading cautions: "Patience, here, may be the answer—if there is the correct concept of what the proper interpretation of patience is."

For Cayce, patience is considerably more than putting up with delays or tolerating obnoxious behavior. Instead, it is a matter of *seeing clearly,* recognizing the spiritual reality penetrating physical reality. Patience allows us to *understand the purposefulness* behind what's going on in time and space. But when misguided people with materialistic views try to influence us, they keep us from this purposefulness—they create "the pit that separateth the soul from that patience."

Accept responsibility to each other. A healthy response for meeting any problem has a social dimension. The key here is responsibility *to* each other rather than *for* each other. Nobody can change anybody else; no soul can bear the blame for another soul's error. However, each of us has a specific responsibility to others: To see in every person the qualities that we worship in our Maker. Unless we take on that effort, we have "not begun to have the proper concept of universal consciousness."

What's more, this social dimension has another feature. Because we serve as examples to those around us, people notice what we say and do, especially how we react to problems. The human tendency to imitate can be used to great advantage here because we have the power to inspire and lift others up by our example. "So live that thy friend, thy foe, thy neighbor, may also—through patterning his expressions after thee—find the way."

Expect a responsive God. Edgar Cayce reminds us of "the greater promise from the foundation of the world." God hears our requests for help when times are difficult, and a response is speedily forthcoming—we should expect it and count on it.

Finally, Cayce's advice to the factory worker reassured her of the benefits to be had by living in a healthy way. To live according to these five points, especially when life is troubling, awakens in us "that peace which each soul seeks, and brings with same healing." Our modern world, decades after this reading was given, has its own stresses and turmoil, but the pattern for living—the road map—equips us to find the health we seek.

THE READING

❖

THIS PSYCHIC READING, 1747-5,
WAS GIVEN BY EDGAR CAYCE ON JUNE 20, 1942.
The conductor was Gertrude Cayce.

GC: You will have before you the entity, [1747] . . . Ohio, who seeks a mental and spiritual reading, with information, advice and guidance that will clear the field for her regarding her stand on many things. You will give the entity that needed at this time, answering any questions that may be asked:

EC: Yes, we have the body, the inquiring mind, [1747].

In giving for this entity a mental and spiritual interpretation of the problems as disturb the body in the present, many phases of those held as tenets or beliefs should be touched upon. But first we would give for the entity that which is the basis for this entity approaching the study of phenomena of every nature that has been and is a part of the experience in the present.

And from same there may be determined that which is not merely idealistic but that as may be a practical, ideal manner of application of the physical relationships with individuals of various degrees of development—of those mental attitudes which should be held in the study of the entity, in the interpreting for individuals of those problems and disturbances which arise in their experience.

Also there may be understood the spiritual and the ideal manner in which the entity may determine or choose within self that as may be adhered to, that as may be questioned, and that as may be discarded in the experience of the entity.

First—there is the consciousness to the body of there being

a physical body, a mental body, and the hope or desire for and the knowledge of a spiritual body. These are one—just as the entity finds in the material plane, or the earth-consciousness, that it is of three-dimensional natures. Also, in the analysis of the various studies and approaches to the mental as well as spiritual understanding, the entity finds that there are three phases of man's relationship or man's comprehension. Hence in the earth there is, in reason, only the three-dimensional attitude. Yet there are the experiences of the entity, as well as of others, of more than three-dimensional concepts.

In the Godhead there is found still the three-dimensional concept—God the Father, God the Son, and God the Holy Spirit.

Hence—if this is acceptable to the entity in its conception of that which has been, which is, which may be—these are still founded in that summed up in "The Lord thy God is One."

Also, in the interpretation of the universe, we find that time and space are concepts of the mental mind, as to an interpretation of or a study into the relationships with man and to the universal or God-consciousness.

Then, there must be another phase in human experience that man also may complete this triune in his study of the mental, the spiritual and the material relationships in this material world.

Patience, here, may be the answer—if there is the correct concept of what the proper interpretation of patience is in the experience of this entity.

Hence these being chosen, they are—then—the basis upon which the reason, the expectation, the application, shall be in dealing with all phases of the experience of the entity in this material relationship.

As is understood, then—Father-God is as the body, or the whole. Mind is as the Christ, which is the way. The Holy Spirit is as the soul, or—in material interpretation—purposes, hopes, desires.

Then, each phase of these has its part to play, its part of influence upon the individual in its relationships to problems, to individuals, to its hopes and fears. For, each has its phase of expression in the activities of the entity.

Hence, as we find, these are then not merely ideals, but they are working, practical, everyday experiences.

Then, as the individual entity meets various problems—with this analysis of the problem—there is the questioning within self as to whether it is purely mental, purely the physical seeking expression, or the desire of the body-fears, the body-temptations, the body's glory, merely the body's satisfaction, or as to whether the problems are purely of the mental. The mind is the builder, for the holding of a problem does not change it one whit—it is what one does about it that makes the change!

Then, to know to do good and not to do it is sin. To know the truth and not give expression is faultfinding in self. Yet know, until an individual entity—in time or space, or in acquaintance-ship or in the friendship of an individual—sees in every other entity that he would worship in his Maker, he has not begun to have the proper concept of universal consciousness.

For, the very fact of an individual having a physical consciousness, no matter his state or status in the material plane, is an indication of the awareness that God is mindful of that soul, by giving it an opportunity to express in the material plane.

And thou art thy brother's keeper. Not that ye should impose or impel another entity by thine own ideas, any more than God impels thee. For, He hath given thee the free will, the birthright; which is as the mind, that makes for the alterations. Hence ye may give expression even as He did, who came into the earth that we through Him might have eternal life.

Then, what is thy attitude?

So live that thy friend, thy foe, thy neighbor, may also—through patterning his expressions after thee—find the way to that mercy which is manifested in Him, who gave "I stand at the door and knock—by thy biddings I will enter—by thy rejection I will leave—I hold no grudge."

This requires that expression then, in time and space, of that patience of which He spoke, "In patience become ye aware of your souls."

This, then, is the attitude that ye shall assume. Give that as is asked of thee in the interpreting of the problems; no more, no less. But ever be ready, as He, to enter, to help, to give when asked, when sought. For, as He hath given, which is the greater promise from the foundation of the world, "If ye call, I will hear, and answer speedily—though ye be far away, I will hear—I will answer."

That is the attitude that the self shall hold towards those problems where there are disputes, discouragings, disappointments. Yea, they oft arise in the experience of all. But think, O Child, how oft thou must have disappointed thy Maker, when He hath given thee the opportunity and calls, "The day of the Lord is at hand," to all of those who will hear His voice.

Put ye on, then, the whole armor of God, the breastplate of righteousness, the sword of the spirit of truth. *Know* in *Whom* ye have believed, as well as in what ye believe. *Live* each day in such a manner as to indicate to everyone ye meet that thou hast an answer for the faith that prompts thee to act in this or that manner.

Be not discouraged because the way seems hard at times. Know that He heareth thee. For as He hath given, "If ye will keep my law—" And what is His law? It is to love the Lord, to eschew evil—which is the whole duty of man—love thy neighbor as thyself.

This brings into the consciousness that peace which each soul seeks, and brings with same healing—not only of body but of mind, and keeps the attunement with the spirit of truth.

Know, too, that His spirit—God's spirit, the Father in the Christ, through the Holy Spirit—beareth witness with thy spirit. And though there comes periods when there are the temptations from all manners of sources, *hear not* those that deny that He hath come in the flesh. Listen to those that bespeak of the cross as the way. Harken not in any manner to those who deny the cross or the cup of bitterness in death.

These be the channels, these be the ways that the blind leading the blind, both fall into the pit that separateth the soul from that patience, that of Abraham's bosom. "By faith are ye healed, not of thyself—it is the gift of God."

Let love be abroad, in thy mind, in thy understanding. For the Lord hath looked on thee and loved thee, and hath shown thee the way. Harken to His voice, "Be not afraid—it is I that would speak to thee and thy heart."

Love the Lord. Love His ways. Be patient, be understanding, and He will bring it to pass in thy consciousness of His walking and talking with thee.

Ready for questions.

Let thy prayer oft be:

Lord, I am Thine. Use me as Thou seest fit—that I may be the greater channel of blessings to those that Thou would, through my effort, bring to Thy understanding. I seek only in the name of the Christ.

We are through.

✢

PHYSICAL FITNESS

• •

This reading, 341-31, one of Edgar Cayce's best, spotlights the universal principles of good health, of which *balance* is key. While the concept of balance sounds simple enough, you need to work to maintain balance in your life so that no part of you gets shortchanged. Understanding balance superficially may tempt you to neatly compartmentalize your life into periods of time that allow you to devote attention to each aspect of your life one by one. But the reading goes deeper than that and shows how the physical, mental, and spiritual interrelate. Their mutual interdependency is the essence of Cayce's message.

Reading 341-31, in fact, seems to emphasize *not* compartmentalization but discovering how the many aspects of life hang together. For example, consider this admonition found in the reading: "Know how to apply the rules of *metaphysical* operations to a corncob." There's really only one universe, in other words, not a metaphysical realm separate from a physical realm. What works in one dimension should work in others as well, and rules governing the mental have counterparts in the physical and the spiritual. What works on a grand scale should work on a less grand scale the same way. As Edgar Cayce puts it in the reading, ". . . each cell . . . each corpuscle, is a whole *universe* in itself." And consider the way human anatomy can depict a psychological truth symbolically: Blood passes through the liver twice for every time it passes through the heart, just as we should "think twice before [we] speak once."

True balance, then, requires sensitivity to *interrelationships*, not a checklist of all the good deeds we can squeeze into a day. Unfortunately, a checklist is how some people try to achieve health; and yet, for all their hectic efforts, they often undermine their own physical well-being.

Cayce's version of what happens to food when it's eaten and then digested is an excellent illustration of his philosophy of health. Physical conditions beyond the digestive organs play an important role, and his son Hugh Lynn, the recipient of the reading, was told to make sure both his physical body and his mind were exercised sufficiently, even when "tired," so that his whole being would respond properly to his diet.

Later, Cayce encouraged Hugh Lynn to try a visualization exercise while he ate—"That thou eatest, *see* it *doing* that *thou* would *have* it do"—a clear illustration of mind-body interaction. In fact, this simple exercise is one of the best ways to verify Cayce's approach of using the mental to enhance the physical.

Even more dramatic, though, is his reference to the placebo effect: "Give one a dose of clear *water,* with the impression that it will act as salts." The impact of mental expectation on the physical body vividly demonstrates the mind-body connection. Edgar Cayce was ahead of his time in pointing out how significant this phenomenon really is.

Also in this reading, Cayce refers to Daniel in the Bible, explaining how food can stimulate states of consciousness. By self-observation, we may have already seen hints of this relationship between body and mind. An area ripe for research, preliminary findings regarding nutrition and mental illness suggest that certain foods, such as sugar and white flour may aggravate mental disorders.

What also makes reading 341-31 special is its *spiritual* component. While many medical researchers today recognize the link between body and mind, spiritual needs must be included as well. We must to have a purpose in life, and to achieve that purpose means appreciating our bodies as gifts from God, as vehicles by which we can serve the divine plan. Engaging the spiritual in a balanced lifestyle also means looking for the spirit living among us, expecting to see God in the midst of the material world, "in the wind, the sun, the earth, the flowers, the inhabitants *of* the earth."

Surely, the principles of Edgar Cayce are right on the cutting edge of today's philosophy of health. But as encouraging as new developments may be, he calls us to an even greater vision.

THE READING

❖

THIS PSYCHIC READING, 341-31,
WAS GIVEN BY EDGAR CAYCE ON MARCH 10, 1931.
The conductor was Gertrude Cayce.

[The first few paragraphs contained specific physical advice rather than general guidelines, and they have been omitted here.]

EC: . . . It would be well for the body to so conduct, so arrange the activities of the body as to be better *balanced* as to the mental and the physical attributes of the body. Take more outdoor exercise, that—that brings into play the muscular forces of the body. It isn't that the mental should be numbed, or should be cut off from their operations or their activities—but make for a more evenly, more perfectly balanced body-physical *and* mental. Know how to apply the rules of *metaphysical* operations to a corncob, or to a fence rail, or to a hammer, an axe, a walking cane, as well as the *theories* of this, that, or other mind, that in nine cases in ten is seen to become a storehouse for mental deficiencies of *physical* energies! Now get the difference! It is not mental unbalance, but a mental body may be so *overused* as to allow physical energies to become *detrimental* forces *in a physical body*; for each energy *must* expend itself in *some* direction, even as a thought that takes form brings in to being a mental image. Is that image in the position of being a *building* force cooperative with the energies of the physical body? Or do they *destroy* some motive force in the physical without allowing an outlet for its activity?

Then, be a well-*rounded* body. Take specific, *definite* exercises morning and evening. Make the body *physically*, as well as mentally, tired and those things that have been producing those conditions where sleep, inertia, poisons in system from non-eliminations, will disappear—and so will the body respond to the diets.

Now, in the matter of diets—*one* activity is necessary, if there is to be a mental diet—or if there is to be a diet for a well-rounded *physically* useful, *mentally* useful, *spiritually* useful body. But there is the lack of vitamins as B and C, in this body. One, the C, stamina for mental energies that are carried in the white tissue in nerve energy and plexus. B, as is of calcium, of silicon, of iron. These would be well-balanced, will those of the food values that carry same be taken, but *unless* the activities physical for the body are such as to put same into *activity* they become drosses and set *themselves* to become operative, irrespective of *other* conditions. (This as aside, but as very well in keeping with the circumstances or conditions.) Vitamins in a body are elements that are combative with, or in opposition to, the various activities of a living organism, and may be termed—and well termed—as those of bacilli of any nature within a human or physical organism. That's what we are talking of, or dealing with in this body.

Now, when these are taken into the system, if they are *not* put to work by the *activities* of the *system*—either physical or mental—

they become *destructive* tissue, for they *affect* the plasm [plasma] of the blood supply or the emunctory and lymph which is another name for a portion of a blood supply in a system.

Then, in the meeting of the diet—be sure the activities, physically, and mentally, are in keeping with; and *do not do* these *spasmodically,* but *be* consistent—for the physical body, the mental body, the spiritual body, is as "Grow in grace, in knowledge, in understanding."

That thou eatest, *see* it *doing* that *thou* would *have* it do. Now there is often considered as to why do those of either the vegetable, mineral, or combination compounds, have different effects under different conditions? It is the *consciousness* of the *individual body!* Give one a dose of clear *water,* with the impression that it will act as salts—how often will it act in that manner?

Just as the impressions to the whole of the organism, for each cell of the bloodstream, each corpuscle, is a whole *universe* in itself. Do not eat like a canary and expect to do *manual* labor. Do not eat like a rail splitter and expect to do the work of a mind reader or a university professor, but be *consistent* with those things that make for—even as the *universe* is builded. In the layers of one is dependent upon the activity of another. One that fills the mind, the very being, with an expectancy of God will see His movement, His manifestation, in the wind, the sun, the earth, the flowers, the inhabitant(s) *of* the earth; and so as is builded in the body, is it to gratify *just* an appetite, or is it taken to fulfill an office that *will* the better make, the better magnify, that the body, the mind, the soul, *has* chosen to stand *for?* and it will not matter so much what, where, or *when*—but knowing *that* it is consistent with that—that is desired to be accomplished *through* that body!

As has been given of old, when the children of Israel stood with the sons of the heathen and all ate from the king's table, that which was taken that only exercised the imagination of the body in physical desires—as strong drink, strong meats, condiments that magnify desires within the body—this builded as Daniel well understood, not for *God's* service—but he chose rather that the *everyday,* the common things would be given, that the bodies, the minds, might be a more perfect channel for the manifestations of *God*; for the forces of the Creator are in *every* force that is made manifest *in* the earth.

Few are able, even as the prophet of old, to see God in battle, in the shedding of blood, in the thunder, in the lightning, in the earthquake, in the various tumults in nature—but *all* may experience Him in the still small voice within! Do *thou* likewise, and the body is the temple *of* the living God, and is a *reasonable* service that we present same holy and acceptable unto Him.

Just as great a sin to *over* eat as to over drink; to over *think* as to over act! *In* that thou buildest, do even as He. Make thine body, thine *mind,* ready for *every* occasion that arises in the life. Think well on what was given, "*Why* could not *we* cast him out? Such is done only—*only*—through fasting and prayer." When thou prayest, enter into thine closet—that is, within self—not shutting oneself away from the world, but closing self to God's *presence,* and pray in secret and the reward will be in the open; for, as was given, "Men do not light a candle and put it under a bushel, but it is set—*set*—on a hill, that it may give *life,* light, unto all."

So, in conducting thine own life—make the physical corrections necessary, yes—but make also thy mind and thine body, thine going in and thine coming out, thine activities day by day, consistent *with*—and the reward will be—an exemplary life, a *goodly* body, an *open* mind, a *loving* spirit!

Few may show forth that even felt in the heart with the liver bad, for twice does the blood pass through the liver to once in the heart. The liver is the clearinghouse both for that of the blood in and out of the heart and lungs. So in the conduct of the life, in the study, think twice before you speak once—for there's only *one* tongue but two eyes. There is only *one* heart but seven lobes in the liver; and in thine hands—use that thou hast, and thine eye will be *single* in service, thine tongue will be loosed in the right direction.

THE WORKSHOP OF MARRIAGE

• •

One of Edgar Cayce's finest readings on marriage was given to a young woman about to be wed. It may be tempting to discount the advice here simply because it was directed at a couple who were years—if not decades—away from a truly deep and mature loving relationship. Yet the fresh innocence of their new love allowed a visionary like Cayce to step back and see the potential of marriage as an ideal. Most partners who came to him asking for advice were already wounded by marital strife.

In the reading, 480-20, Cayce emphasizes how marriage partners are *complements;* a weakness in one, for instance, is likely to be counterbalanced by a strength in the other. The woman is described by him as having strong *leadership* tendencies, the implication being that her husband is weak in that area. Seen from one perspective, this type of filling in the holes for the other partner can work out well; but it also can create challenges in the marriage that must be met creatively, and with considerable self-awareness, or otherwise such a strength-weakness pairing can undermine the relationship. So while Cayce warns the woman not to let her natural strength as a leader overshadow, or even overwhelm, her husband's efforts to develop leadership qualities in himself, Cayce also warns her not to abandon her own skills and allow herself to become subservient to her husband. And while a delicate balance is required for both the partners *and* the relationship to flower, the psychology of coupling sometimes leads to just such a paradoxical, uneven pairing. For example, one partner may excel at something and so it's easy for the other partner to feel that he or she could never be as good at it, so "Why bother?" Maybe it's financial planning, or sociability, or playfulness. But when one partner ends up *carrying* responsibilities for both partners alone, the result can be resentment on the part of *both* partners.

Cayce as marriage counselor picks up on another key issue for healthy husband-and-wife dynamics: Loving relationships are especially vulnerable to *perceived* negligence. The person we love most deeply is usually the one who can hurt us most deeply, particularly if we feel unappreciated or invalidated by that person. Often unintended, such negligence can become a major "stumbling block," as Cayce puts it, to the marriage. Open, honest communication is the key.

Cayce also emphasizes the importance of taking an interest in the activities of your partner "as though they were a part and parcel and portion of yourself." But, once again, a delicate balance is needed because each partner needs a sense of *autonomy*. Few marriages could thrive if the partners did everything together; there needs to be room for individuality. The key here is *valuing* your partner's interests, and that kind of support goes a long way toward building a healthy marriage.

Halfway through the reading, Edgar Cayce hones in on two factors that can determine whether a marriage will be healthy—"an effectual, helpful experience in life," as he describes it. First, there needs to be an element of the *sacred* in the relationship. *Sacred* is such a powerful word, with connotations of calling up spiritual forces; but, in effect, that is just exactly what we do. Second, we need to avoid *self-indulgence*; put another way, we need to avoid *willfulness*, a need to get what we want without regard for what the other person wants. Such willfulness, such self-indulgence, can sabotage any sacredness in the marriage.

There is considerable detail in the reading about *the home* as well. In fact, we might say that Edgar Cayce places as much stock in the creation of a loving home as he does in the creation of a loving relationship. This emphasis may sound a bit old-fashioned to us today, in our era of broken homes and magazine covers touting the latest remedy for *fixing* a relationship. But to Cayce, the home was a big deal, and perhaps it's worth closer scrutiny on our part as we ponder how to heal the troubled society we live in. Not only is the home a haven for the couple, it's also where others can experience the loving *vibrations* generated by the couple. It serves as a haven for family, friends, even strangers. It's a "garden of beauty" that blesses many.

A final bit of advice comes just before the question-and-answer exchange at the end of the reading, and it neatly summarizes Cayce's philosophy of how to create a healthy marriage: *Be joyous*. There will be problems in a marriage, naturally, but never forget the power of living joyfully. And when problems come, turn inward, and for this reason alone both partners need an active inner life. By having a clear, strong connection to the spirit inside ourselves, we are able to have a clear, strong connection with our partner.

THE READING

❖

THIS PSYCHIC READING, 480-20,
WAS GIVEN BY EDGAR CAYCE ON JULY 22, 1935.
The conductor was Gertrude Cayce.

GC: Entity, [480]. Considering her past and present development, together with opportunities in this present life, you will advise her regarding her adjustment to the new life before her. You will answer the questions that may be asked regarding her coming marriage and information given in her life reading through these sources.

EC: Yes, we have the entity known as or called in the present [480], and the information that has been given through these channels respecting the physical, the mental and the attributes necessary for change in the spiritual or soul development.

In the approach, then, to those changes that are eminent in the mind of this entity in the present, well that all these conditions be taken into consideration; remembering ever as this:

Only counsel may be given, only those conditions that are as ideal without being idealistic, those conditions that are as necessary influences without there being other than the choice of the entity in making for the application of same in the experience.

For as the ways are chosen before thee, you each may find in the new associations and relations the ability to make the best conditions, the surroundings, the experiences that will bring into the experience of each that which will be the most helpful in the soul and development mentally of each; provided the adjustments are made in those directions, with the thought of that necessary in the experience of each to make for such.

As indicated, these will find that they are a complement one to another in a great many ways.

The natural tendency of the entity, [480], is to be the leader, the impelling influence. Do not let this, then, overshadow the abilities or the activities of the mate in *any* way or manner. This does not mean to become, from the mental or the material side, as subservient to his ideas; but let each give and take, knowing that this is to be a fifty-fifty proposition, with you each supplying that which is best within yourselves.

When the necessities are such as to require waiting and patience even, in those things that may at the time appear to be as negligence on the part of the one or the other, do not rail at such times or allow those things to become stumbling blocks; but always *reason* well together.

In those things that pertain to the social life, be considerate one of the other. *Know* that there is the necessity of you each being as interested in the activities of the other as though they were a part and parcel and portion of yourselves. Not in a *demanding* attitude, but you each living your own life, each having your own interests, each having your own responsibilities; and each supplying those necessary influences or forces in each association as to make for a harmonious cooperative activity in such social activities as may be had in every phase of the experience.

Let each budget the time. Let each give so much to the recreation for the body, for the mind, for the social activities, for the necessary activities for the supplying of the needs in their varied relationships. And be *cooperative* one with another in such things.

Let also there be time for the recuperative forces necessary in the experience, those that may be added as elements in the entertainment, the necessary forces for the adding to the *effects* of the abilities in all phases of human experience as correlated to the coordinating of the lives one with another.

The marital relationships, as we have indicated, will become an effectual, helpful experience in the life of the entity; as also in the life of the mate, if the coordinations of their activities in such relationships are made as to be sacred in their notions, their ideas, their activities being not for self-indulgences but as a union of that necessary for the creative forces and influences in the experiences of the life of each, as to bring the crowning influence to the experience of each.

In the establishing of the home, make it as that which may be the pattern of a heavenly home. Not as that set aside for only a place to sleep or to rest, but where not only self but all who enter there may feel, may experience, by the very vibrations that are set up by each in the sacredness of the home, a helpfulness, a *hopefulness* in the air *about* the home. As not only a place of rest, not only a place of recreation for the mind, not only a place as a haven for the bodies and minds of both but for all that may be as visitors or as guests. And remember those injunctions that have been in thine experience in many of thine sojourns, and be thou mindful of the entertaining of the guests; for some have entertained angels unawares. Make thine home, thine abode, where an angel would *desire* to visit, where an angel would seek to be a guest. For it will bring the greater blessings, the greater glories, the greater contentment, the greater satisfaction; the glorious harmony of adjusting thyself and thy relationships one with another in making same ever harmonious. Do not begin with, "We will do it tomorrow—we will begin next week—we will make for such next year." Let that thou sowest in thy relationships day by day be the seeds of truth, of hope, that as they grow to fruition in thy relationships, as the days and the months and the years that are to come go by, they will grow into that garden of beauty that makes indeed for the home.

In *every* association, whether one with another in thy relationships or with thy own friends, or with the strangers that enter, let thy activities be such that there may come more and more of that which is *directed* by the spirit of *hopefulness, helpfulness,* in thy attitudes one to another.

And as these grow to the harvest in life, the *Lord* may give the increase.

If ye have builded such that hate, envy, malice, jealousy are the fruits of same, these can only bring dissension and strife and hardships. But if the seeds of truth and life are sown, then the fruition—as the life goes on together—will be in harmony. And He, the Father, being thy guide in all will bless thee, even as He has promised from the beginning. For in the fruit of thy bodies may many be blessed, if ye will but seek that *through* the union of thy purposes, of thy desires, with their import in things spiritual, such may come to pass.

Not that the life is to be made long-faced, that no joy is to enter in! *Rather* be ye *joyous* in thy *living,* in thine association, in thy activities, ever. For joy and happiness *beget* joy and happiness; unless the import be of a *selfish* nature.

But when doubts and fears and troubles arise (as they must, as they will in the experience of all), come ye rather together before the throne of grace and mercy, as may be found in the meditation before the Lord. Take thine troubles to Him, not to thy fellow man! For *He* is merciful when *man* may be unkind, jealous, hard-hearted, set, determined. But let thy yeas be yea in the Lord; let thy nays be nay in the Lord.

And in adjusting thyself in these ways and manners ye may bring to thine experience the greater glory of the Father in the earth.

Ready for questions.

Q In what former incarnation did I know [633]?
A These will be given in their proper order.
Q What is our greatest purpose together in this life?
A Harmony!
Q How may I express and live up to the highest ideals in marriage?
A As has been indicated.
Q As my life reading [480-1] gave that I might attain to the best in this experience through music or the play, how may I co-ordinate same with marriage and express the highest in both?

A For in the home is the music of what? As indicated, it is an emblem of the heavenly home. And as these are made into the harmonious experiences that may come in the associations, they may bring indeed the music of the spheres in the activities as one with another, and those that must be contacted in the highest of man's achievement in the earth—the *home!*

We are through for the present.

❖

A SUMMARY
of Edgar Cayce's Approach to Healthy Living

While some of the most remarkable Cayce readings about the physical body involves cures for serious illnesses, his greatest contribution may well have been in helping people to *stay* healthy. Maintaining health requires the careful, consistent application of certain fundamental principles, among them the need for balance, and an awareness of the creative power of our attitudes and emotions in shaping the condition of our physical bodies. But healthy living also means having positive, supportive, loving relationships with other people. And the key to such relationships is to first have a strong relationship with the spiritual forces within ourselves.

CHAPTER FOUR

HOLISTIC HEALING

❖

ALTHOUGH EDGAR CAYCE IS WELL KNOWN FOR SOME OF HIS unorthodox remedies for treating various ailments, we cannot understand his approach to holistic healing in a cookbook fashion. Not only are there individual differences from person to person; there is also the crucial need to treat the attitudes, motivations, and emotions of the patient.

To understand Cayce's holistic healing, let's examine his underlying principles about healing and the integration of body, mind, and spirit. When we understand those principles, then his suggestions for treatment are much more likely to be effective. The first reading in this chapter, 1120-2, is typical of the many thousands of readings Cayce gave in spelling out how the various systems of the body coordinate and how they can be brought into better alignment with each other.

The second reading, 1189-2, looks at psychosomatic illness and health—that is, the interplay of body, mind, and spirit to create our physical condition. The recipient suffered from chronic fatigue, and Cayce gave an especially eloquent discourse on how the various aspects of ourselves interact to influence health.

Next is a series of excerpts from a wide variety of readings—a "sampler" of sorts. Although Edgar Cayce gave readings on hundreds of different ailments, the *essential* scope of this book allows us just a glance at his work. The excerpts demonstrate how he approached four everyday ailments: the common cold, headache, indigestion, and sinusitis. As a bonus, a lengthy excerpt about rejuvenation is included because of Cayce's optimistic outlook about the body's potential for longevity.

COORDINATING BODY SYSTEMS

•   •

Most people interested in Edgar Cayce's work probably have never read one of the health readings in its entirety. Our knowledge of his pioneering vision of the body is based almost entirely on excerpts or books written by experts *about* the material. But there's much to be gained by carefully studying a complete reading.

Each reading, of course, was geared to the particular needs of the recipient; each focused on a specific malady and recommended treatment tailored to the individual. But despite the fact that each health reading was customized, reading 1120-2 contains useful information for nearly all of us. It's an example of Cayce the health adviser at his best. This reading's universal value lies in the fact that the twenty-nine-year-old man's symptoms resemble those so many people suffer in today's stressful world, and that it demonstrates so clearly Cayce's model for how the body works.

The man, who received a first reading some months earlier, now was requesting additional advice because of chronic fatigue and periodic headaches. (Cayce saw clairvoyantly that the symptoms all traced back to imbalances in the man's second and third dorsal, or thoracic, vertebrae, just a few inches below the base of the neck.) Getting such a reading from a psychic was, no doubt, an unconventional and controversial move, and Cayce even warns that his theories will likely be disputed, presumably by the man's regular doctor.

The reading begins with a rather positive picture: The man is in generally good health. However, his bothersome symptoms, if left uncorrected, later could develop into much more serious problems. The very structure of the reading reveals a key element in Cayce's model of how the body works when he addresses the status of three principal systems:

The circulatory system (or "blood supply"). When the circulation of the blood is hindered, it affects the body's capacity to assimilate both oxygen and nutrients. What's more, the circulatory system (including the lymph system) must be working effectively for the body to properly rid itself of waste products. (Cayce often used the word *emunctory*, which means "waste removal.")

The nervous system (or the "nerve forces"). There are two primary subsystems involved: the *cerebrospinal*, which includes large portions of the brain, spinal cord, and nerves connected to the spinal cord, and which make both sensory awareness and voluntary control of the muscles possible; and the *autonomic nervous system*, which, although it has control centers located in the brain, generally operates outside of conscious awareness. The autonomic system, in turn, has two subsystems: the *sympathetic*, which largely relates to the activation of internal organs; and the *parasympathetic*, which is more concerned with the quieting and regenerative processes in the body.

In the readings, Cayce was concerned especially with the

junction points where the cerebrospinal and sympathetic interact—the *ganglia* alongside the vertebrae of the spinal column. When there is misalignment, or *subluxation,* of these vertebrae, the resulting imbalance between the two systems can produce a wide variety of problems for the internal organs. The reading presents a succinct primer on the topic, and it shows why Cayce so often recommended osteopathy or chiropractic adjustments.

The array of internal organs. Edgar Cayce usually hones in on just a few organs that are related to the disturbance especially. Surprisingly, in some health readings the organs mentioned seemingly have nothing to do with the problem at hand since no pain or discomfort has been experienced there; for example, the liver and kidneys are mentioned in a high percentage of the readings.

Anyone studying Cayce's material likely will find that it's not so easy to get through the descriptions and diagnoses for these three systems. But don't be dismayed if you don't entirely understand what Cayce is saying; instead, look for key themes. One of them certainly is the *interconnectedness* of the systems, which is becoming accepted more widely in medical circles today, overshadowing a long-standing tradition that the body's systems operate independently. Now we have the new field of *psychoneuroimmunology,* demonstrating that the mind, nervous system, and immune system are directly linked.

Another key theme in Edgar Cayce's health model is that many ailments are a *reflex*—that is, a reaction to something that's out of balance elsewhere in the body. Notice, for example, how Mr. 1120's digestive problem are described as a reflex instead of a problem with the organs themselves.

Even without the same symptoms, there is solid advice to us all in this reading about maintaining balance overall to promote health. Furthermore, we see clearly how Cayce understood the body, and we see the type of strategy he used to treat it.

THE READING

✣

THIS PSYCHIC READING, 1120-2,
WAS GIVEN BY EDGAR CAYCE ON APRIL 17, 1936.
The conductor was Gertrude Cayce.

EC: Yes, we have the body here, [1120], present in this room.

Now, as we find, the general physical forces of the body in many ways appear to be well. And the reactions in most of same are good. Yet we find there are hindrances, disturbances and impulses the correction of which now would not only be a helpfulness to those conditions that disturb the body at times in a greater degree than is shown in the immediate, but would assist in preventing disturbances that would be of a much more violent nature to deal with—if allowed to become more and more a condition to be reckoned with by a perfectly normal functioning body.

These have to do, as we find, with impingements that exist in the nervous system, as will be seen by their effect upon the body as well as in the disturbances or nature of same as produced.

Then, these are the conditions as we find them with this body, [1120] we are speaking of:

First, *in the blood supply,* from the disturbed condition in the nervous system (that is, the cerebrospinal impulse), (more than the sympathetic) there are hindrances with the *manners* of assimilation. Thus there are those tendencies for a slowing of the circulation in its return from the extremities, or through the arteries into the veins.

Hence we have in the metabolism of the system an unbalancing, but with the corrections of that which has produced same in the first there would be a more helpful condition in creating a normal equilibrium.

In the nerve forces themselves of the body, we find: As has been indicated, here is the basis or the cause of the disturbances.

In some time back there was a hindrance in the ganglia of the 2nd and 3rd dorsal, that has produced there the tendency for a lack of proper incentive for its coordination with the vegetative or sympathetic nerve system as *well* as an excess of activity in the deeper nerves as from the junction there of the cerebrospinal and sympathetic with the organs of assimilation.

Let it be understood, then, by the body, the manner in which this disturbance arising there affects the system (for it will be disputed to the body):

Each segment connects with a centralized area between the sympathetic and the cerebrospinal systems, or in the spinal cord impulse itself. In *specific* centers there runs a connecting link between the segments. And such a one exists in this particular center as we have indicated.

In each of those areas called a ganglion there is a bursa, or a small portion of nerve tissue that acts as a regulator or a conductor, or as a director of impulses from the nerve forces to the organs of the body that are affected by this portion of the nervous system.

Not that any one organ, any one functioning of an organ, receives all its impulse from one ganglion or one center along the spine; but that these slowing up by a deficiency in the activity because of pressure produce—as here—a lesion, or an attempt of the blood flow (that is, the lymph and emunctory flow) to shield any injured portion or any pressure. This ofttimes increases the amount of pressure to other portions of the body.

Hence we have an incoordination with the activities in other portions of the body. But with the correction or removal of pressure from such an area, the affected portions will be relieved; that is, as in this body here, the effects to the sensory forces—as the throat, the nasal passages, the eyes, that are affected by this lack of the blood flow.

For, remember, though the heart beats—it is governed, or the circulation is governed by nerve impulse that acts as a supervisor or an overseer would, in conducting to the activity of the system that which not only supplies the nutriment for its individual functioning but also the eliminations of drosses from such used activity, as well as supplying nutriment from that assimilated by the circulation in its entirety for the recuperation and rebuilding.

And remember, these conditions are constantly going on in the system at all times.

What, then, are the conditions produced by this subluxation, in this particular body?

There are times, even with the full-blooded circulation or full quantity that exists, when the outer portions of the body (that is, through the superficial circulation) become as deadened for a period; a few moments is sufficient to make for pallidness to the body; easily tired by walking of any great amount; easily tired at times—or even more so—(than by walking at certain periods) by sitting around; or worrying about or being over-anxious about conditions brings headaches, fullness in the throat, upsetting at times of the digestive forces and the reactions to the whole of the assimilating system, as *well* as producing for the general forces of the body a tendency towards acidity throughout the system. So, the eliminations even through the alimentary canal become involved.

Now, in taking those things that assist in producing a stimu-

lation to either the eliminations or to cause a balance in the
acidity and alkalinity of the body, or so that we make for an increased flow or a draining of conditions through the lymph flow
through the head or soft tissue of throat and head, the condition
is allayed. But the *causes* of these effects, the causes of those
things that upset the digestive forces, the causes of that which
has made for a disturbance through the eye, the ear, nose,
throat, in their relative relation one to another, arise from those
areas indicated—as we find.

In the functioning of the organs themselves:

As to the brain forces, when there is a *physical* coordination
as related to their activity with the system, we find that—as we
have indicated for the body through its *mental* development—
the body's mental abilities and associations are able to segre-
gate, able to make for definite impressions upon activities in
given directions. But if these are hindered by the tiring that
comes on, or those disturbances through the organs' functioning as indicated, these naturally will become *laggard*—or the
abilities of the body will become hindered.

In the throat, bronchi, lungs and larynx—as we have
indicated—there occurs at times, as a tendency from this improper pulsation, and especially from the specific ganglia referred to, the more susceptibility of the body to congestions
through such areas; though organically these are very good.

Heart's activity is as we have indicated.

Digestive forces again are disturbed or upset at times, nervously; but organically, as for their balance, as a coordinant
tendency through the system, very good. And when such corrections are made, we would find these disturbing reactions would
be overcome.

As to the activity of the spleen, the pancreas, the liver, the

gall duct area: When foods are assimilated, these organs function for or in producing the juices or fluids that act upon elements in the foods that are assimilated in an acid and alkaline
content from the stomach itself. With these hindrances, there
becomes at times the tendency for these to become acid.

Hence through the alimentary canal disturbances arise at
times; but these are reflex, as we find, as may be indicated,
rather than being organic or even functional in these portions of
the system.

Then, in meeting the needs of these conditions, as we find:

First we would begin with the use of the hydrotherapy activity that would not only give periods for specific exercise but *at*
such periods have a massage and an adjustment in those *particular* areas indicated; that is, the upper dorsal, specifically in the
3rd and 2nd, coordinant with the cervical area, to the base of
the brain.

Also we would add with same an electrical vibration as a portion of such treatments.

And we will find the bodily functionings, the muscular
forces, the whole general outlook, will be brought to a normal
force in this body, [1120].

Ready for questions.

Q What type of electrical treatment should be given?
A Either the violet ray or the *alternating* current of a sinusoidal
vibration that is *hand* applied.
Q Should these adjustments be made osteopathically or chiro-
practically, or just how?
A As indicated, in the proper regulated hydrotherapist treatment we have the masseurs that would make such an adjustment when these are taken.

Use these as at intervals; once a week, or twice a week one week, once a week the next week, twice a week the next week, then once a week; and then whenever there are those tendencies for the tiredness or sluggishness through the activity of the liver or the eliminations, or pains to the head or even a heaviness there.

And, as we find, we will keep the body fit.

Q These treatments will relieve the tiredness?

A This, as we have indicated, is what these are for! When we remove those pressures that cause these conditions, then we remove that feeling, see?

Q What treatment should be used for the scalp?

A The electrical treatment with the violet ray for this particular body, we find, would be the *most* beneficial.

Q Will this prevent the hair falling out?

A As indicated, there have been those tendencies for the superficial and the deeper circulations to be disturbed. They are breaking away, they are not coordinating. A stimulation to any portion of the body for greater activity, by not too much but as using the comb of such a hand violet ray machine through the hair and head, will make for such stimulation as to make more growth of the hair and also a better growth of the hair.

Q What about general exercise, golf and tennis?

A Well, he'll find his golf stroke will improve a great deal if he will remove this pressure between the shoulders as indicated!

These, to be sure (the exercise), are helpful conditions.

Do these.

We are through for the present.

❖

BODY-MIND-SPIRIT HEALING

• •

Fatigue, frequent emotionally upset, loss of interest in life: these are common complaints today. In fact, chronic fatigue syndrome is one of the most mystifying ailments of our time. Are these symptoms caused by an undetected virus? Or might the origins be more complex?

Reading 1189-2 provides an interesting slant on chronic fatigue, a condition that was already known more than sixty years ago but didn't receive the publicity it does now. A twenty-four-year-old woman sought clairvoyant advice from Edgar Cayce about some all-too-familiar-sounding symptoms. Dispirited, she had lost her sense of drive and ambition. She was melancholic, drained of creative energy, bordering on an emotional breakdown. She also had several other unnamed physical complaints. The woman submitted this question to Cayce: "How may I best overcome the spells of emotional hysteria which interfere so seriously with my work?"

As we might expect, Cayce diagnosed the condition from a holistic point of view and recommended steps to promote balanced healing. Of special interest is what was causing it all. Her high ideals somehow always brought a sense of profound disappointment that troubled her soul. Other people failed to measure up, and, due to her overly sensitive nature, a feeling of rebellion was stirred up inside her. That rage caused imbalances in her body and hence her ailments.

It's a paradox of the human condition that high ideals can make us vulnerable. When we expect a lot—from ourselves or from someone else—we increase the likelihood that things are going to come up short. The flavor of this irony is found in Luke 12:48 ("To whom much has been given, much will be expected"), the psychology of Carl Jung ("The brighter the light, the darker the shadows"), or any number of other sources. All these insights say that the closer we come to the Ultimate, the more severe the test will be, the more vulnerable we are.

How did the reading counsel the woman to work through her own healing? What might Cayce advise today for a similar condition?

First, he counseled, pay attention to your ideals. Clarify your values. Make sure you are rooted in something more than just the material reality of this world. Anchor yourself in the reality of the invisible world, in that which is timeless.

Next, recognize that disappointment can easily be your own projection onto other people. We're bound to be disillusioned by others, true, but the paralyzing disappointment suggests something else is going on just beneath the surface. No doubt you have some very good reasons for feeling let down, but that the letdown should be so devastating, Cayce suggests, is because "you have been disappointing." The woman somehow had become so disconnected from her own ideals that she failed to apply them to herself in her interaction with other people.

The reading is very specific about how the woman's loss of solidarity with her ideals had happened, and could happen to us. She was inclined to "accede to wishes or desires of others, [in order] to hold or keep their respect." Her sense of direction in life—what psychologists would call one's *locus of control*—resided outside herself. This very displacement led to disappointment in herself (perhaps unconsciously so), which, in turn, led to disappointment in others and melancholic dispiritedness, which led to a chain-reaction loss of drive, fatigue, and near breakdown.

Edgar Cayce's reading holds out great hope for turning the woman's condition around. It required working at several levels concurrently. First was getting in touch with the *living* quality of her ideal, emphasizing vibrancy, activity, and a sense of being alive: ". . . a *living* God, a *living* hope, a *living* faith—an *activative* experience!" Disappointment, despair, and depression make the spirit sluggish; what's needed is movement and purposeful activity.

Cayce's second recommendation was to stimulate well-being. For the woman, a drugless approach was emphasized, although today someone with similar symptoms might choose one of the newer medications, a psychotropic drug, especially if the symptoms are deemed psychological. Cayce proposed hydrotherapy and "electrical" therapy, the latter apparently referring to one of the then novel low-voltage devices described by him in other readings and *not* harsh electroshock treatment.

Third, Cayce asked her to use her free will to achieve some disciplined, balanced rhythms to her day: ". . . let the body make out a schedule for itself." A certain amount of time was to be devoted each day to improving her attitude about her relationship to God, a certain amount of time improving interpersonal relationships, and a certain amount to physical exercise *and* relaxation. Anyone willing to make some choices and formulate a plan such as this and then put it into action is bound to see some results. And no doubt a big part of the therapy is having control over one's life.

Overall, we can appreciate this reading because it deals not only with a common, contemporary issue but also because it's such a fine example of Edgar Cayce's holistic approach to healing. While so much of what is called *holistic* is really just a collection of nontraditional remedies, here we see insightful, coherent treatment that truly deals with the body, mind, and spirit.

THE READING

❖

THIS PSYCHIC READING, 1189-2,
WAS GIVEN BY EDGAR CAYCE ON JUNE 7, 1938.
The conductor was Gertrude Cayce.

EC: Yes, we have the body, [1189].

Now as we find, in considering the particular disturbances which exist with this body—and these with the view of bringing normalcy and a revivifying of purposes, desires or ambitions—the body *whole* must be taken into consideration; that is, the physical, the mental, and the spiritual attributes of the body.

For while each of the phases of a body-development is met within its own environ or phase, there are experiences which arise within a body—as we find within this body—when all of these must be considered as they coordinate or cooperate one with another.

And as is then to be understood, these *must* coordinate and cooperate—body, mind, soul—if there is to be the best reaction in the physical, mental or spiritual.

Hence the injunction—from the spiritual aspects, and O that every soul would gain the concept, know and be conscious within—that "The Lord Thy God Is *One!*"

Now with this body we find there has been an exceeding upset in the ideals of the body-mind; coming from disappointments in individuals and in the reaction to that which is the ideal of the entity within itself.

And being of a supersensitive nature, it has (the mental) *rebelled* at these conditions.

Now the expressions of these reactions are within the *physical* forces of the body.

Hence we have been gradually on the border of a nervous breakdown, as it would be called by most pathologists or psychologists.

Yet through the emotions these have produced, as we find, *definite* reactions in the physical forces of the body; as related to the nervous system, both cerebrospinal and sympathetic. And those areas that find greater distress are where the cerebrospinal and the sympathetic or imaginative centers coordinate with the physical reactions of the body.

Hence we have had periods of uncontrollable melancholy. We have had periods of the uncontrollable overflow of the ducts that express emotions; inability of perfect assimilation—which immediately upsets the metabolism of the whole physical body.

These then, as we find, are both pathological and psychological conditions that disturb the equilibrium of the body.

These are not as faults, these are not as conditions that may not be corrected; yet—from the very nature of their affectation through the emotions—both the physical *and* the mental are to be taken into consideration in giving counsel or advice for corrective forces for this body.

First:

Who is to say as to what must be any individual's ideal? But know, O Soul, that it must be founded in spiritual, unseen, everlasting things!

What are these?

Faith, hope, love; without thought of self.

For when self or the own ego becomes disappointed, know that you have been disappointing *in* your relationships to that which produces or may produce same.

Not that it is always necessary to accede to wishes or desires of others, to hold or keep their respect, love, hope or faith. But know in *whom* as well as in what you believe! And if thy faith is founded in the spiritual, the Creative, the constructive forces, it brings peace and harmony.

Then let thy heart, thy mind, determine within itself.

See and be in that attitude as given of old; letting others do as they will or may, but for thee ye will cleave to a *living* God, a *living* hope, a *living* faith—an *activative* experience!

Thus, as ye do this, the other things may pass.

As you find, there has been created an inactivative force—other than repellent—between the sympathetic nervous system and the judgments; or the cerebrospinal nerve reaction of positive fact or nature.

Hence as we will find, change of scene and of environment will be well.

But *first* we would have the low electrical forces that would *attune* the bodily forces to coordinate one with another.

Then also we would have the hydrotherapy and the electrical forces.

Do not resort to drug of *any* nature. For upon same as to bring those appetites that would become—the vibrations of the mental and spiritual will only rebel, or so feed upon same as to bring those appetites that would become—to the mental and spiritual forces of the entity—repellent in their end.

Work and associate with those influences or forces wherein there is help being lent or given to others. This will also create an atmosphere, an attitude for the body mentally and physically that will be constructive.

For the very nature of the entity, and of the impelling influences that we have indicated for the body, is to be *busy!*

Then let it be in *constructive* forces, but keep busy—no matter in what direction, keep busy!

As we find, these adhered to will bring about the better reactions.

At first it may appear that these are not very definite, but let the body make out a schedule for itself in this manner:

"So much time each day (*and do it!*) I will give to the improvement of my mental concept of my relationships to Creative Forces of God.

"So much time each day I will give to *physical* relaxation and exertion for expression, for the activities to produce the proper coordinant relationships between mind and the body.

"So much time I will give (*and give it!*), each day, to putting into *practice* that which is *perceived* and *conceived*," as to thy relationships to the Creative Forces, thy relationships to thy fellow man.

And not necessarily those in high places, nor altogether those who have lost hope. For the body, mind and soul needs the encouragements as well as the concrete forces of example where hope has been and is lost, that must be revived by thy activity.

Keep in the open oft, and in thy activity.

And we will find—before the season has gone—a new outlook upon the experiences in this life!

Ready for questions.

Q How should the low electrical forces be used?

A Those of the direct current; as in the low galvanic or the low violet, or the like.

Q How often would you suggest the hydrotherapy treatments?

A Once or twice a week in the beginning, and then gradually farther apart.

Do these things as we have indicated, and as we find we will bring that as described.

Q Who would you recommend to follow these suggested treatments?

A Choose this for yourself.

Q How may I best overcome the spells of emotional hysteria which interfere so seriously with my work?

A As indicated. *Doing* something! but considering body, mind *and* purpose of soul!

Q How may I overcome constant fatigue physically which results in disinterestedness in people and in my work?

A As indicated; in the manners that have been outlined.

Q How may I regain my former drive and ambitions?

A Just as has been given. There must be reestablished, as it were, the *ideal;* and things that have made the body and mind, and the very physical forces afraid, must be wiped away as a tear.

We are through for the present.

❖

SAMPLES OF EDGAR CAYCE'S ADVICE FOR HEALING

Several hundred ailments are addressed in the some nine thousand health readings Edgar Cayce delivered over the years. Dozens of people sought treatment for some of them, and from their multiple case histories emerged a general pattern of treatment for each. Nevertheless, we need always remember that Cayce's readings were for individual people, and that what he said was a little different from one individual to the next. Presented here is a sampler of how he approached several common conditions. Readers wishing more detail about a given condition can contact the Association for Research and Enlightenment (www.edgarcayce.org), founded by Cayce in 1931, which contin-

ues to work with those wishing to research and apply his suggestions.

THE COMMON COLD

On rare occasions, Edgar Cayce was asked to give a general reading on a specific ailment. Here's an excerpt from a reading on the
common cold.

Each body, as so oft considered, is a law unto itself. Thus
what would be beneficial in one for prevention might be harmful to another; just as what might have beneficial effects upon
one might prove as naught to another.

The cold is both contagious and infectious. It is a germ that
attacks the mucous membranes of nasal passages or throat. Often it is preceded by the feeling of flushiness or cold sensations,
and by spasmodic reactions in the mucous membranes of the
nasal passages.

Then, precautionary or preventative measures respecting the
common cold would depend upon how this may be fully judged
in the human body, or as to what precautionary measures have
been taken and as to what conditions exist already in the individual body.

First: A body is more susceptible to cold with an excess of
acidity OR alkalinity, but MORE susceptible in case of excess
acidity. For, an alkalizing effect is destructive to the cold germ.

When there has been at any time an extra depletion of the vital energies of the body, it produces the tendency for an excess
acidity—and it may be throughout any portion of the body.

At such periods, if a body comes in contact with one sneezing or suffering with cold, it is more easily contracted.

Thus precautions are to be taken at such periods especially.

To be sure, this leaves many questions that might be asked:

Does draft cause a cold? Does unusual change in dress? Does change in temperature? Does getting the clothes or the feet damp? Etc.

All of these, to be sure, AFFECT the CIRCULATION; by the depletion of the body-balance, the body-temperature or body-equilibrium. Then at such times if the body is tired, worn, overacid or overalkaline, it is more susceptible to cold—even by the very changes produced through the sudden unbalancing of circulation, as from a warm room overheated. Naturally when overheated there is less oxygen, which weakens the circulation in the life-giving forces that are destructive to ANY germ or contagion or such.

Then if there is that activity in which the body becomes more conscious of such conditions, this of itself USES energies oft that produces PSYCHOLOGICALLY a susceptibility!

Consequently, as we find, this is one of the most erratic conditions that may be considered as an ill to the human body.

Much at times may also depend upon the body becoming immune to sudden changes by the use of clothing to equalize the pressures over the body. One that is oft in the open and dresses according to the general conditions, or the temperatures, will be LESS susceptible than one who often wraps up or bundles up too much—UNLESS—UNLESS there are other physical defects, or such conditions in the system as to have reduced the vitality locally or as a general condition through the system.

So much, then, as to the susceptibility of an individual or body to colds.

Then, precautions should be taken when it is known that such tendencies exist; that is, weakness, tiredness, exhaustion, or conditions arising from accidents as of draft, dampness of clothes, wet feet or the like, or contact with those suffering with a cold.

As is known, all vital forces are activities of the glandular system; and these are stimulated by specific glandular activity attributed to the functioning of certain portions of the system.

Then, when exposed to such—under the conditions as indicated, or the many other phases of such that make up the experience of an individual, these would be the preventative measures:

The use of an ABUNDANT supply of vitamins is beneficial, of ALL characters; A, B, B-1, D, E, G and K. . . .

Hence it may be said that the adding of vitamins to the system is a precautionary measure,—at all seasons when the body is the most adaptable or susceptible to the contraction of cold, either by contact or by exposure or from unsettled conditions.

The diet also should be considered,—in that there is not an excess of acids or sweets, or even an excess of alkalinity, that may produce such a drawing upon some portion of the system (in attempting to prepare the assimilating system for such activity in the body) as to weaken any organ or any activity or any functioning as to produce greater susceptibility.

Hence there should be kept a normal, well balanced diet that has proven to be right for the individual body,—if precautionary measures are to be taken through such periods.

Also there should be precautions as to the proper clothing, as to drafts, as to dampness of feet, as to being in too hot or too cold a room, as to getting too tired or exhausted in any way or manner.

Precautions in all these directions to keep a near normal balance are measures best to be taken towards preventing the contracting of cold.

When once the cold has attacked the body, there are certain measures that should always be taken.

First, as has so often been indicated, REST! Do not attempt to go on, but REST! For, there is the indication of an exhaustion somewhere, else the body would not have been susceptible. Then, too, the inflammation of the mucous membranes tends to weaken the body, so that there is the greater susceptibility to the weakened portions of the body throughout the special influence of the lymph and emunctory activity,—such as the head, throat, lungs, intestinal system. Then, if there has been an injury in any structural portions of the body, causing a weakness in those directions, there becomes the susceptibility there for the harmful effects from such.

Then, find or determine next where the weakness lies. Is it from lack of eliminations (which causes many ailments)?

Hence quantities of water, as well as an alkalizer, as well as a booster to assimilating forces, are beneficial things towards producing a balance so that the cold and its consequences may be the more readily or easily eliminated or eradicated.   902-1

HEADACHES

Edgar Cayce often thought that headaches originated in the gut. Repeatedly, he refers to the *caecum*, which is the pouch at the beginning of the large intestine. In this reading, we see recommendations for cleansing the large intestine, as well as for adjusting the spine osteopathically. Diet, anxiety, and emotional imbalance also are identified as contributing factors.

For, when there are any types of headaches (and they may arise from many sources) there is distress somewhere in the physical being of the body that is the source of the cause of same. One may have a type of headache from a stomach ailment, another may be from poor digestion or poor eliminations;

and these apparently cause pressures in varied portions of the head—or the reflex nerves of the brain center itself.

Here we have a type that is sometimes called migraine, or that really means "we don't know the source of same."

In this particular body we find the combination of disturbances. These are more severe when there is an overanxiety about any emotional influence in the experience (in this body), whether conscious or unconscious, or in those periods when something aggravates the body in its mental activity. These arise, then, from a condition existing in this body bordering on the pancreas, on the activity of the spleen upon the body.

When such conditions occur, the body will find, by the application of the hand on the body that there is a cold area just across the diaphragm, as compared to the rest of the body.

The expression in the nerve reflexes we find associated with certain ganglia in the cerebrospinal system, where the sympathetic nerves and the nerves of the central nervous system coordinate. In this particular body, these occur from the 6th to the 8th dorsal. These, then, are the areas where stimulation is needed for the association or coordination, for the relieving of those reflexes, or those pressures that cause reflexes in the brain centers themselves; so as to relieve these tensions in this body.

But the sources of these pressures arise from the conditions in the colon and in the caecum area.

Then, in going about to remove these pressures,—we would have osteopathic treatments and colonic irrigations. Because these conditions have been existent with the body for a long period, there will be required a series of these treatments periodically—if we would keep these coordinations in the areas to prevent the reacting upon reflexes of the nerve forces that cause these disturbances for the body.

Remove these pressures in the colon by high colonic irrigations. Keep these up, though it may bring on a mild attack during the first or second period. Keep these up until all of the mucus is entirely removed, for this is the source of the pressure—in a part of the caecum area. These colonics in the beginning should be given not more than fifteen days apart, until five or six have been given. And these must be scientifically given, not a "slap dab" job. For, these are conditions where the special areas in the caecum center are to be purified.

Continue also occasionally to relax and stimulate the centers in the cerebrospinal system that supply nerve energies to the areas through pancreas and the spleen area as it connects with same along the whole alimentary canal, to the areas outlined. These treatments should be given osteopathically or neuropathically, and be given about twice a week until ten or twelve have been given. Then they may be made farther apart. Or go for two or three weeks without any, and then have another series.

Do these and we should stimulate the activity to refrain from these headaches. For, we will not only remove the causes but we will supply energies from the body to replace these with normal reactions.

Of course, foods have their effect. Keep away from too much sweets, or mixed fruits or candies—for this body.

In the activities mentally, keep optimistic—even when everything goes wrong.

Do that.   3329-1

INDIGESTION

Here again, the reading presents a snapshot of how Edgar Cayce made specific recommendations for a particular ailment. Notice how the description of this forty-one-year-old man's problem emphasizes that more is going on than just eating the wrong foods. An overly acidic condition prevails in the body overall; and, what's more, there is a lack of coordination between the kidneys and liver. Too much of the circulating blood is tied up in the abdominal organs, and not enough is available for the body's extremities.

In that of the lower digestive system, being an over-acidity from the conditions existent in system, naturally there are the resultant forces thrown into the intestinal tract, and THROUGHOUT this causes distress to the body.

In the activity of the eliminations as thrown off through the kidneys, or through the HEPATIC circulation as a whole—the liver, as indicated, congestion. Hence the excretory and secretive system not ALWAYS working in accord one with another, for often the greater portion of the blood supply is in THIS portion of system, with insufficient in the extremities. This causing the laxness of the circulation.

In the kidneys, these express themselves in the character of the urine, or of the eliminations as are thrown through same, and will be found that these may be altered or changed considerably by the diet, or even by the AMOUNT of water that would be taken into the system.

In meeting the needs of the conditions of this body, not only must the specific conditions be considered, but also the building UP, or of the GENERAL debilitation as has existed on account of the conditions, so that—in aiding one we do not OVERTAX the other. The diet, of course, would be among the first things to be considered.

In meeting the needs, then, we would do this:

As medicinal properties that will aid the system, we would

follow those of the alkaline, and especially of Chalk-Bismuth, and such, in the system.

The water that is taken—MOST of same should carry those of elm, and this should be prepared just before taking, but should ALWAYS be cool, or cold.

Just before the MEALS are taken, that of a MILD tea of Saffron should be able to coat the whole of the stomach proper. This will aid digestion.

Also those of the food values should be practically, or in a practical manner—they will be found necessary to be changed, see—for these will necessarily alter the conditions in system, and when there is found disagreement in any portion, alter these. The fruits and cereals should be those that are of EASY digestion. Occasionally there may be taken rice cakes, with honey—but the honey should NOT be other than that WITH the honeycomb. Not strained honey. Ovaltine may be taken as a drink at times. No tea, no coffee. In the character of MILKS—this will not always agree with the system, for curds would be produced from same that would be bad. Then, these may be altered by the CHARACTER of the milk at times as may be taken. That of the goat's milk, or of the dried milk, or of such, may be used occasionally. This with the cereals, or with the foods, or with the first morning foods.

Of the noon—these should consist chiefly of those of the liquid diet, and should NOT be too EXCESSIVE in ANY manner. Beef JUICE may be taken; but NOT the flesh itself. Small quantities, often sipped, would be the better for THIS body; that is, near the noon hour, see?

In the evenings—these may be altered to those that are blood and nerve building, and may be changed to any of the characters of foods that are ALKALINE REACTING! Eggs may be taken at this time, provided the YOLK only is prepared, either in the form of hard and WELL MASHED afterward, mixed with any of the oils—olive oil, also those of cod-liver oil, should be part of the diet. Ready for questions.

Q What quantity of elm and saffron should be used?

A For each glass of water a pinch between the finger and thumb of the ground elm, stirred well, with a small lump of ice in same; prepared about two to three minutes before it is drunk. Of the saffron—this should be made as a tea, STEEPED—as a tea—and NOT too strong. This may be altered according to that—when this is taken, it should be preferably warm, and just before the meal—see? So that, that as first taken, in the system—or into the stomach—forms a coating over the whole of same. If these are found to produce DISTRESSES at any time, NOT the QUALITY of the stuff but the QUANTITY should be decreased; for these will be effective, as will also be found Magnesia and Bismuth will be effective in CHANGING the conditions in the system. Do that. Charcoal should be effective also, to reduce the amount of gas.

Well that the irrigations of oil be occasionally used for the lower portion of the system, so that the colon may be cleansed properly, and that the STRAIN as has been induced by the lack of blood supply through this portion of the system may be increased. BUILD up the general system.

The manipulations as would be given in this condition would be for the strengthening of the whole nerve system, that the body may relax thoroughly when it rests—for the BUILDING properties for THIS body will be found in rest and sleep.

5545-1

SINUSITIS

Sinusitis, a complex condition, can be caused by different things in different people. For the twenty-seven-year-old woman in this reading, Edgar Cayce notes that an inadequate blood supply has resulted in a supersensitivity to external irritants. As with many of his health readings, he mentions ingredients and remedies that are not familiar to us today. You can obtain more information about their availability by contacting the Association for Research and Enlightenment.

Also there are those tendencies, from this lack of the supplying to the blood force, for inflammation or weakness through the mucous membranes; causing the nasal passages, the antrum, and the soft tissue of the head and throat to become supersensitive to environs or activities about the body.

These should be taken into consideration also, and we will find that the body may resist cold and those inclinations for sneezing and irritation that arise at times through these portions of the body.

As to applications for bettered conditions, then:

We would be more careful as to the budgeting of the time. Take time for rest and recuperation. Take time for activities in which the exercising of the body-physical makes for resuscitation and not for detrimental conditions.

Refrain from stimulations as of ANY influence of carbonated drinks or intoxicating beverages or any carrying malt in same; that is, as a stimulant. Malt as an active principle in the DIGESTIVE system would be very well, yet—as we find—even this may be taken in a better form for the body,—as we will suggest.

Also: Have at least six to ten general osteopathic treatments, to RELAX the body; especially through the areas from the 9th dorsal to the 1st cervical, and in the latter portion of such treatments coordinating the areas from the lower portion of the sacral and lumbar to the lst cervicals.

Then, as to the diet:

Here we find that citrus fruit juices in quantities, regularly, will be helpful. Drink at least a pint of orange juice, with the juice of half a lemon squeezed into same, each day; for periods of ten days,—then leave off for a period of ten days, and then take again for another ten days, and so on.

With the meals take ADIRON; one tablet with each meal, or three tablets each day,—one at each meal. Take a whole bottle of sixty tablets in this manner, leave off a few days, and then take again,—and so on, continuing to take same for several months in this manner,—and then gradually lessen the periods of taking same, provided the system has been replenished sufficiently that there is not the fatigue when leaving same off.

Prepare an inhalant in a large-mouthed, dark glass bottle, with two vents through the cork,—and these vents corked with smaller corks. Let the bottle be at least a six to eight ounce container.

To 4 ounces of Pure Grain Alcohol, add—in the order named:

Oil of Eucalyptus................20 minims,
Compound Tincture of Benzoin................15 minims,
Rectified Oil of Turp................5 minims,
Rectified Creosote................3 minims,
Tolu in Solution................30 minims.

Shake the solution when it is to be inhaled night and morning, or when there is a tickling or coughing, or the inclination for sneezing at other times also,—that is, when these occur any time during the day; but inhale regularly of mornings upon arising, and of evenings when retiring. Inhale into one nostril, holding the other, then into the other side; also into the throat,—letting the fumes go into the lungs,—not swallowing the inhalant, but inhaling the fumes, see? Hold either side of the nostril as it is inhaled in the other nostril.

Do these, and we will bring better conditions for the body.

2186-1

REJUVENATION

Although it's not an ailment or disease, the topic of rejuvenation surfaced often in the readings of Edgar Cayce. He felt the human body could live to be at least 120 years old if people were just willing to pay the price required to keep balanced and fit. In this reading, a thirty-seven-year-old man asked Cayce to tell him how he could extend his life expectancy greatly. Here are key principles of longevity, such as cell renewal, the theory that, essentially, the body rebuilds itself every seven years. So even with the man's weaknesses, according to Cayce, he still has the potential to live 120 or more years!

And that which bespeaks of longevity in a body bespeaks of each cell, each atomic structure, each of the corpuscles being able to reproduce itself WITHOUT those tendencies or inclinations of racial or environmental conditions, but as one purified or cleansed for that continuity of experience within itself.

Knowing these tendencies, these weaknesses, does not then indicate that there are those bugaboos continually before the entity. For, these are left behind when ye do that ye know to do, and leave undone those things ye must or else pay the price of neglect, over-indulgence, gratification for the moment that there may be the satisfying of an appetite or tendency as may exist in the body!

Here we find the necessity for care, for exercise, for constant checking up on the bodily activities; not daily, necessarily,—but we remember that the body-physical alters in its expression continually, and by the end of a cycle of seven years it has entirely replaced that which existed at the beginning of the period seven years ago. Replaced with what? The same old tendencies multiplied, the same old inclinations doubled—or eradicated?

This depends, then, upon those activities as related to the influences or tendencies which exist. For, as may be told by any pathologist, there is no known reason why any individual entity should not live as long as it desires. And there is no death, save in thy consciousness. Because all others have died, ye expect to—and you do! These are a part of thy consciousness, in what? In the mental, in the spiritual,—and the physical reacts to same.

This is the condition that exists, then, with this body; a weakness, a tendency,—not a disease but a dis-ease,—in the hormones of the blood plasm; that tends—with cold, congestion, overacidity, or the improper balance of foods for the plasm's reproduction—to cause in sinew, in bone, a plastic or static condition.

As far as the blood count is concerned, in numbers, in protoplasm cells, or red blood, white blood and the leucocyte, we would find few bodies better balanced than this individual entity.

As to the plasms in the nerve reflexes from brain, and the coordination of the gray and white matter,—only at times do we find these show a variation.

Frustration will at times cause, to this body, a reaction that becomes rather aggravating to the body afterwards. At the moment it is too much disturbed to even know the cause of same, but it blesses itself out, or someone else, after same is passed!

This is a reflex from the hormone supply, the inability to supply in the brain circulation sufficient of the quick activity to the impulses there, under stress.

These are merely tendencies in the body.

As to spiritual tendencies and inclinations,—these may not be given. For, these are choices of the soul itself.

The tendencies as to the ideal are well. As to whether ye keep same, this ye determine in thine own mind. But ideals are not your mind,—ideals are principles acted upon BY the mind. But remember, just as that expectancy—because your great, great, great, great grandfather died you will die too—is there, and is part of the expectancy of every cell of your body! It can be eradicated, yes. How? By that constant activity within self of expectancy that this condition does not HAVE to happen to you!

That is as the spirit. And as the spirit builds, as the spirit forms in its activity in mind, the mind becomes then the builder. The mind is not the spirit, it is a companion to the spirit; it builds a pattern. And this is the beginning of how self may raise that expectancy of its period of activity in the earth. And this is the beginning of thy ideal. Of what? Of that the soul should, does, will, can, must, accomplish in this experience!

And by what authority? WHO, WHAT do you put in authority in thy earthly experience? In spirit, then in mind?

As to the manner of eradicating these fluctuations, these confusions,—do not confuse these with that as of a "front," as of a defense. But merely to know that you are right, to know in activity that you are right, has paved the way for self to control ANY situation that may arise,—whether of a mental confusion or of a combination of confusions from the mental and spiritual situations.

Hence again the mental rests upon its conception and choice of its ideal in spirit, and as to Who and What is the authority in same.

As to the physical conditions, that are a part of the patholog-ical effects in the body:

At certain periods have those tests as to acidity, albumin, the balance in chyle activity through the body, as to glandular re-actions; and these give then the positive or negative flexes in the body.

Knowing the tendencies, supply in the vital energies that ye call the vitamins, or elements. For, remember, while we give many combinations, there are only four elements in your body,—water, salt, soda and iodine. These are the basic elements, they make all the rest! Each vitamin as a component part of an ele-ment is simply a combination of these other influences, given a name mostly for confusion to individuals, by those who would tell you what to do for a price!

In those activities, then, add—in the proper balance—that which will maintain this equilibrium. And if you set your life to be a hundred and twenty, you can live to be a hundred and twenty-one!

2533-6

SUMMARY
of Edgar Cayce's Approach to Holistic Healing

• •

Healing is best understood in terms of *systems*. First, we need to understand that the various systems of the physical body—the nervous system, the circulatory system, the endocrine system, and all the internal organs—are interconnected pro-foundly. A disorder in one system can produce symptoms in an-other. But just as surely, achieving balance and harmony in one system can benefit the others.

This systems approach applies to the bigger picture as well. Each of us is made up of a body, a mind, and a spirit that are interconnected. For healing to be total and lasting, we need to work to integrate all three aspects of ourselves. We not only need to promote physical healing for the body, we need to transform the attitudes and emotions that govern it, and we need to discipline ourselves to keep clearly in focus the spiritual ideals that guide it.

CHAPTER FIVE

THE SOUL'S JOURNEY:
REINCARNATION AND LIFE PURPOSE

✦

T HE SECOND-LARGEST CATEGORY OF EDGAR CAYCE'S READINGS
addresses self-understanding and the journey of the soul to
find a purpose in life. With nearly two thousand *life readings* in all,
they include details about past life experiences and ways to discover your soul's purpose and how to deal with karmic patterns
that are holding you back.

Reincarnation was always a problematic topic for Cayce, in
part because he himself had been slow to warm to the idea. Not
surprisingly, initially many people he did readings for were new to
his work and probably had the same reaction. But for the twenty
years that he gave life readings, 1924 to 1944, he was well ahead
of the Western world's modern-day familiarity with the concept.

Reincarnation was always presented by Cayce as a series of
human lives, not different species, as with some Eastern religions.
Even more significant, his approach retained the flavor of his

early Christian faith. He suggested that even though we can learn, and our souls can grow from one lifetime to the next, the cycle can be stopped only by adhering to the *law of grace*—the power to reconcile and heal that comes from God's merciful love rather than due to our own efforts. We can make *little steps* forward in developing the soul (or back, since free will leaves room for rebellion and separation from God). But the truly *big step* toward enlightenment comes only through willingness to surrender to that spark of the divine that has always lived in us.

In this chapter, we explore three readings that illustrate Edgar Cayce's approach to the journey of the soul, and, specifically, his theory of reincarnation.

The first reading was given for a group interested in proving the validity of reincarnation.

The second, one of his so-called *mental-spiritual* readings, of which there are some eleven hundred in number, offers advice about holistic living. These discourses rarely dealt with the specifics of past lives but nonetheless included the concept of reincarnation. This specific reading includes a succinct statement about the mission of every soul, but one devoid of metaphysical details, with no intricate scheme about higher dimensions, no complex explanations of how reincarnation, karma, and grace work. These topics can be found in other readings. Our *essential* Cayce material comes down to more practical, simple matters: Can the soul learn to be more *patient* and *tolerant* in the fullest sense? Can the soul learn to live in a way that actually *applies* what it knows? Can the soul learn to *be present in the moment* so that it can receive and meet lovingly whatever arises?

The final discourse for this chapter is a life reading given for a six-year-old boy. While it doesn't have as many details about past life experiences as most other life readings do, it nevertheless is one of the finest examples of Edgar Cayce as spiritual philosopher and life coach.

HOW AND WHY TO STUDY REINCARNATION

· ·

By 1937, Edgar Cayce had given life readings to hundreds of people, a few of which included details about past lives right here in the United States—what were called *American incarnations*. Because they included names, dates, and locations, not surprisingly some of his more enthusiastic followers wanted to conduct further research to corroborate evidence, even to provide convincing "proof." (Several have tried since 1937, sometimes with tantalizing results, but nothing that could be held up as definitive.) Nevertheless, reading 5753-2 is an articulate statement about the search for truth—on any topic, really—and the care we must exercise when looking into past life experiences.

Cayce first reminds the group that what constitutes the truth for one person may not be adequate for another. There is a certain quality of *relativity to the evidence,* and, ultimately, it is only *personal* experience that can convince one completely. What's more, he warns that we shouldn't pursue knowledge just for knowledge's sake but only as applicable to our lives in some practical way. The following passage from the reading captures the very essence of his thinking about what makes any endeavor worthwhile: "Only that which produces or makes for experiences that may make a citizen a better citizen, a father a better father, a mother a better mother, a neighbor a better neighbor, is constructive."

In fact, Edgar Cayce comes down rather hard on curiosity seekers, such as those compelled to know one's name or place of birth in a past life. "And to find that ye only lived, died and were buried under the cherry tree in Grandmother's garden does not make thee one whit better neighbor, citizen, mother or father!"

If we really want to explore the reality of past lives, it's found in the social and moral dimensions of everyday life. We experience ourselves as souls who have been in the world before, and now we are willing to take some responsibility for the mess the world is in today. It's a matter of opening our hearts to the suffering all around us and seeing our role in it. It's a matter of knowing that we "in the present may correct it by being righteous—THAT is worthwhile!" By being compassionate toward others, we begin to remember who we really are, and part of that remembering is a broader awareness of what it means to be a soul.

Edgar Cayce even invites us to study the life of King David, who he says committed most every sin in the book, but only once, since he always learned from his mistakes. "Well that ye pattern thy study of thyself after such a life!" In living life passionately and fully, taking risks and making mistakes, and yet learning from his mistakes, David discovered that karma and grace don't have to wait until the next lifetime but are here to guide our living today.

Reading 5753-2 no doubt was a far cry from what the research group hoped to hear from Cayce. They wanted methodology, and instead they got a discourse on what makes life really worthwhile—this and any other life.

THE READING

✤

THIS PSYCHIC READING, 5753-2,
WAS GIVEN BY EDGAR CAYCE ON JUNE 29, 1937.
The conductor was Gertrude Cayce.

GC: You will have before you the New York Research Group, members of which are present here, and their desires and purposes to study and secure evidence to check the American incarnations of those who have had life readings through Edgar Cayce. You will advise this group as to the best methods for undertaking this study with a series of Readings to secure further data on individual records. Answer questions.

EC: Yes, we have the group as gathered here, the members of the New York Research Group, as a group, as individuals; with the desires, the purposes for research as evidence of incarnations of individuals.

In giving that as we find that may be helpful in such an experience, first they of the group should each determine within their own mind WHAT is evidence; and then be sure that is NOT evidence to thy neighbor.

For we are not all of one mind, and evidence or knowledge is an individual experience—and must be experienced.

Know that from the conscious mind only that which is drawn by comparison is evidenced in that consciousness.

Incarnation is not of the material, though—as the mind—manifests through the material.

Hence while it is part and parcel of the material, its evidence is rather in what is done about it.

Again the group should as individuals determine within themselves as to what they will do with same, when there has been proof-positive to them.

Do not gain knowledge only to thine undoing. Remember Adam.

Do not obtain that which ye cannot make constructive in thine own experience and in the experience of those whom ye contact day by day.

Do not attempt to force, impel or to even try to impress thy knowledge upon another. Remember what the serpent did to Eve.

In the studies, then, know WHERE ye are going. To gain knowledge merely for thine own satisfaction is a thing, a condition, an experience to be commended, if it does not produce in thine experience a feeling or a manner of expression that you are better than another on account of thy knowledge. This becomes self-evident that it would become then a stumblingblock, unless ye know what ye will do with thy knowledge.

As to the manners of interpreting—these may be observed, these may be made constructive by the study of those influences that in the associations and dealings with thy fellow man ye have had weaknesses, inclinations. These are mental, not material things, though they may have brought material activity. Warnings, constructive activity in warnings, then may prove to be of helpful experience in the activity of any individual group.

That this should not include documentary data or evidence, to be sure, is well; for documentary evidence to the mind of the masses is nil. Only that which produces or makes for experiences that may make a citizen a better citizen, a father a better father, a mother a better mother, a neighbor a better neighbor, is constructive.

And to find that ye only lived, died and were buried under the cherry tree in Grandmother's garden does not make thee one whit better neighbor, citizen, mother or father!

But to know that ye spoke unkindly and suffered for it, and in the present may correct it by being righteous—THAT is worth while!

What is righteousness? Just being kind, just being noble, just being self-sacrificing; just being willing to be the hands for the blind, the feet for the lame—these are constructive experiences.

Ye may gain knowledge of same, for incarnations ARE a FACT!

How may ye prove it? In thy daily living!

Using the experience of David the king as an example, what was it in his experience that caused him to be called a man after God's own heart? That he did not falter, that he did not do this or that or be guilty of every immoral experience in the category of man's relationship? Rather was it that he was sorry, and not guilty of the same offence twice!

Well that ye pattern thy study of thyself after such a life!

There may be an excuse—yes, there may be a forgiveness for those that err once; is there for twice, is there for thrice? Yea—though ye forgive, if ye would be forgiven! For that is the law.

Then, such a study is WELL—if ye know whither ye go.

If ye do NOT know whither ye go, ye had better leave it alone!

❖

THE MISSION OF THE SOUL

• •

Once we have grasped the idea that life is purposeful, and that each of us has a distinct purpose in life, it's only natural to wonder, How am I doing? Am I doing what I'm here to do? Am I making it?

The fifty-seven-year-old man who received the following reading had the benefit of Edgar Cayce's psychic counsel to help answer those questions. He had gotten assistance from Cayce twice before, and now he was asking for a penetrating assessment of his inner and outer development, a sort of *spiritual audit*. He was presented with a profound description of the spiritual tasks we *all* face, a picture of the human soul and its essential job while in the material world.

To develop the soul requires an ideal; spiritual growth occurs within the context of having chosen a purpose. It doesn't just happen to us, like losing baby teeth or finding that first gray hair; it requires initiative. More specifically, Cayce recommends certain ideals: *patience* and *tolerance*. What is it about these ideals that contributes so significantly to the mission of the soul? Patience and tolerance force us to shift gears and to look at life in a new way, requiring that we *go beyond* appearances. In other words, our consciousness shifts and we see and feel things in a different way.

When we're patient, we have a new sense of time; when we're tolerant, we see the behavior of other people in a way that leaves room for understanding and forgiveness. Neither quality makes much sense from a materialistic point of view; for example, the appearance we're going to miss the boat if we don't hurry up, or that people are going to get the best of us if we let them get away with it. But even though patience and tolerance don't always seem very logical, they are qualities that awaken us to the realization that we are indeed souls. It's that awareness that is so very key to our mission here on earth.

To examine this concept further, let's return to questions addressed in earlier chapters: What exactly is the soul? When we begin to awaken spiritually, what is it that we realize about ourselves? Edgar Cayce suggests two answers in particular: *immortality* and *individuality*. As he says in this reading, we start to sense "the continuity of life . . . [that] which lives on and on"; and, furthermore, we awaken to our own uniqueness and freedom, "that which is individual of each and everybody as it finds expression in the material world."

Easier said than done: It's not easy being patient and tolerant, even occasionally. But Cayce promises that if we don't succumb to the fatigue of loving service—if we don't become "weary in well-doing"—then we're given the *crown of life*. This lovely metaphor refers to a distinct state of consciousness that comes as a gift as we sincerely try to live the mission of the soul, a gift which he defines as *the ability to know that one is in accord with divine protection*. That is to say, we're not cut loose and left adrift in the material world; the spirit is with us, protecting us, as we live our mission.

And while our task is simple, it's not an easy one. Any soul's mission is to apply and live out *what you know,* and meet *creatively* with all your resources *what comes to you.* The second point is found again and again in this particular reading, it's a theme, a refrain:

- "[D]oing with a might in the Lord that thy hands find to do."
- "Tend His lambs, those that are in thy way, those thou meetest day by day."
- "That that is given thee put to use."

Statements of this sort are powerful reminders that we don't have to go out looking for challenges to prove ourselves, to restlessly search for spiritual opportunities. Life brings them to us.

At first, something in us may not be satisfied with answers like that. "The mission of the soul" somehow sounds more grand, suggesting deeds of cosmic proportions, not something as mundane as patience and tolerance when dealing with everyday difficulties. But as you read Edgar Cayce's message in the reading below, see if it doesn't stir something up in your own soul, something that knows the deepest truths often require only the simplest explanations.

THE READING

⟡

THIS PSYCHIC READING, 442-3, WAS GIVEN BY EDGAR CAYCE ON JANUARY 26, 1934.

The conductor was Hugh Lynn Cayce.

HLC: You will give a mental and spiritual reading for him, giving the reason for entrance into this cycle of experience and detailed guidance for the development and expression of his inner soul faculties in this present life.

EC: Yes, we have the entity here, [442].

In considering the activities of the mental and soul body of an entity, in relations to its activities or its purposes in any given experience, something of that which has been builded in the soul development is necessary to be referred to as comparison, that there may be presented in a comprehensible way and manner that for mental and soul expansion in any given activity.

In this entity, [442], we find in the varied experiences or appearances through its activity in the environs, more of the developments than of retardments. While in varied experiences there are seen periods when indecisions and the particular activity made for rather the retarding, in the whole we have found that with the application of that which has become apparent in the present experience—as to what has been set as the ideals and principles by which the application of life in a given appearance or experience may be in a direction or in accordance with the entity's own judgments—the development has been in accord with an ideal. Making for, then, in self, patience—which has been pointed by Him who is the Giver of life as being the qualification in every entity's experience through the application of which every entity becomes aware of possessing a soul, that birthright which is the gift of the Father to each and every entity that may be presented before the Throne of Thrones, before the Holy of Holies, in a holy and acceptable way and manner.

In righteousness, then—as is found in patience, that has become the worthy attribute of the soul of this entity, in tolerance and in patience, has come the awareness of the continuity of life—and that the soul is that which is individual of each and every body as it finds expression in the material world, which lives on and on in those environs that have been created by what that soul has seen and comprehended in its experience as being according to those directions as He, the Father, the Lord of all, would have each and every soul be.

Then, as we find in the experiences of this entity, these have become worthy attributes, as these are well pleasing in His eyes; so that there may only be given that injunction, "Be not weary in well-doing, for he that endureth unto the end shall wear the crown of life." The crown of life here means being aware of those abilities within self to know that the self, the ego, the I, is in accord with, is aware of, the divine protection that has and does come to each and every soul that fulfills its mission in any experience.

What, then, ye ask, has been the mission of this entity, this soul, in this experience? That, with that which has gone before, there may be given the opportunity as to what the soul would do about that it knows is in accordance with, in keeping with, what His injunctions have ever been to His fellow man; that ye make thy paths straight, that ye do unto thy fellow man as ye would have your fellow man do unto you; love the Lord thy God, eschewing evil, keeping the heart joyous in the service and in the tasks that are set before thee day by day, doing with a might in the Lord that thy hands find to do. For, His ways have ever been that ye grow in the grace and in the knowledge and in the understanding of the Lord and His ways. Not that ye rest idly by when there is work to do, but just being kind, just being patient, just being long-suffering with those who would err according to thine own conscience, yet in thine own life, in thine own dealings with such ye show forth that love, that patience that He hast shown with the sons of men since He has called into being *bodies*—physically—that are known in the material world that these may furnish a channel through which those things that are known and accepted as being the qualifications of a spiritual life may *find* manifestations, and thus bring forth their fruits, their meats, ready for repentance.

For, while in humbleness of heart yet, in gladness does each soul find those things, those loads to be met day by day. And as there is the step taken here and there in the meditations (for, as He has given, "As oft as ye ask in my name, *believing,* it shall be done unto you"), He is faithful in His promises; for, as He has given, "I will not leave thee comfortless, but ye shall be quickened—even as the spirit in thee makes thee alive, makes thee aware of the joys that are thine through the service that thou may render to thy fellow man, in justness, in mercy, in just being kind, just being gentle to those here, there, that have become and do become thy lot to be measured with." For, there are no such things as perchance, but the law of demand, the law of supply, the laws of love are ever, ever in thine own hands day by day. For, when there comes the needs that thou shouldst show forth thy love that has been shed on thee in thy activities in a material world, the opportunities that may be measured to thy fellow man are shown. For, as He has given, "Inasmuch as ye have done it unto the least of these, my little ones, ye have done it unto me."

Hence, in thy steps, be acquainted with the Lord. Seek, in thy secret places, that He knoweth thee aright. And there will come those answers as thou meditatest in thine inner self as to what, where and how thou shalt measure thy steps day by day. For, justice and mercy and peace and harmony are as His gifts to those that seek His face. He has given, "If ye love me, keep my commandments." His commandments are not grievous, neither do they deny thee any influence, any material things that will make for joy in thine own experience. Rather do the fruits of mercy, peace, justice and harmony make for such in thine own experience.

Hence, follow in the ways that are set before thee, knowing that He will call thee by name. And he that *He* names is redeemed in His sight. And there is nothing to fear save self. For, as has been given, "I am persuaded there is nothing in heaven, in earth, in principalities or in powers, that may separate the soul from the love of the Father save the waywardness, the indecisions, the unkindnesses that the self may inflict upon self or the fellow man."

Keep the way. Feed His sheep. Tend His lambs, those that are in thy way, those thou meetest day by day. Let thine own light so shine that they may know that thou walkest, that thou talkest, oft with thy God.

THE SOUL'S TALENTS AS A
TWO-EDGED SWORD

• •

Reading 4087-1 is about training children; but it's also about the challenges any of us face trying to fulfill the potential in our lives or help others fulfill theirs. Another excellent example of how reincarnation works, it can teach us about our own lives, especially regarding our talents.

The many life readings Edgar Cayce gave for children are among his most fascinating. There is something very special about this six-year-old boy, whose parents turned to Cayce for help in 1944. With his life stretching before him so full of possibility and promise, the past and future came together because of Cayce's ability to perceive clairvoyantly the deep patterns of the soul.

From background notes, we know a little about the boy and why his parents sought help. Several incidents led them to believe that he was an unusual soul with a remarkable psychic talent, and his ability made for an interesting challenge for the family: How could he fulfill the purpose for which his soul had been chosen *and* still lead a normal life? This challenge was compounded by the fact that the parents were having troubles in their marriage, and, in fact, many of the paragraphs are directed to them rather than the boy.

Cayce first validates the reports of the boy's psychic experiences, indicating right away that in more than one past life he had had the same ability. There is even a brief description of how this ability operates within him to produce *precognition* ("visions of things to come") or *clairvoyance* ("things that are happening"). The triggering mechanism is the *kundalini*, or "life-force," rising spontaneously in the sixth center (the *pineal* center) from the second center (what Cayce sometimes called the *lyden* center, associated with the cells of Leydig).

The spontaneous occurrences to which the boy was subject were a way of visiting ancient patterns on his soul, especially as related to the Old Testament. Cayce describes a very specific past life that is even mentioned in I Kings 13. First, a little background will help us interpret his advice.

Nearly a thousand years before the birth of Christ, and just after the death of King Solomon, Jeroboam successfully led a revolt in which the ten northern tribes established their own nation of Israel, with Jeroboam as the first king. Jeroboam, in an effort to keep his people from journeying to Jerusalem to worship, set up shrines locally, many of which fostered cults at odds with Judaism. It was against this background that an unnamed prophet (this very boy, according to Cayce) confronted Jeroboam. Among the signs that the prophet employed to prove he was God's spokesman was an ability to wither the king's hand and then restore it.

The problem for this prophet (this boy) was *whom to trust*. In his divinely inspired mission to confront Jeroboam, he also had been given other specific instructions, which he failed to fulfill. A person also claiming to be a prophet lied to him and persuaded him to disregard the instructions, which resulted in the prophet/boy's undoing and violent death (see I Kings 13:15–25). Cayce's advice: ". . . he is not to listen at all of those who may counsel him as to the manner in which he is to use the abilities . . . but [instead] to trust in Him who is the way." Apparently, there was still the potential for the boy's soul to be led astray.

Cayce then refers to another lifetime in which the boy's soul misunderstood or misused his paranormal gifts. Again, Cayce identifies the boy as the reincarnation of a biblical character, and, again, it's a rather minor personage but a key player anyway in a powerfully instructive story (see Acts 8:18–24 for details). A man named Simon, who lived in Samaria, desperately wanted the power to heal by laying on of hands, as Peter and John did. He offered to buy the power from Peter—something that hits uncomfortably close to home in our era of commercialism. The lesson learned by the soul, about spiritual gifts and money, applied to Cayce's own life and the boy's.

But what do these stories from sixty years ago teach us today? They tell us about the right use of our abilities, and how we have carried abilities from previous lives to the present one. The talent need not be one as dramatic as the boy's or some biblical character's; the principles of reincarnation, karma, and growth of the soul work the same way for everyone.

Attached to any talent is some kind of temptation. Think about your own talent. Maybe you've a talent for art, finance, or just plain persuasion. Perhaps it's an aptitude for understanding what other people are feeling or a knack for solving problems. No doubt such a talent will play a big role in your fulfilling what you came to earth to do, just as the boy's psychic ability did.

One key to successfully helping the soul to grow in this lifetime is to *recognize* potential misapplications of talent. It's not necessary to remember past lives specifically; all we need to do is develop sensitivity to the patterns in our soul generally, to sense the little tugs of temptation that cross our path when we apply our talent. Edgar Cayce didn't mean to scare the boy or us away from using our gifts. He just wanted the boy and us to keep in mind how a gift can be a two-edged sword.

THE READING

❖

THIS PSYCHIC READING, 4087-1,
WAS GIVEN BY EDGAR CAYCE ON APRIL 15, 1944.
The conductor was Gertrude Cayce.

GC: You will give the relations of this entity and the universe, and the universal forces; giving the conditions which are as personalities, latent and exhibited in the present life; also the former appearances in the earth plane, giving time, place and the name, and that in each life which built or retarded the development for the entity; giving the abilities of the present entity, that to which it may attain, and how. You will answer the questions, as I ask them:

EC: Yes, we have the records here of that entity now known as or called [4087].

As we find, there are great possibilities but there are also great problems to be met with the training and the direction for this entity through the formative years.

For as we find this entity has more than once been among those who were gifted with what is sometimes called second sight, or the super-activity of the third eye. Whenever there is the opening, then, of the lyden (Leydig) center and the kundaline forces from along the pineal, we find that there are visions of things to come, of things that are happening.

Yet in the use of these through some experiences, as we will find, the entity is in the present meeting itself. For the entity was the prophet who warned Jeroboam. Read it! You will see why he is not to listen at all of those who may counsel him as to the manner in which he is to use the abilities that have been and are a portion of the entity's experience; but to trust in Him who is the way.

Do not get away from the church! In the church keep these activities, that there may be surety in self that has to do or to deal with only the use of such insight, such vision, to the glory of the Father as manifested in the Son.

Do not use such for gratifying, satisfying, or even encouraging the entity to use such. But do train the entity in the use of divine purpose, divine desire. For if the purpose and the desire is right, we may find that the entity may—as in the experience before this—use the activities for the benefit of his fellow man.

For in the use of the power that has been a portion of the entity's consciousness there may come help to many.

For in the experience before this the entity attempted to buy same from Peter. Hence that tendency, that realization that the misuse of same may bring destructive forces into the experience.

In that experience the entity being warned, as he asked "Pray that I may be forgiven for the thought that such might be purchased," he was forgiven. For as it was indicated, "What thou shalt bind on earth shall be bound in heaven, what thou shalt loose on earth shall be loosed in heaven." There we find that the entity through that experience used the ability granted through such for a greater understanding, a greater interpretation. For all of God that any individual may know is already within self. It is in the application and the practice of same within self, in its relations to its desires, its hopes, its fears, and to its fellow man. For as ye sow, ye must reap.

Before that the entity was the prophet of Judah who was sent to Jeroboam to warn him, and who brought about the withering of the hand, and also the healing of same; yet turned aside when faced with that in which the mind said "A more excellent way."

There are no short cuts. What God hath commanded is true. For the law of the Lord is perfect and it converteth the soul.

Here the parents have a real, real obligation. They have a real, real opportunity. So live in self that thine own lives may be an example to this entity through its formative years. So teach, not let it be given to someone else—so teach, for it is thy responsibility, not the priest's, not a teacher's, NOT a minister's responsibility, but thine. Don't put it off. Don't neglect, or else ye will meet self again.

In the training let it first begin with self, as with the entity [4087]. Joseph he should be called. Let the training begin with that indicated in Exodus 19:5—"If thou will harken to the voice, He hath a special work, a special mission for thee—but thou must harken to the voice within, that ye present thy body as a living sacrifice, holy and acceptable unto Him, which is a reasonable service." For they who have been called, who have been ordained to be messengers have the greater responsibility; not as a saint—for there is more joy in heaven over one sinner than ninety and nine who are so-called saints, or those who are themselves satisfied with that they do.

Then study that interpreted in Romans. Ye will find it is not from somewhere else, not from out of the blue, not from overseas, not from before the altar. For thy body is indeed the temple and there he may indeed meet his Maker. There indeed may he meet himself. There indeed may he open the door of his own consciousness so that the Master may walk and talk with him.

Do not discourage, do not encourage the visions—until the first lessons are learned.

Then there will be the needs that THOU, as well as others, take heed to the warnings this entity may be sent to give.

We are through for the present.

❖

SUMMARY
of Edgar Cayce on Reincarnation and Life Purpose

* *

Edgar Cayce's understanding of reincarnation has a certain compatibility with the Judeo-Christian tradition. A succession of lifetimes makes it possible for the soul to move toward oneness with God while taking responsibility for its choices and constantly *meeting itself* in the circumstances of material life. But according to Cayce, karma is something more than debts to be paid; it's a matter of *soul memory*, even memory stored in the unconscious mind. We tend to replay old memories and repeat old patterns until our free will consciously decides to create new patterns of thinking, feeling, and acting. Literally remembering the details of past lives is not what is important; rather than getting distracted by that, it is far better to focus on the challenges and opportunities in our *current* lifetime, employing reincarnation as a tool for understanding how and why everything happens for a reason.

Another significant aspect of Edgar Cayce's theory of reincarnation is that for each lifetime the soul comes into the material world, it has a mission that includes work to help transform itself for the better as well as work that transforms the world for the better. Finding and using the soul's talents is the key. Cayce suggests that with self-study, we can intuit the soul purpose and even articulate a personal mission statement.

CHAPTER SIX

SOUL DEVELOPMENT AND SPIRITUAL GROWTH

❖

I N DESCRIBING THE GROWTH OF THE SOUL, EDGAR CAYCE IS sometimes criticized for lacking sophistication, for leaving out esoteric principles and relying too often on spiritual basics. But are we ready to deal with the details if we aren't ready to deal with the fundamentals? There are no doubt more complex ways of defining the mission of the soul and its steps along the way to spiritual evolution. In fact, Cayce sometimes does just that. But in certain readings—the ones that really are the more *essential* Edgar Cayce—he does us a favor by stripping away the metaphysical and focusing on what it takes to be successful spiritually.

In this chapter, we explore the heart of the development of the soul as Cayce saw it. We start with a remarkable reading, 518-2, that eloquently addresses the question of what truly makes life worthwhile. What is the nature of *greatness* in life? Cayce articulates the basic goal of living as the nurturing of *a way of being in life,* a way that is open to God, and other people, and that finds the greatest meaning and joy by being a blessing to others.

Next, we take an overview of the sequence of spiritual growth that Edgar Cayce developed for individual and group study, the "A Search for God" series, which many people feel is the heart and soul of his teachings. Although more fully permeated with language from the southern Protestant tradition than elsewhere, the wisdom is universal nonetheless. It's a demanding, powerful program for awakening a higher level of consciousness in ourselves.

WHAT IS GREATNESS?

• •

The modern world pushes us into believing that greatness lies in notoriety. If something is well known, well advertised, or a part of everyday conversation, then it must be special. Nothing could be further from Edgar Cayce's definition of greatness, of a life well lived. To him, *service done with humility* characterizes worthwhile living.

This theme weaves throughout this mental-spiritual reading, 518-2, which was done for a twenty-five-year-old woman who was searching for a deeper sense of purpose in life. Just eighteen months earlier, Cayce had given her a life reading that was full of past-life scenarios and advice that largely confused her. "I think my life reading is wonderful, but I don't understand it," she had written to him later. This second reading was to clarify the first. It's a fine statement of the universal principles governing the growth of the soul, with a special emphasis on joyful service undertaken with patient humility. To some scholars, the fourth paragraph (see page 193) is his most incisive illumination of the universal purpose of life: It's a journey toward becoming conscious, and cleansed, so that we can become companions with our Creator.

Ms. 518 must have been inspired by these sentiments, but she probably also wondered how such lofty ideas fit the more mundane problems she faced. In her first reading, she said she was perplexed about her choice of career. Rather than focus on career in the second reading, Cayce focuses on *a way of living* that leads to the development of the soul no matter what career path she takes. This emphasis on a way of life may remind us of Tao, or "the way." Cayce's version of the way sees joyful service displacing self-centered desires.

What can block service and the growth it brings? Sin, in the language of traditional theology. Hardly a concept that many of us would want to address seriously because of all the baggage that comes with it, Cayce addresses it head-on. Selfishness, grudges, and wrath were patterns in the woman's soul that kept her spiritual identity—her *individuality,* or the *I AM,* as it's called here—separated from God. And he warns against another kind of obstacle, *willfulness,* which focuses on private fulfillment. We *all* must guard against such selfishness, as much today as in Cayce's time. We're off the mark when we "intentionally turn our back" on spiritual opportunities, particularly in social relationships. With that clear warning, reading 518-2 returns to more hopeful themes, especially that great joy comes to anyone who makes an effort to lift the consciousness of anyone else.

Edgar Cayce even offers a two-part statement about what makes for greatness in life: that it is knowledge based, "That ye might know the Lord and *His* goodness"; and that it has a service component, that we "become as a messenger in thy service and thy activity before thy fellow man." Note that service, however patient or humble, doesn't stand alone. Its context comes from knowledge and understanding. Have you ever unintentionally caused more harm than good in an ill-conceived effort to serve? Without knowledge and understanding, you aren't going to achieve the helpful results you hoped for.

THE READING

❖

This psychic reading, 518-2,
was given by Edgar Cayce on August 13, 1935.
The conductor was Gertrude Cayce.

GC: Mental and spiritual reading, giving the original purpose of entrance into this solar realm of experience, trace the mental and spiritual development from the beginning through the various stages of experience, and give such guidance as the entity needs in awakening her psychic soul faculties and in using same for the highest spiritual development in this life. You will answer the questions she has submitted, as I ask them.

EC: Yes, we have the entity and those experiences in the mental and soul forces of same, as may be applicable in the experience in the present; that may make that necessary for the entity's development and to bring the influences that are necessary for the understanding.

In tracing the experiences of the entity, and in giving purposes, aims, desires, let these be set as the law; or as the ideal manner of approach to any of such conditions:

First, the entering of *every* soul is that it, the soul, may become more and more aware or conscious of the Divine within, that the soul-body may be purged; that it may be a fit companion for the *glory* of the Creative Forces in its activity.

The activity for this entity, then, is the same; that it may have the opportunity. For it has been given that the *Lord* hath not willed that any soul should perish. But with every temptation He hath prepared a way; so that if he or she as the erring one will turn to Him for that aid, it may find same.

Then again, in the appearances, do not look or seek for the phenomenon of the experience without the purpose, the aim. *Use* same as a criterion, as what to do and what not to do. Not that it, the simple experience, has made or set *anything* permanent! For there is the constant change evidenced before us; until the soul has been washed clean through that the soul in its body, in its temple, has *experienced* by the manner in which it has acted, has spoken, has thought, has desired in its relationships to its fellow man!

Not in selfishness, not in grudge, not in wrath; not in *any* of those things that make for the separation of the I AM from the Creative Forces, or Energy, or God. But the simpleness, the gentleness, the humbleness, the faithfulness, the long-suffering, *patience!* These be the attributes and those things which the soul takes cognizance of in its walks and activities before men. Not to be *seen* of men, but that the love may be manifested as the Father has shown through the Son and in the earth day by day. Thus He keeps the bounty, thus He keeps the conditions such that the individual soul may—if it will but meet or look within—find indeed *His* Presence abiding ever.

The soul, the individual that purposely, intentionally, turns the back upon these things, choosing the satisfying of the own self's desire, then has turned the back upon the living God.

Not that there is not to be joy, pleasure, and those things that maketh not afraid in the experience of every soul. But the joy in service, the joy in labor for the fellow man, the joy in giving of self that those through thy feeble efforts may have put before them, may become aware in their consciousness, that *thou* hast been with, that *thou* hast taken into thine own bosom the law of the Lord; and that ye walk daily with Him.

What, ye say then, was the purpose for which ye entered in at this particular experience? That ye might know the Lord and *His* goodness the more in thine inner self, that ye through this knowledge might become as a messenger in thy service and thy activity before thy fellow man; as one pointing the way, as one bringing—through the feeble efforts and endeavors, through the faltering steps at times, yet *trying*, attempting to do—what the conscience in the Lord hath prompted and does *prompt* thee to do.

As to thy music, in this thy hands may bring the consciousness of the harmonies that are created by the vibrations in the activities of each soul; that each other soul may, too, take hope; may, too, be *just kind*, just gentle, just patient, just humble.

Not that the way of the Lord is as the sounding of the trumpet, nor as the tinkling of cymbals that His might be proclaimed; but in the still small voice, in the hours of darkness that which lightens the heart to gladness, that which brings relief to the sufferer, that which makes for patience with the wayward, that which enables those that are *hungry*—in body, in mind—to be fed upon the bread of life; that they may drink deep of the water of life, through thy efforts.

These are the purposes, these are the experiences that bring in the heart and in the soul the answering of that cry, "Why—why—have I come into this experience?"

Be ye patient; be ye quiet and *see* the glory of the Lord in that thou may do in thine efforts day by day.

Do that thou *knowest* to do, *today!* Then leave the results, leave the rewards, leave the effects into the hands of thy God. For *He* knoweth thy heart, and He hath called—if ye will harken.

❖

"A SEARCH FOR GOD" AND THE
DEVELOPMENT OF THE SOUL

• •

A series of 130 readings given by Edgar Cayce between 1931 and 1942 is the closest thing he offered to a curriculum for spiritual growth. Presented to a small group of his closest supporters who wanted to know more about developing their own intuition and spiritual consciousness, the readings became the basis for small group and individual study and research worldwide.

The curriculum is not as obviously sequential as, say, a math or foreign language curriculum might be. While there are distinct lessons, each with four or five readings to elaborate on the meaning of the spiritual quality addressed, oftentimes Cayce looked at a topic from an unusual angle, as in his notion that *patience* is far more involved than just *waiting compliantly* and instead involves one of the three fundamental dimensions of a soul's experience in the material world.

It is hard to do justice to "A Search for God" so briefly as follows, but you certainly get a taste, a snapshot of the essence of the first twelve of twenty-four lessons in the series and commentaries that go with them.

1. COOPERATION

Cooperation may seem like a curious place to embark on the path to spiritual growth, but it makes sense if we consider that not much can get done without it. There is no group unless the members of the group cooperate. At a personal level, there is no health—physical, mental, or spiritual—unless the various aspects of ourselves learn to cooperate.

At its most essential, cooperation is a matter of not letting an egotistical sense-of-self control the situation. Not easy, of course, but a good starting point toward self-understanding.

In relationships with other people, drop any feelings of superiority, thinking you know better than other people, that your agenda is more important. As the series lesson on "Cooperation" put it: "In whatever state we find society, let us meet it upon its own level; as we look up, we lift it. That is cooperation." But even more than meeting people halfway, cooperation is an opportunity to be "a channel of blessings" to others.

Q Before we can have cooperation, do we not have to offer ourselves?

A In cooperation IS the offering of self to be a channel of activity, of thought; for as line upon line, precept upon precept, comes so does it come through the giving of self; for he that would have life must GIVE life, they that would have love must show themselves lovely, they that would have friends must be friendly, they that would have cooperation MUST cooperate by the GIVING of self TO that as is to be accomplished—whether in the bringing of light to others, bringing of strength, health, understanding, these are one IN Him.

262-3

2. KNOW THYSELF

The next step is honest self-appraisal. But the ancient injunction to *know thyself* is not just a single step on the path of soul growth but instead is ongoing. Without self-observation, we surely will fall prey to self-deception as we move on to the steps that follow.

Knowing oneself requires being honest. You cannot be true to another person, or to God, unless you can be true to yourself.

Without being true to the self, rare is the individual who is capable of integrity.

Edgar Cayce proposes this challenging experiment: "Stand aside and watch self pass by." This is not an invitation for out-of-body travel but instead refers to an internal process that is accomplished with one's will and attention, a *witnessing consciousness*. Even more challenging, dare to observe objectively and nonjudgmentally your own inner world of thoughts and feelings, the part of yourself that others cannot see.

Q How may I learn to know self as I am known?

A Being able to, as it were, LITERALLY, stand aside and watch self pass by! Take the time to occasionally be sufficiently introspective of that, that may happen in self's relation to others, to SEE the reactions of others as to that as was done by self; for true—as it has been said—no man lives to himself, no man dies to himself; for as the currents run to bring about the forces that are so necessary to man's own in these material things, so are those forces in self active upon those whom we act upon. Being able, then, to see self as others see you; for, as has been given, "NOW we know in part, then shall we know even as we are known." Then, in Him so let thy life be in Him, in thought, in deed, that "Ye that have known me have known the Father also" may be truly said of self. Stand aside and watch self pass by! **262-9**

3. WHAT IS MY IDEAL?

Ideals are central to Edgar Cayce's vision of personal growth, and it's no surprise that he would place clarifying one's ideals early in the "A Search for God" sequence.

It's important to distinguish between an *idea* and an *ideal*. Ideas arise from our experience of physical life and our personality. In contrast, ideals come to us—that is, they are not "man-made," as Cayce puts it—from deep within our soul as our unconscious life begins to stir and slowly reveal itself to us. As we experience it, an ideal *chooses us* just as much as we choose it. If we pay attention to this awakening, nurture it, and look for it to emerge even more fully, then we have adopted a spiritual ideal.

And what ideal does Cayce especially encourage us to pay attention to, nurture, and invite into our lives most fully? The ideal of wholeness, of oneness, of unity. As unique as the individual soul is, it can never become the whole; in other words, it can never become God. But it can strive to be as one with the divine— we can "attain to such an ideal," Cayce tells us.

Though there may be many ideas in the approach to the one, the differentiations are lost in the purpose of the ideal. An ideal, then, CANNOT, SHOULD not, WILL not, be that that is man-made, but must be of the spiritual nature—that has its foundation in Truth, in God, in the God-head, that there may be the continual reaching out of an individual, whether applied to the physical life, the mental life, or the spiritual life; knowing that FIRST principle, that the gift of God to man is an INDIVID-UAL soul that may be one WITH Him, and that may know itself to be one with Him and yet individual in itself, with the attributes OF the whole, yet NOT the whole. Such must be the concept, must be the ideal, whether of the imaginative, the mental, the physical, or the spiritual body of man. All may ATTAIN to such an ideal, yet never become the ideal—but ONE WITH the ideal, and such a one is set in Him. 262-11

4. FAITH

Questions of faith, belief, and doubt are vital to spiritual growth, and they have been debated by theologians for centuries. While belief and doubt are two sides of the same coin, faith exists outside their back-and-forth polarity.

As long as we confine our spiritual seeking to what we believe already, we never break out of the box of materiality. The conscious personality has a vested interest in there being certain truths in life in order to hold on to its worldview. Oftentimes, one's beliefs are so strong and persistent that they take on the appearance of truth.

But belief always attracts its opposite: *doubt*. Doubt drives the analytical mind, and is the basis for the scientific method, and it views life in terms of physical reality alone. The rationality of the logical mind is shaped by doubt.

Faith, on the other hand, is the *experience* of the unseen reality of life. Faith is a direct, personal encounter with the nonmaterial side of life, and having faith is a crucial step along the spiritual path and a hard step if we don't feel a connection to some spiritual ideal. When one has experienced the power of faith, belief and doubt become irrelevant.

Q Please explain by illustration: "Most say they believe, and yet begin at once to explain as to how this means in the mental rather in the material source."

A As has just been outlined as to how faith, as an attribute that came into being as the Son—in which the faith is magnified as to make those active forces in will, and the growth of the soul. So, as is seen in individuals as would say, "Yes, I believe— but" "but" meaning there is that doubt, that by the comparison of some individual, individuals or circumstances in their experience, when, where, or how, that individuals spoke yet acted in a manner as if that did not exist! Then, creating that doubt for self, applying to self, brings about that as is the opposite of faith, or else partakes of that within the conscious mind that begins with the lessons that must be answered by the attributes of the physical consciousness, that seek for a demonstration through those senses of the body that makes for an awareness to the physical being; yet, as is seen, these are the manners in which the variations to individuals reach those various conditions or circumstances in their experience.

262-15

5. VIRTUE AND UNDERSTANDING

Virtue is hardly a popular term in the today's world, somehow sounding disconnected from reality. Edgar Cayce tries to redeem it, suggesting that virtue is the integrity we bring to our purpose in life once we've found it. Without virtue, we never really grow in our understanding of our purpose.

Once we come to know our spiritual ideal, it's possible for us to truly have faith, to truly perceive the nonmaterial. But what do we do with the capacity to experience the spiritual world directly? We still must live in the material world, afterall, with its practical demands. With virtue, we are able to hold on to the feelings and insights stimulated by faith; we are able to maintain our integrity of purpose and intention. And with integrity, understanding begins to blossom, an understanding of how the material and nonmaterial are both part of the same whole.

Q Please give us that which we need in understanding and beginning work on our next lesson, on VIRTUE AND UNDERSTANDING.

A In the beginning of the study of this lesson, would be well that each individual of the group, or students of same, review that as has been the preparation for the study of the attributes that are now to be set before such students. In the beginning was that as would apply to the individual's cooperation with a group, or concerted effort on the part of individuals with one mind, or aim, or purpose. The understanding, or looking into self, and the preparation of self in the light of that of the cooperation. Then as to become active with that as had been gained. Then the basis with which an entity approaches the forces within each individual, that there may come forth those works, that are through the activity OF that force of faith in the material activities of an individual. Then there begins as in this: Adding to thy faith, virtue and understanding. Virtue, in this study, then, is to be as the criterion with which thine faith is to be put into active service; for without that pureness of the virtue of self's own mental, material and spiritual self, there can come little understanding.

262-18

6 . FELLOWSHIP

Having experienced faith, and embraced virtue, now we can establish a personal relationship with the Creator through fellowship. While some think of *fellowship* in terms of other people, Edgar Cayce uses the term *brotherhood* instead and reserves fellowship for our relationship to God. Cayce was asked in reading 262-22, "Please explain the difference between fellowship and brotherhood." His answer: "One to God, the other to man."

These two experiences are closely tied, of course: Fellowship, the personal relationship to God, allows us to express love to others. And that show of love reminds us of the essential relationship we have with the divine within us.

Q Can brotherhood exist among men without true fellowship?
A Fellowship is first brotherhood, a pattern of—or a shadow of—what fellowship is; for, as has been given, all one sees manifest in a material world is but a reflection or a shadow of the real or the spiritual life. Brotherhood, then, is an expression of the fellowship that exists in the SPIRITUAL life.

262-23

7 . PATIENCE

Patience, as we have seen earlier, is crucial to Edgar Cayce's teachings. He viewed it as one of the fundamental measurements of the experience of life, along with time and space. Patience, in fact, is a measure of our understanding of *the purposefulness* of what happens to us in time and space.

Patience is an inward quality, however. While we outwardly measure experiences in terms of time (when it happens) and space (what happens and where), patience is more subtle: It means being spiritually attuned, allowing us to experience what Cayce calls a "purposeful life." We are able to put others first ("preferring the other"), and see the essence of God even in those behaviors that annoy us. No wonder we find Cayce often saying "in patience become ye aware of your souls" (1747-5).

Q In learning the lesson of PATIENCE, please advise how we may overcome the little harassing annoyances that come in our daily lives.

𝒜 As was given of Him, as ye seek, know there is that Comforter present that will speak for thee under EVERY condition; for, as He gave, "I will not leave thee comfortless. Be NOT afraid." Be MAD, but sin not! In thine UNDERSTANDING gain the presence of Him ever as thy companion, in every act, in every word; for every thought must be accounted for, and in grace—His grace is sufficient—will there be that constant, prayerful attitude for a purposeful life; forgetting self, preferring another above self. Lose self in Him. THESE will answer. Not as an outward, but an INWARD growth—that makes for the beauty of the soul that has patience SHINING through.

𝒬 When we reach the development of ceasing to see faults in those we contact, is it then we can say we have patience?

𝒜 When we see rather Him that we worship even in the faults of others, THEN we are at the BEGINNING of patience.

262-24

8. THE OPEN DOOR

Edgar Cayce's explanation of the universal Christ Consciousness and his description of the life of Jesus are among the most essential of his teachings. The next chapter, "Esoteric Christianity," explores the various elements of his Christology. "A Search for God," however, focuses on one element in particular: the image of Christ as the open door. The seeker must use free will to open that door, to choose life over death, and to allow Christ Consciousness to come in.

Consider the door. It allows passage through a wall without destroying it. The wall protects us, but we need to pass through it to get in and out. If we apply the door to human nature, we see that there is a wall between the finite and the infinite. The average individual could not stand the elimination of that wall because the infinite could be overwhelming, and in one lacking sufficient wisdom, could be employed selfishly and destructively. The door allows us to selectively experience the infinite without being swallowed up by it.

Then turn to the 30th of Deuteronomy and ye will read "Today there is set before thee good and evil, life and death, choose thou." The will, then, in self is the gift of thy Maker, thy Creator; that ye might understand and approach Him, putting thy trust, thy hope in His hands. For thy brother, even Jesus who became the Christ—by making intercession, by offering Himself as the sacrifice that made possible man's approach to God through Him—has promised, "I stand at the door of thy heart, of thy consciousness. If ye open, I will enter, if ye will listen to that still small voice within." For thy body is the temple of the living God, and there He has promised to meet thee. There ye may find the answer. Ye have the ability. Will you listen?   3506-1

9. IN HIS PRESENCE

In "A Search for God," we might expect the awareness of God's presence to enter as soon as we "open the door." Edgar Cayce suggests that we don't feel the divine presence as often as we might simply because we "keep it as a thing apart"—that is, we objectify God as a superhuman being who is separate from us rather than *beingness* that resides within us and all around us.

So how can we be more open? While the answer will differ from person to person, a good starting point is to release some of our worries. A worrying mind is a barrier; it slams that open door shut. Instead, we must nurture joy and gladness in life, even in the face of adversity.

Q Please expand on how we may come into the realization of His presence.

A As we have given above, the greater fault from the realization is that it—His presence—is kept as a thing apart. HE wills that all should come to the knowledge of His presence abiding with all. We come to this knowledge and consciousness by doing those things that are conducive to bringing into every atom of our being that which gives the attributes OF His presence in the earth; and in DOING this do we come to know His presence.

Q Please expand on how we may prepare ourselves that we may abide in His presence.

A This would refer rather to the individual experience; for in the preparations of self there are varied consciousnesses, and what to one might be necessary to another would be secondary . . . As we may experience by that abiding presence, what are the fruits of same? WORRIES pass away, joys take their place . . . Then, when ye abide in His presence, though there may come the trials of every kind, though the tears may flow from the breaking up of the carnal forces within self, the spirit is made glad . . .   262-33

10. THE CROSS AND THE CROWN

Of these twelve lessons in the series, this is the one that people have the most difficulty understanding and applying. Perhaps it's so tough because, like any system of spiritual transformation, it requires that we surrender our own view of the world. We must surrender our fears and our own plans for getting what we think we want.

To describe this *letting go,* Edgar Cayce uses the biblical imagery of the cross, although the same principle can be found in ancient wisdom from many traditions. The crown is the new consciousness that emerges when we let go.

So, each in their respective lives, their own experiences, find their cross overcoming the world, overcoming those things, those conditions, those experiences, that would not only enable them to meet the issues of life but to become heirs with Him of the Crown of Glory.

What, then, is this Crown of Glory? Does this bespeak only of those things, those conditions, that have to do with the spiritual life? Did the overcoming give the authority? Did the overcoming make this Son of man the Lord, the Glory, the Crown of Life?

So He, as the pattern for each, makes the way clear, the way open that each soul—as it meets the crosses, endures the temptations and overcomes them—may become an heir, JOINT heir with Him to the Crown of Glory; with power temporal, power mental, power spiritual to become the Sons and Daughters of God, as many as are called—and all that fulfil that purpose for which they, as individuals, are called—and carry on in that manner, overcoming, meeting, bearing within themselves. Not in sorrow, not in wailing, but in the JOY of the Lord.

Then, the first of the signs that may be given—to as many as have met the cross, as have endured, is given that which enables them—in whatsoever state they find themselves in meeting their crosses—to do so in the JOY of the Lord. Happiness and joy go hand in hand.   262-36

11. THE LORD THY GOD IS ONE

One of the qualities emphasized throughout "A Search for God" is the *interconnectedness* of life. The emphasis in this lesson is on how we look at our material lives and how we try to live practically, applying the inner lessons that have been absorbed.

The challenge is making all the aspects of our lives work in harmony. Our job, our marriage, our friends, our health may pull us in different directions, and the competition for our time and energy may leave us feeling that our integrity and consistency are lacking. On other occasions, the difficulty is in reconciling our inner values with the demands of making it in the outer world of business and human relationships.

Edgar Cayce teaches us in the series, and in individual readings such as this one for a thirty-five-year-old lawyer, that God is the source of everything we experience. In that light, it really is possible to integrate all the various elements of our lives; in fact, it is even our birthright, as Cayce often said.

Q Am I mentally lazy, and can you suggest how I can best arouse my mental energy to help me live a full life, both as far as my marriage and my business are concerned?

A We would concern self principally now with the BUSINESS; for when the life has adjusted itself the marriage relations, the business relations, the material relations and the spiritual relations are of ONE measure, and should be the same experience in the life of all. When life is made into such a manner that the life is one, all thoughts are one. So, it has been given how to make the business relationships not only interesting but worth while, helpful, remunerative; and builded upon that principle, that policy, will make those relationships in every walk of life as not idealistic things but RE-

ALITY; for life IS real, life IS earnest! The grave is not the goal; for life is ONE! It is in Him! Lose not thy birthright in Him for secular things.   912-1

1 2 .   L O V E

Love is the capstone of this first set of twelve lessons of "A Search for God." It is the product of all the inner work done in the first eleven lessons. Love is not just about having personal relationships, however. It is an entire way of life. Edgar Cayce waxed poetic in the following passage in painting a picture of the loving life.

EC: Yes, we have the group as gathered here, as a group and as individuals—and their work in preparation of the lesson Love.

Each may find in this that which is being sought by each, in the study of the lesson and that which each seeks to manifest in the lesson. As each goes forth to make manifest, each may find that sought.

The first, in that expressed in a baby's smile; in the hope, the light, the seeking, the manifestation of that which is love undefiled.

The next may see it in the rose, as it seeks—with that it has to do with—to make manifest that beauty in expression that may GLORIFY its Maker.

The next may find it in friendship, in that which speaks without thought of self, that which makes for the expressions of love GLORIFIED through the friendliness that comes with friendship.

The next may find it in that as reasons for the beauty of a song, in the harmony that shows forth in the expression of the soul within; whether in instruments or the soul raised in praise to the Giver of light.

The next may find it in the expressions of the duty that may be the lot of one that, without thought of self, shows forth in the acts of life that first thought of the duty from a material stand-point, yet the LOVE made manifest from wholly showing forth His life, His love, till He come again!

The next may find it in the manner of speech under the var-ied circumstances that arise in the experience of all, through that association which comes in the daily walks of life, and in the encouragement that may be given through the kind word spoken; the giving of the cup of water to anyone seeking, to those that thirst. This may show to such a one the love that is manifest in "God is love."

The next may find it in whatever the hands find to do, that done well, in all phases of one's experience, that lends self in the daily walks of life, doing the best with that which presents itself, in the glorying of the expressions, "As ye do it unto the least of these, my little ones, ye do it unto me."

The next will find it in the glory that comes in the satisfac-tion of a contented heart, in knowing that each day has brought an opportunity that has been taken advantage of by self in show-ing the kindness here, going out of the way in self's own life to make the lot of a neighbor more joyous, brighter, in the activi-ties of the daily life.

The next may find it in looking forward to those days that may come, for the filling of those places that may be made or given in the lives spent in the service of Him who may call that thy face be that which may bring the knowledge of thine life, thine heart, spent in His service day by day. **262-45**

SUMMARY
of Edgar Cayce on the
Development of the Soul

• •

S oul development involves maturing into a certain way of being in life: present, patient, helpful, loving. It has nothing to
do with one's level of psychic ability or one's place in the world.
Instead, it's learning how to put aside one's personality and willfulness and instead awaken to one's individuality and willingness
to serve God. Edgar Cayce's "A Search for God" focused on developing character and spiritual consciousness. Success depends
on our willingness to actually *practice* the teachings. Soul growth
is possible only through application.

CHAPTER SEVEN

ESOTERIC CHRISTIANITY

✧

Edgar Cayce challenges us to see the life, the teachings, and the importance of the historical Jesus in a whole
new light. He indicates that there is lost wisdom about the events
of Jesus's life and the very meaning of his coming two millennia
ago. He presents Jesus as the incarnation of a soul, who, in many
ways, is very much like us, including having past lives, sometimes
as known figures from history. And Cayce proposes that to fully
understand the meaning of Christ, we must recognize, awaken in
ourselves, and live an internalized Christ Consciousness.

And while his ideas about Jesus and the Christ Consciousness
are radical, in many other ways Edgar Cayce was rather conservative theologically. It would be misleading to call him a fun-
damentalist, and yet his teachings assert many of the more
traditional views of Christianity, including the Immaculate Conception, the Virgin Birth, the Resurrection, the Second Coming,

and various miraculous events recorded in the Old and New Testaments. There is also the feeling of his endorsing Christianity as the pinnacle of religious movements, even though Cayce himself professed an embracing and inclusive attitude toward the religions of the world.

Perhaps most difficult for Christians to accept is Cayce's distinction between Jesus—the man, the soul—and the Christ, as a spiritual power, and a universal consciousness. Instead of seeing Jesus Christ as virtual first and last names of a being who was radically different from us, Cayce called Jesus our "elder brother"— that is, someone who is on the same path as we and yet is more mature than we are and more awakened. In the esoteric Christianity of Edgar Cayce, Jesus is the life *pattern* for us to emulate, whereas the Christ is the *spiritual power* that we invoke to guide and heal us.

Cayce also proposed that Jesus had esoteric teachings for his closest followers that are only hinted at in the biblical accounts. Their flavor is evoked in the Gospel of Thomas, discovered at Nag Hammadi, Egypt, in 1945, just after Cayce's death.

One example is the Lord's Prayer. Cayce indicates that it is special not only because it is the only prayer that we have a record of as coming directly from Jesus; there is a deeper meaning and purpose to its words. It is a kind of *mantra,* in that the words have a universally evocative power. The various lines of the prayer are keyed to the seven spiritual centers, the *chakras,* and when properly applied it has an awakening effect on the chakras. The correspondence is as follows:

"Our Father who art in heaven" = the seventh chakra
  (the highest).
"Hallowed be Thy name" = the sixth chakra.

"Thy kingdom come, Thy will be done" = the fifth chakra.

"In earth as it is in heaven" = *earth* refers collectively to
  the four lower chakras, *heaven* refers to the three
  upper chakras.

"Give us this day our daily bread" = the first chakra
  (the lowest).

"Forgive us our debts as we forgive our debtors" = the
  third chakra.

"Lead us not into temptation" = the second chakra.

"But deliver us from evil" = the fourth chakra.

"For Thine is the kingdom and the power and the glory
  forever" = sequentially, the fifth, sixth, and seventh
  chakras.

But just knowing these correspondences is not enough. The prayer has the power to enlighten only to the extent that we experience the *meaning* of each line of the prayer while attending to the body. It is what in the passage below Cayce calls "the response to the mental representation." That is, something can happen in the mind, or the "mental body," that connects us to the essential meaning of the words.

For example, while the meditator says "Forgive us our debts [or trespasses] as we forgive our debtors [or those who trespass against us]," the whole point is to *feel* the meaning underlying the words. Can the meditator feel forgiveness toward others, and then, in turn, feel forgiven him- or herself? If so, then Cayce suggests there is an "opening of the center," an awakening of the spiritual potential that resides there. And with that opening comes energy, which may not be felt immediately by the meditator but which causes something profound to happen inside the meditator. A connection has been made to greater vitality in life, what Jesus referred to as "the bread ye know not of."

Q Does the outline of the Lord's Prayer as placed on our chart have any bearing on the opening of the centers?

A Here is indicated the manner in which it was given as to the purpose for which it was given; not as an ONLY way but as a way that would answer for those that sought to be—as others—seekers for A way, AN understanding, to the relationships to the Creative Forces. It bears in relationships to this, then, the proper place.

Q How should the Lord's Prayer be used in this connection?

A As in feeling, as it were, the flow of the meanings of each portion of same throughout the body-physical. For as there is the response to the mental representations of all of these in the MENTAL body, it may build into the physical body in the manner as He, thy Lord, thy Brother, so well expressed in, "I have bread ye know not of."   281-29

AWAKENING TO A PERSONAL
RELATIONSHIP WITH CHRIST

• •

No Cayce reading is any clearer than 5749-4 about the promise held out to each of us that we can have a direct, personal relationship with Christ. It was delivered to some of the members of the original "A Search for God" group on a summer afternoon over seventy years ago. Three of those present had their own experiences they were hoping to have interpreted by Cayce. They wondered if their communication with Christ was actually just that.

From the moment Edgar Cayce began, it was clear that this reading was going to be remarkable. In well over ninety-nine percent of the other readings, his own superconscious mind offered the information, but reading 5749-4 seems to be one of those rare occasions when he *channeled* the consciousness of some other being—in this case, the apostle John. There is a certain ambiguity about how much of the reading is John and how much is Cayce, but in at least three places John announces himself specifically.

What makes the reading so special, however, is not so much the unexpected communication from John as the promise it offers: Anyone who sincerely wants to make direct contact with Christ, *and* acts in such a way as to reflect that desire, can expect to make contact.

Where is Christ, anyway? Where is he found? This reading speaks to those questions directly. Yes, it's natural for the physical, conscious mind to think in terms of time and space; they are the familiar categories that help us understand things. But it gets frustrating trying to pin Christ down to a location so that we can go there and make personal contact. He is not on the earthly plane in corporeal form. Instead, Cayce suggests that if we need to locate Christ spatially, then we should understand him as being "in the individual entity"—that is, he's found within us, and it is a relationship that becomes conscious through attunement.

Attunement is the essential factor that makes personal relationships possible. Christ Consciousness is a universal consciousness residing in every soul. And it is the consciousness of an extraordinary historical being who lived twenty centuries ago in the physical dimension and who still exists as an active, living presence in the spiritual dimension.

How do we get in contact with him? By means of a resonating vibration of sorts that is possible when we reach a state of wholeness, a condition in which we feel in sync with ourselves so that our desires and our talents are in alignment. We've probably all had times when we experienced that kind of wholeness, and perhaps then we also intuited just how connected we are with the spiritual.

Attunement is central to many Cayce readings, including these on meditation and healing. Attunement involves the body, the mind, and the free will achieving harmony with the spirit. It's tempting to leave out the body and believe that contacting Christ is purely a psychological matter. But as this reading points out, attunement gets right down to each atom physically.

The mind factor includes two keys: *faith*, which is knowing that Christ can and will communicate with us directly and which has a potent, attuning effect on us; and *surrendering fear*, as when Christ, in initiating contact, so often says, "Be not afraid," words which may be necessary because something in us shies away from such an encounter. Fear more than any other emotion can block attunement.

The third attunement factor is the right use of free will, which is something often ignored but which Cayce puts right at the heart of his advice. If any of us wants a relationship with Christ, we've got to actively work to "[make] the will of self one with His will." More than anything else, it means letting our deeds reflect our beliefs and faith. It means applying what's in our hearts. The promise offered in this reading—actually, the reaffirmation of the promise in the Bible—is that Christ will come to anyone who wants it of his or her own free will and then "acts in love to make [it] possible."

Deep down inside, each of us knows just what that means. *Oh, if only I knew for sure exactly what Christ wants me to be doing*, we may protest. But in the quiet place of knowing, a place we often don't like admitting knowing about, we're absolutely certain of what's required. We know that we must take the time to be present for other people and really hear what they are saying, rather than being caught up in the busy demands of our own "things to do." We know we must invest quality and excellence in all our efforts, especially those that affect other people. And, just as surely, in that quiet place of knowing, it has been revealed to us that we are quite capable of putting the Christ spirit first in our lives. What's asked of us is not outrageous, not unreasonable, "not grievous." It's within our reach.

THE READING

✦

THIS PSYCHIC READING, 5749-4,
WAS GIVEN BY EDGAR CAYCE ON AUGUST 6, 1933.
The conductor was Gertrude Cayce.

GC: You will have before you the Norfolk Study Group #1, members of which are present in this room, who seek more knowledge of, and that a reading be given on, Jesus the Christ. We would appreciate all knowledge that might be given on Him at this time, after which you will answer the questions that may be asked by each individual present.

EC: Yes, we have the group as gathered here; and their work, their desires. We will seek that as may be given at this time.

"I, John, would speak with thee concerning the Lord, the Master, as He walked among men. As given, if all that He did and said were written, I suppose the world would not contain all that may be said."

As He, the Christ, is in His glory that was ordained of the Father, He may be approached by those who in sincerity and earnestness seek to know Him—and to be guided by Him. As He has given, by faith all things are made possible through belief in His name.

Believest thou? Then let thine activities bespeak that thou wouldst have, in spirit, in truth.

Seek, then, each in your own way and manner, to magnify that you, as souls, as beings, would make manifest of His love, in the way He will show thee day by day.

As He came into the world, as man knows the world, then He became as man; yet in the spirit world He seeks to make manifest that sought by those who do His biddings.

For, as He gave, "If ye love me, keep my commandments. These are not new, and are not grievous, that ye love one another—even as the Father loveth me."

Q [993]: Please explain why during meditation last Monday noon I had the longing to seek more knowledge of, and a reading on, Jesus the Christ.

A The inner self approached nearer the attunement of the consciousness of the Christ presence. The Christ Consciousness is a universal consciousness of the Father Spirit. The Jesus consciousness is that man builds as body worship. In the Christ Consciousness, then, there is the oneness of self, self's desires, self's abilities, made in at-onement with the forces that may bring to pass that which is sought by an individual entity or soul. Hence at that particular period self was in accord. Hence the physical consciousness had the desire to make it an experience of the whole consciousness of self.

Seek this the more often. He will speak with thee, for His promises are true—every one of them.

Q [560]: Please explain: While meditating I had the realization of the forces within and the forces without being the one and the same force. Then as if someone said: "Why not look to the within?" When I turned to the within, I received a realization of the Christ which seemed to take form in body.

A In this the body-consciousness experienced much that "I, even John, experienced when I looked behind me from the cave and saw that the without and within are *one*," when the desires of the heart make each atom of the physical body vibrate with the consciousness of, the belief and the faith and the presence of, the Christ life, the Christ Consciousness.

Life is an essence of the Father. The Christ, taking up the life of the man Jesus, becomes life in glory; and may be glorified in each atom of a physical body that attunes self to the consciousness and the *will* of the Christ Spirit.

Q [69]: Is the Celestial Sphere a definite place in the universe or is it a state of mind?

A When an entity, a soul, passes into any sphere, with that it has builded in its celestial body, it must occupy—to a finite mind—space, place, time. Hence, to a finite mind, a body can only be in a place, a position. An attitude, sure—for that of a onement with, or attunement with, the Whole.

For, God is love; hence occupies a space, place, condition, and *is* the Force that permeates all activity.

So, Christ is the ruling force in the world that man, in his finite mind—the material body, must draw to self of that sphere of which the entity, the soul, is a part, of whatever period of experience, to be conscious of an existence in that particular sphere or plane.

Q Is Jesus the Christ on any particular sphere or is He manifesting on the earth plane in another body?

A As just given, all power in heaven, in earth, is given to Him who overcame. Hence He is of Himself in space, in the force that impels through faith, through belief, in the individual entity. As a Spirit Entity. Hence not in a body in the earth, but may come at will to him who *wills* to be one with, and acts in love to make same possible. For, He shall come as ye have seen Him go, in the *body* He occupied in Galilee. The body that He formed, that was crucified on the cross, that rose from the tomb, that walked by the sea, that appeared to Simon, that appeared to Philip, that appeared to "I, even John."

Q Wherever He is, how may I contact Him so that I may see Him and hear Him speak?

A The making of the will of self one with His will makes a whole attunement with Him. He *will*, with the making of self in accord and desiring same, speak with thee. "Be not afraid, it is I."

Q [585]: Was the vision I saw early one morning several months ago a vision of the Master?

A A passing shadow, yes. Pray rather to the Son, the Father through the Son, that He walks with thee—and He *will* walk and talk with thee. Be *not* satisfied with *any* other. He may oft give His angels charge concerning thee, yet know the Master's touch, the Master's voice; for He may walk and talk with thee. *He* is the Way; there is no other. He in body suffered; for himself, yea—for thee also. Wilt thou turn, then, to any other?

Q When Jesus the Christ comes the second time, will He set up His kingdom on earth and will it be an everlasting kingdom?

A Read His promises in that ye have written of His words, even as "I gave." He shall rule for a thousand years. Then shall Satan be loosed again for a season.

Q [379]: How may I raise my vibrations so as to contact the Christ?

A Making the will, the desire of the heart, one with His, believing in faith, in patience, all becomes possible in Him, through Him to the Father; for He gave it as it is. Believest thou?

Then, "according to thy faith be it done in thee."

We are through.

✣

A CLAIRVOYANT VIEW OF
JESUS THE MAN

• •

A mong the various readings about the life of Jesus, Edgar Cayce sometimes tried to paint a graphic picture of certain biblical events. It was almost as if he were trying to do what modern parapsychologists call *remote viewing*. He acted as a clairvoyant reporter, offering details about a given story in the Bible, and in such a way that it becomes more alive to us.

Of course, none of Cayce's clairvoyant experiences can be proved. But it's interesting to note that he sometimes did something similar when reading for someone several hundred miles away. Before giving an answer about a specific health concern or interpreting a dream or doing what that particular reading called for, he might speak in detail about what was happening right at that moment in that person's life. For example, "not bad-looking pajamas," or "Yes, she is now waiting on a lady in front of a glass [window] with a knot on the post . . . and [now] the two are sitting together." In most instances, the person later confirmed that the details were very accurate.

And so we have evidence of Edgar Cayce's skills as a remote viewer. Whether he could also travel back in time clairvoyantly is an open question, but readings like 5749-1 below certainly present a provocative and, for some people, inspirational picture.

THE READING

✥

This psychic reading, 5749-1,
was given by Edgar Cayce on June 14, 1932.
The conductor was Gertrude Cayce.

EC: The Lord's Supper—here with the Master—see what they had for supper—boiled fish, rice, with leeks, wine, and loaf. One of the pitchers in which it was served was broken—the handle was broken, as was the lip to same.

The whole robe of the Master was not white, but pearl gray—all combined into one—the gift of Nicodemus to the Lord.

The better looking of the twelve, of course, was Judas, while the younger was John—oval face, dark hair, smooth face—only one with the short hair. Peter, the rough and ready—always that of very short beard, rough, and not altogether clean; while Andrew's is just the opposite—very sparse, but inclined to be long more on the side and under the chin—long on the upper lip—his robe was always near gray or black, while his clouts or breeches were striped; while those of Philip and Bartholomew were red and brown.

The Master's hair is 'most red, inclined to be curly in portions, yet not feminine or weak—STRONG, with heavy piercing eyes that are blue or steel-gray.

His weight would be at least a hundred and seventy pounds. Long tapering fingers, nails well kept. Long nail, though, on the left little finger.

Merry—even in the hour of trial. Joke—even in the moment of betrayal.

The sack is empty. Judas departs.

The last is given of the wine and loaf, with which He gives

the emblems that should be so dear to every follower of Him. Lays aside His robe, which is all of one piece—girds the towel about His waist, which is dressed with linen that is blue and white. Rolls back the folds, kneels first before John, James, then to Peter—who refuses.

Then the dissertation as to "He that would be the greatest would be servant of all."

The basin is taken as without handle, and is made of wood. The water is from the gherkins [gourds], that are in the wide-mouth Shibboleths [streams? Judges 12:6], that stand in the house of John's father, Zebedee.

And now comes "It is finished."

They sing the ninety-first Psalm—"He that dwelleth in the secret place of the Most High shall abide under the shadow of the Almighty. I will say of the Lord, He is my refuge and my fortress: my God; in Him will I trust."

He is the musician as well, for He uses the harp.

They leave for the garden.

❖

THE SECOND COMING

• •

The second coming of Christ is perhaps the most significant of all the prophecies made in the Cayce readings. It was a topic of deep personal interest to Edgar Cayce the man, too. The following reading, 5749-5, was given to help him prepare for a scheduled lecture on the subject.

The Cayce readings, of course, are hardly alone in looking for such a great event. "Many . . . have preached concerning this Second Coming," as he puts it. What is special about this reading are some of its themes about the *meaning* of Christ's return.

Note the unusual way this reading begins. The opening paragraphs serve to introduce Cayce himself, as if he were some master of ceremonies introducing a speaker. It's not clear who, or even what, this introducer is—another aspect of Cayce's soul, a spirit speaking through an entranced Cayce, or something else. In this introduction is a remarkable label for Cayce and his work: "forerunner of . . . Christ Consciousness." We might presume that this phase refers both to the teachings found in the readings and to the clairvoyant sensitivity Cayce demonstrated.

Also mentioned is Cayce's visionary dream, which came during another reading that very morning. (This phenomenon happened many times, that one aspect of his mind could give a reading while another aspect dreamed.) In the dream, he was traveling on a luxurious train with a white and gold interior with several famous evangelists, each deceased, heading for a place where John, the Beloved Disciple, would be teaching. The dreaming Cayce asked one of the evangelists if he remembered him. To which the evangelist replied, apparently referencing in a symbolic way that he, Cayce, was still alive in the physical world: "Oh yes, but you are not just like we are. . . . You are on this same train with us right now, but don't forget you have to go back and don't you get too far away." This dream was directly related to Edgar Cayce's concerns about the meaning of the Second Coming.

The heart of reading 5749-5 begins on page 228 with the paragraph that opens, "Ye, my brethren." It includes many elements central to Cayce's theological position on Christ. For example, Christ is the first to conquer death (that is, to "put on immortality"). And he came not to judge and condemn us, since we condemn ourselves already by our willfulness and our separation from God.

As if to answer definitively the question about Christ's possible return, Edgar Cayce presents a theme that is echoed later in the reading: Christ has come once before, and he will come again in any age when there is need. In the history of humankind, there have been windows of opportunity, periods of possible break-through. He intervenes directly in our affairs whenever we are ready to attain a new level of understanding and application of the one basic principle, that our creator is spirit, and any worshipful approach of that creator must be based on right understanding and truth.

In reading 5749-5, Cayce also presents the broad view of Christ as being intimately involved in human evolution for many millennia. Instead of a single remarkable visit to earth through the body and personality of the man we know as Jesus, Cayce's Chris-tology describes him as a guide and sustainer of long standing. In this light, we might be more accurate in wondering about *another coming* instead of only a second one. With each coming, human-ity is nudged back toward the divine plan for spiritual evolution—what Cayce refers to here as "continued activity toward the proper understanding and proper relationships . . . [to] Him."

Christ and his influence have been experienced in different ways in different eras. Not always has it been a direct incarnation, although in 5749-5 there are clear references to the possibility of his coming again "in body," "in the flesh." But it has sometimes been his spirit inspiring and directing men and women who have served as leaders of their people. The work of such individuals is bound to upset those whose values and ideals are rooted in mate-rialism ("contention in the minds and hearts of those that dwell in the flesh"). The Christ impulse counteracts the forces of selfish-ness, prejudice, hate, and the other shortcomings listed by Cayce near the end of the reading.

We might well ask ourselves two questions about the possibility of another coming of Christ . First, are we at a time in human his-tory that is ripe for Christ's influence to engage us directly once again? That is, are we ready for a breakthrough, a quantum leap to some new application of the divine plan to evolve toward oneness? Many would argue yes and point to certain promising signs—for example, the evident potential for science and spirituality to come together, which surely would be a breakthrough for humanity. Another hopeful sign is the ecumenical outlook of many religious leaders, a deep appreciation of and respect for the value of *all* traditions, again another breakthrough.

Second, what can each of us do as individuals to make a return of Christ possible? This is not the only reading in which Edgar Cayce claims that preparations were made in advance of Christ's coming two thousand years ago, and such preparation would be needed just as much today. Christ's return becomes reality only "as there is prepared the way by those that have made and do make the channels for the entering in." Our little acts of tolerance and kindness play a big role in paving the way for such a coming.

THE READING

❖

This psychic reading, 5749-5,
was given by Edgar Cayce on May 1, 1934.
The conductor was Gertrude Cayce.

GC: You will have before you Edgar Cayce, present in this room, and his inquiring mind in relation to the talk which he expects to give next Monday evening on the "Second Coming." You will give what he should present at this open meeting on this subject.

EC: That which crowds in at the present may be well for those present, but would it be well for those in open meeting? From this experience, though, there may be gathered that which has been given and that which may be helpful to many in the comprehension of that which is the experience of those that seek through such channels to have for themselves the experience that may be had by those here in this room in the present.

Be mindful then, each of you, of that ye may inwardly experience in that which may be given you.

For, those experiences that have been told you of the vision [E.C's dream of that a.m.] of the gathering of those that were known to many in this present land and in the lands abroad were in reference to just those things that may be said respecting the Coming.

Many of these have ministered, have preached concerning this Second Coming. Not a one but what has at some time left the record of his contemplations and experiences in those environs, whether made in the heart and mind of his hearers or in the written word; yet here today, in what ye call time, ye find them gathering in a body to *listen* to that as may be given them by [Edgar Cayce?] one who is to be a forerunner of that influence in the earth known as the Christ Consciousness, the coming of that force or power into the earth that has been spoken of through the ages.

Listen, while he speaks! [Edgar Cayce?]

Ye, my brethren, in your ignorance and in your zeal have often spoken of that influence in the earth known among men as the record made by those that would influence the activities in the religious or spiritual life of individuals through the ages, as a record of the Son of man as He walked in the earth. Rather would ye listen and harken to those things as He spoke when He made those inferences and illustrations as to how those had closed and did close their ears to what was actually going on about them; yet they knew Him not! He, our Lord and our Master, was the first among those that put on immortality that there might be the opportunity for those forces that had erred in spiritual things; and only through experiencing in a manner whereunto all might be visioned from their greater abilities of manifesting in the various phases, forms and manners as they developed through that ye know as matter, could they come to know how or why or when there was made manifest in any realm spirit that was good and spirit that was in error. For, He gave thee, had ye not *known* the Son ye would *not* be condemned in thine own self. For, condemnation was not in Him, but "ye are condemned already." And in the coming into the influence of those that would open themselves for an understanding might there be the approach to Him. He has come in all ages through those that were the spokesmen to a people in this age, that age, called unto a purpose for the manifestation of that first idea.

Readst thou how the sons of God came together, and Satan came also? "Hast thou considered my servant? Hast thou seen his ways?" And the answer, even from the evil force, "Put forth thine hand—touch him in those things that pertain to the satisfying of desire that is flesh, and he will curse thee to thy face." Then, "He is in thine hand, but touch not his soul—touch not his soul!"

So we see how that the coming into the earth has been and is for the evolution or the evolving of the soul unto its awareness of the effect of all influences in its experience in the varied spheres of activity; and that only in Him who was the creator, the maker, the experiencer of mortality and spirit and soul *could* this be over come.

Then, the necessity. For, has it not been said, has it not been shown in the experience of the earth, the world, from any angle it may be considered, that He has not willed that any should be lost—but has prepared the way of escape in Him, the Maker?

But who is the worthy servant? He that has endured unto the end!

Then, He has come in all ages when it has been necessary for the understanding to be centered in a *new* application of the same thought, "God *is* Spirit and seeks such to worship him in spirit and in truth!"

Then, as there is prepared the way by those that have made and do make the channels for the entering in, there may come into the earth those influences that will save, regenerate, resuscitate, *hold*—if you please—the earth in its continued activity toward the proper understanding and proper relationships to that which is the making for the closer relationships to that which is in Him *alone*. Ye have seen it in Adam; ye have heard it in Joshua, Joseph, David, and those that made the preparation then for him called Jesus. Ye have seen His Spirit in the leaders in all realms of activity, whether in the isles of the sea, the wilderness, the mountain, or in the various activities of every race, every color, every activity of that which has produced and does produce contention in the minds and hearts of those that dwell in the flesh.

For, what must be obliterated? Hate, prejudice, selfishness, backbiting, unkindness, anger, passion, and those things of the mire that are created in the activities of the sons of men.

Then again He may come in body to claim His own. Is He abroad today in the earth? Yea, in those that cry unto Him from every corner; for He, the Father, hath not suffered His soul to see corruption; neither hath it taken hold on those things that make the soul afraid. For, He *is* the Son of Light, of God, and is holy before Him. And He comes again in the hearts and souls and minds of those that seek to know His ways.

These be hard to be understood by those in the flesh, where prejudice, avarice, vice of all natures holds sway in the flesh; yet those that call on Him will not go empty-handed—even as thou, in thine ignorance, in thine zealousness that has at times eaten thee up. Yet *here* ye may hear the golden scepter ring—ring—in the hearts of those that seek His face. Ye, too, may minister in those days when He will come in the flesh, in the earth, to call His own by name.

We are through.

S U M M A R Y
of *Edgar Cayce's Esoteric Christianity*

• •

Edgar Cayce invites us to consider a new way of understanding Christ. At the heart of his Christology is a distinction between *Jesus*, the most recent incarnation of a soul who had many lifetimes on earth, and the universal *Christ Consciousness*, the awareness of the oneness of all life. Jesus is "our elder brother" in the sense that he is a soul like us who has been on the long, difficult journey of growth of the soul. And Christ Consciousness is not something far off but instead resides already in the unconscious mind of each soul, waiting to be awakened by free will.

CHAPTER EIGHT

SOCIAL VISION

✢

EDGAR CAYCE BECAME FAMOUS IN THE LATE 1960s WITH SUCH books as *The Sleeping Prophet* that crowned him a prognosticator in the Nostradamus mold and as the visionary of a new world order. Had he lived to see his legacy understood in this way, he probably would have been uncomfortable—not because his readings lacked prophetic insight and social vision, but because they made up such a tiny percentage of his life's work. He would wish us to place less weight on the prophecies, more on his pioneering work with holistic healing and his simple, direct methods for achieving personal spirituality.

Even though only about one percent of the readings address world events or social issues, they are an important part of his teaching and essential in understanding his message to the world. He saw the problem as people who were trying to force "one portion of the world to think as another" (3976-8). This sort of intolerant coerciveness was bound to lead to suffering on an unprecedented planetary scale unless counterbalanced by a more humane vision. *He saw how the world could evolve in a constructive way.*

In this chapter, we explore several of Cayce's famous visionary readings. They have been saved for last because it keeps them in perspective, having already examined the other elements of his philosophy. Taken out of context, these readings can mislead the reader who is looking for the sensational in Cayce's work.

Two key principles are worth keeping in mind.

First, Cayce's prophecies have a long-term perspective. Admittedly, some, especially the early ones, targeted 1998 as a pivotal year. For the most part, they didn't come true. Instead, Cayce's insights unfolded and even changed somewhat as he grew older and his vision matured. It makes more sense to look at his later work and invest it with more credence than the earlier work. For example, many of the predictions from the late 1920s and the mid-1930s involved catastrophic changes to the earth. From the late 1930s to early 1940s, we find the changes predicted are more likely to be gradual than sudden. Here's a case in point from September 1939:

Q Three hundred years ago Jacob Boehme decreed Atlantis would rise again at this crisis time when we cross from this Piscean Era into the Aquarian. Is Atlantis rising now? Will it cause a sudden convolution and about what year?

A In 1998 we may find a great deal of the activities as have been wrought by the gradual changes that are coming about. These are at the periods when the cycle of the solar activity, or the years as related to the sun's passage through the various spheres of activity become paramount or Catamount [?] [Tantamount?] to the change between the Piscean and the Aquarian age. This is a gradual, not a cataclysmic activity in the experience of the earth in this period.   1602-3

Looking further into Cayce's long-term perspective, one interesting passage deals with the year 2158. In March 1936, Cayce had a dream on a train coming back to Virginia from an ill-fated trip to Detroit where he was briefly thrown in jail for practicing medicine without a license. In a reading after that, he was asked to interpret the dream, and he said it had two meanings: to give Cayce himself hope that his legacy would be remembered and available two hundred years hence; and to offer a prophetic picture of what the world might be like in the mid-twenty-second century. Here is the dream:

I had been born again in 2158 A.D. in Nebraska. The sea apparently covered all of the western part of the country, as the city where I lived was on the coast. The family name was a strange one. At an early age as a child I declared myself to be Edgar Cayce who had lived 200 yrs. before. Scientists, men with long beards, little hair, and thick glasses, were called in to observe me. They decided to visit the places where I said I had been born, lived and worked, in Kentucky, Alabama, New York, Michigan, and Virginia. Taking me with them the group of scientists visited these places in a long, cigar-shaped, metal flying ship which moved at high speed. Water covered part of Alabama. Norfolk, Virginia, had become an immense seaport. New York had been destroyed either by war or an earthquake and was being rebuilt. Industries were scattered over the countryside. Most of the houses were of glass. Many records of my work as Edgar Cayce were discovered and collected. The group returned to Nebraska taking the records with them to study.

294-185

The second key to Cayce is the difference between prediction and prophecy. Prediction is about what will happen in the future.

Prophecy is about what *could* happen if things don't change, especially as seen in the Old Testament, so dear to Cayce's heart and which surely influenced his own work. A prediction says "Here is the way it's going to be," a prophecy says "The future can still be worked out but here's what will happen if you don't use your free will and start making things different." Prophecy empowers the individual, and that is exactly what Cayce wants to do with these readings.

In June 1940, for example, as World War II raged in Europe and simmered in the Pacific, Edgar Cayce was asked what was going to happen to America. The question came from a group of sixty-four people who had come to Virginia Beach to see him. The answer came in the reading as a promise: They had the power to directly influence the course America would take, but only if they prayed with conviction and then acted on those prayers. This is prophecy in the deeper sense of the word.

Let thy voice be raised, then, as in praise to thy Maker; not in word alone but rather in the manner in which ye meet thy fellow men day by day. For the prayer, and the living of same by those sixty and four who are here gathered, may even save America from being invaded—if that is what ye desire.   **3976-25**

And so with these two key principles in mind, keeping a long-term perspective, and knowing the difference between prediction and prophecy, we are equipped to explore the Cayce readings.

DEALING WITH CHANGE

• •

Many of Edgar Cayce's readings were delivered during some of the most tumultuous times in history. Reading 1723-1 was given in the summer of 1938, yet what makes it especially relevant for us today is its theme of how to deal with change from a spiritual perspective.

In 1938, the world was still in the throes of the Depression, and in the United States, despite Roosevelt's New Deal programs, severe economic hardship was the norm. Too, war loomed on the horizon in Europe. In fact, World War II began just ten months after Cayce gave this reading.

The message about dealing with change was delivered not to an economic pundit or political leader of the time but to a common fellow instead, a twenty-five-year-old who drove an oil truck. While the man's estate was a modest one even for his time, the themes were universal and speak to our time as well.

Two themes in particular stand out. First is the dynamic tension between that which changes and that which is changeless. It's something which each of us must wrestle with, how to be a part of the exhilarating process of change and yet stay connected to the changeless, the eternal. Second is the power granted us by the exercise of free will, the ability to change ourselves, the tough work of choosing daily to be the best we can be.

The reading opens with a description of Mr. 1723's personality traits. First, the bad news. The comments are brief but blunt, and it probably wasn't easy for him to accept: "material-minded, hard-headed, stubborn." Then the good news, which is considerably longer. Using the language of astrology to describe temperament, Cayce portrays the man's strengths and weaknesses, then gives him some hopeful advice about using his talents constructively. He presents him a vision of what his soul is here on earth to contribute.

Bridging the good and the bad news is some insight about habit. The only thing that gets in the way of our spiritual progress is our *inclinations*—that is, "what we lean towards doing," just like a ball will roll down a hill due to the momentum innate to the incline of that hill unless we stop the ball and make it roll back up. Any of us can change because free will makes change a real option. And each of us has had some experience with change personally, so we know it's possible.

What makes all this information about habits important is this psychological principle: In times of change, either our strengths or our weaknesses come to the fore. The choice is up to us. Think about what happens in times of natural catastrophe, economic chaos, or war. For some people, it sparks loving deeds of extraordinary caliber; for others, it triggers pitiful acts of selfishness. Think about your own experience: In times of stress, do your best or worst qualities come out? The better you get to know yourself, the more likely you will exercise your free will to make sure it's your best and not your worst. The more potently clear your spiritual ideal, as Cayce points out, the more likely the results will be good.

For Mr. 1723, the reading specifically identifies *kindness* as key to his ability to change. And in learning to change, he can discover the reality that is changeless, even in the face of a world shifting so fast that he can't keep up with it. Sounds a lot like now.

So how do we connect with this elusive changeless side of life? By doing deeds that are so kind and loving they create something that "lives on and on in the heart and soul." Inward, meditative retreat isn't enough if we want to make a connection to the changeless. We need to be *good for something,* to reach out to those in need with a kind word, a moment of attention, some hope. Unpretentious as it sounds, that's the key to dealing with change, and it's the essence of Edgar Cayce's social vision.

❖

THIS PSYCHIC READING, 1723-1,
WAS GIVEN BY EDGAR CAYCE ON NOVEMBER 1, 1938.
The conductor was Gertrude Cayce.

GC: You will give the relation of this entity and the universe, and the universal forces; giving the conditions that are as personalities, latent and exhibited in the present life; also the former appearances in the earth plane, giving time, place and the name, and that in each life which built or retarded the development of the entity; giving the abilities of the present entity, and that to which it may attain, and how. You will answer the questions he submits, as I ask them:

EC: Yes, we have the records here of that entity now known as or called [1723].

In giving the interpretation of the records as we find them, these are chosen with the desire and hope to make the experience a helpful one in the entity's application of self in the present toward a mental and spiritual development with reference to the material—which should be the result of such application.

Then, in viewing the records generally—but without respect to what the entity has done or may do regarding the urges which arise—we find the inclination for the entity to oft be called material-minded, hard-hearted, stubborn, and without any thought of these things which bespeak of affections for affection's sake.

These as given are inclinations. The entity has altered and may alter such inclinations—or they arise as conditions which may be magnified, and thus—though bringing material gains, even at times positions of importance—unless there is the development of the milk of human kindness within the experience it may be, it may become a very lonesome, a very disturbing experience throughout this sojourn.

In the interpreting of the astrological aspects, which are as reference to the interims of experiences, not all experiences are given but rather those which have the greater bearing upon the entity in this present period of activity in this sojourn.

And as first indicated, these are given with the desire that the warnings, the information may be made to be a helpful influence in the entity's application of its dealings with its fellow man.

Jupiter we find as the greater ruling influence. Hence in any endeavor in which the entity's activities are to serve the masses or groups of people, the entity will find a channel through which the greater material and mental as well as spiritual forces may arise.

Hence in those channels where there is the sale of products which are to have their effect or activity among the many—or the gathering of data as a statistician, or records of any nature. All of these become a part of the entity's development, and channels through which the greater influence may come for greater helpful experiences; provided those characteristics as indicated become a part of their application.

In Mercury we find with the adverse influence in Venus, with Mars as well as Saturn, there are the influences which become a part of the entity's environs or surroundings.

Hence of high mental abilities is the entity—with the liking for or desire for study—the liking or desire for knowledge. But such knowledge as statistics, such knowledge as of the natures where the influences or activities of individuals or groups are to be maintained, is not to be used wholly for self in self-aggrandizement or self-advantage taken over others.

To be sure, it may be used in such measures as to bring

greater material opportunities, greater material successes, but at the behest—and not at the advantage taken over less fortunate ones or those who have not applied themselves.

In Venus we find the necessity for the cultivation of influences wherein not merely ideals or idealistic principles are held, but ideals to be adhered to—in mental, in material, but based upon spiritual attributes. These are to be cultivated. So, the doing and being virtuous for the very *nature* of that impelling influence which it brings into the experience of the entity is necessary for cultivation in the activities.

These in their first applications may bring some disturbing influences, yet to know that obligations are opportunities as well as duties, as well as privileges, is a lesson the entity should learn—and it will make for greater contentment, greater peace and happiness in its experiences as it deals with the changing influences and forces which arise.

Then know that while the life is in a changing world, with changing friendships, changing environs and changes of every nature—unless there is accomplished that which lives on and *on* in the heart and soul, little has been or may be accomplished by self in its dealings with its fellow man.

Be acquainted, then, with that home beyond. Take time not merely to be holy or good, but good for something—good in that ye bring each day some new hope, some new opportunity, some new experience in the life of someone—a boy, a child, a babe, an old person who has lost the way in one manner or another. Thus ye will gradually build those steps which may carry you beyond the vale of those who see only the material blessings. For ye will know of Whom, in Whom ye have heard that "His words passeth not away."

So, though changes come, though the heavens may be in turmoil, though the earth and all the activities may be in riot, thy deeds done in such a way and manner will not change but live in the heart and the mind in such a manner as to bring that peace and harmony which comes only to those who take thought of just being kind to the other fellow!

Know that if you would be forgiven, if you would have friends, if you would know peace you must *make* friends, be kind, be joyous, be *content*—but *never* satisfied! For that longing which arises to better thyself is not merely that thy body may take ease, or that ye may gratify the appetites thereof! but it is rather that glory of the hope within for the greater knowledge of the spiritual life to *grow* and *bloom* in thy workaday life.

For only that character of spiritual thought that is a practical thing, that may be lived and experienced day by day, is worthy of thy acceptation.

And it is thy nature—but cultivate it! For this will bring greater opportunities physically, mentally, and open the door of thy consciousness to the unseen forces that make men *not* afraid!

❖

THE SPIRIT OF NATIONS

• •

Twenty-nine discourses between 1921 and 1944, the so-called World Affairs readings, contain some of Edgar Cayce's most significant comments on the international scene, including clairvoyant perspectives on and prophecies for individual nations. In June 1944, just after D-day, came reading 3976-29, delivered at the annual gathering of the leaders of Cayce's organization. It was prompted by the request for information about the *group vibrations* of specific nations—that is, the *spirit* of a nation and its people.

Compared to the familiar stereotypes—the reserved nature of the English, the French love of life, the Japanese work ethic—Cayce's descriptions cut deeper, portraying national group consciousnesses in light of collective karmic fault and collective aspiration. As we study the reading, it's important not to be overly judgmental about the faults of given nations, because we may have had a role in the making of those faults: For Cayce, reincarnation suggests that each of us has contributed to national group consciousness in some lifetime or another.

The reading opens with the *cosmic picture*. Before individual nations were established, souls faced a spiritual choice. On the one hand was companionship with God, his intentions for us; and on the other hand was the impulse to defy God. That spirit of defiance brought confusion to the world and out of that confusion emerged the nations.

As each nation's consciousness evolved over time, so, too, a consensus slowly arose among its people. It's what we might call the *spirit of a nation*—that is, what that nation aspires to and holds dear.

Cayce suggests America as a good illustration of this spirit. Although our national consciousness has had much less time to emerge than many other nations, one central value is clear: freedom. Inherent in freedom, however, is the possibility for error, since freedom so closely aligns with free will, and free will can be exercised improperly. So easily when helping another nation that *helping* becomes *coercion* of that nation and its people. This is something to which America has been especially vulnerable.

What's more, free will can be misused in subtler ways. Edgar

Cayce asks us to consider the words of Jesus: "He shall know the truth and the truth then shall make him free." The key to freedom is to *live* and *apply* the truth in one's own life. By implication, Cayce is saying that Americans often fail to live or apply the truth, especially the most important truth of all: *In God We Trust.*

But why is America so at fault? People all over the world fail to trust in God. Why did Cayce single out America? Because it's what the founders and leaders have aspired to. To hold up freedom as a national ideal makes America even more accountable to properly use free will, whether that means respecting the freedom of all people or just remembering that our nation was founded on the principle of trust in God.

Reading 3976-29 goes on to identify the shortcomings of nations other than America, although in less detail. The English would seem to hold up the idea that they are a little bit better than everybody else. The French err by overindulging the body. The Italians are given to dissension (for which Cayce even offers a prayer that "a few might just agree, that a few even might declare their oneness with the higher forces"). The Chinese are isolated and self-satisfied. And the East Indians apply what they know in an exclusively inward way.

This reading also includes two of Cayce's most dramatic prophecies. First, Russia is depicted as the hope for the world, although not because of any merits of communism but because of its leadership and the opening up of friendly relations with America. With the collapse of the old Soviet Union and the establishment of more freedoms in the new Russia, it looks like Cayce's prophecy may eventually be fulfilled. Perhaps he perceived a broader spiritual trend, one that will have several false starts before the collective will of Russia and America can make a new kind of relationship permanent.

Edgar Cayce's second dramatic prediction is that China would one day be the cradle of Christianity, at least in the *application* of its doctrines if not the doctrines themselves. Is China's opening up to the West and adopting its ideas and lifestyle a sign of this new role? Probably not. Even though the reading was given in 1944, and even though Cayce wasn't specific, sixty years wouldn't seem to qualify as "far off as man counts time," as he intoned. So even more extraordinary changes may be in store for China in the twenty-first century and beyond.

THE READING

❖

THIS PSYCHIC READING, 3976-29,
WAS GIVEN BY EDGAR CAYCE ON JUNE 22, 1944,
AT THE THIRTEENTH ANNUAL ARE CONGRESS.
The conductor was Gertrude Cayce.

GC: It has been indicated through this channel that much might be given regarding what the vibrations of nations, as individuals, might mean. You will give such information concerning these vibrations and their relations to the spirit of the various nations, particularly in connection with the seven sins and twelve virtues in the human family, which will be helpful to us as an organization and as individuals in our attempt to be channels of blessing to our fellow men. You will then answer the questions, which may be submitted, as I ask them.

EC: When there came about the periods of man's evolution in the earth, what was given then as to why man must be separated into tongues, into nations, into groups? "Lest they in their fool-ish wisdom defy God." What is here then intimated? That man, seeking his own gratification of the lusts of the flesh, might even in the earth defy God. With what, then, has man been endowed by his Creator? All that would be necessary for each individual soul-entity to be a companion with God. And that is God's desire toward man.

Thus when man began to defy God in the earth and the confusion arose which is represented in the Tower of Babel—these are representations of what was then the basis, the beginnings of nations. Nations were set up then in various portions of the land, and each group, one stronger than another, set about to seek their gratifications. Very few—yea, as ye will recall, it even became necessary that from one of these groups one individual, a man, be called. His ways were changed. His name was changed. Did it take sin away from the man, or was it only using that within the individual heart and purpose and desire even then, as man throughout the periods of unfoldment put—in his interpretation—that of material success first? It isn't that God chose to reserve or save anything that was good from man, so long as man was, is, and will be one who uses that living soul as a companion with God. That's God's purpose. That should be man's purpose.

In the application of this principle, then, in the present day what has come about? Each nation has set some standard of some activity of man as its idea, either of man's keeping himself for himself or of those in such other nations as man's preparation for that companionship with God. For remember, there are unchangeable laws. For God is law. Law is God. Love is law. Love is God. There are then in the hearts, the minds of man, various concepts of these laws and as to where and to what they are applicable. Then, just as in the days of old, the nature of the flesh, human flesh and its natures, has not changed, but the spirit maketh alive. The truth maketh one free. Just as man has done throughout the ages, so in the present, as one takes those of the various nations as have seen the light and have, through one form or another, sought to establish as the idea of that nation, of that people, some symbol that has and does represent those peoples in those days of the fathers of the present land called America.

What is the spirit of America? Most individuals proudly boast "freedom." Freedom of what? When ye bind men's hearts and minds through various ways and manners, does it give them freedom of speech? Freedom of worship? Freedom from want? Not unless those basic principles are applicable throughout the tenets and lines as has been set, but with that principle freedom. For God meant man to be free and thus gave man will, a will even to defy God. *God* has not willed that any soul should perish, but hath with every trial or temptation prepared a way of escape.

There have come through the various periods of man's unfoldment, teachers proclaiming "This the way, here the manner in which ye may know," and yet in the Teacher of Teachers is found the way, He who even in Himself fulfilled the law. For when God said, "Let there be light," there came Light into that which He had created, that was without form and was void and it became the Word, and the Word dwelt among men and men perceived it not. The Word today dwells among men and many men perceive it not.

Those nations who have taken those vows that man shall be free should also take those vows "He shall know the truth and the truth then shall make him free."

Then what is this that would be given thee today? Here is thy lesson: Hear ye all! Beware lest ye as an individual soul, a son, a daughter of God, fail in thy mission in the earth today; that those ye know, those ye contact shall know the truth of God, not by thy word, bombastic words, but in long-suffering, in patience, in harmony, that ye create in thine own lives, for it must begin with thee. God has shown thee the pattern, even one Jesus, who became the Christ that ye might have an advocate with the Father, for the Father hath said "In the day ye eat or use the knowledge for thine own aggrandizement, ye shall die." But he that had persuaded the spirit, the souls that God had brought into being, to push into matter to gratify desire for self-expression, self-indulgence, self-satisfaction, said "Ye shall not surely die," or what were then the activities of man—for as had been said, "A day is a thousand years, a thousand years as a day."

What was the length of life then? Nearly a thousand years. What is your life today? May it not be just as He had given, just as He indicated to those peoples, just as He did to the lawgiver, just as He did to David—first from a thousand years to a hundred and twenty, then to eighty? Why? Why? The sin of man in his desire for self-gratification.

What nations of the earth today vibrate to those things that they have and are creating in their own land, their own environment? Look to the nations where the span of life has been extended from sixty to eight-four years. You will judge who is serving God. These are judgments. These are the signs to those who seek to know, who will study the heavens, who will analyze the elements, who will know the heart of man, they that seek to know the will of the Father for themselves answer "Lord, here am I, use me, send me where I am needed."

Just as have been those principles of your present conflict. "Send help, for man's heritage of freedom will be taken away." By whom? He that hath said, "Surely ye will not die." There are those two principles, two conflicting forces in the earth today: the prince of this world, and that principle that says to every soul, "Fear not, I have overcome the world and the prince of the world hath nothing in me." Can ye say that? Ye must! That is thy hope; that "The prince of this world, Satan, that old serpent, hath no part in any desire of my mind, my heart, my body, that I do not control in the direction it shall take." These are the things, these are the principles.

What then of nations? In Russia there comes the hope of the world, not as that sometimes termed of the Communistic, of the Bolshevistic; no. But freedom, freedom! that each man will live for this fellow man! The principle has been born. It will take years for it to be crystallized, but out of Russia comes again the hope of the world. Guided by what? That friendship with the nation that hath even set on its present monetary unit "In God We Trust." (Do ye use that in thine own heart when you pay your just debts? Do ye use that in thy prayer when ye send thy missionaries to other lands? "I give it, for in God we trust"? Not for the other fifty cents either!)

In the application of these principles, in those forms and manners in which the nations of the earth have and do measure to those in their activities, yea, to be sure, America may boast, but rather is that principle being forgotten when such is the case, and that is the sin of America.

So in England, from whence have come the ideas—not ideals—ideas of being just a little bit better than the other fellow. Ye must *grow* to that in which ye will deserve to be known, deserve to receive. That has been, that is, the sin of England.

As in France, to which this principle first appealed, to which then came that which was the gratifying of the desires of the body—that is the sin of France.

In that nation which was first Rome, when there was that unfolding of those principles, its rise, its fall, what were they that caused the fall? The same as at Babel. The dissensions, the activities that would enforce upon these, in this or that sphere, servitude; that a few might just agree, that a few even might declare their oneness with the higher forces. For theirs was the way that seemeth right to a man but the end is death. That is the sin of Italy.

The sin of China? Yea, there is the quietude that will not be turned aside, saving itself by the slow growth. There has been a growth, a stream through the land in ages which asks to be left alone to be just satisfied with that within itself. It awoke one day and cut its hair off! And it began to think and to do something with its thinking! This, here, will be one day the cradle of Christianity, as applied in the lives of men. Yea, it is far off as man counts time, but only a day in the heart of God—for tomorrow China will awake. Let each and every soul as they come to those understandings, do something, then, in his or her own heart.

Just as in India, the cradle of knowledge not applied, except within self. What is the sin of India? *Self*, and left the "ish" off—just self.

Then apply in thine own life truth. What is truth? It might have been answered, had an individual entity who stood at the crossways of the world waited for an answer. Yet that soul had purified itself and had given the new commandment that "ye love one another!"

What is it all about then? "Thou shalt love the Lord thy God with all thine heart, thine soul, thine mind, thine body, and thy neighbor as thyself." The rest of all the theories that may be concocted by man are nothing, if these are just lived. Love thy neighbor as thyself in the associations day by day, preferring as did the Christ who died on the cross rather than preferring the world be His without a struggle.

Know, then, that as He had His cross, so have you. May you take it with a smile. You can, if ye will let Him bear it with thee. Do it.

We are through for the present.

✣

EARTH CHANGE PROPHECIES

• •

E dgar Cayce is often associated with predictions about the
earth going through great upheaval; a careful count reveals
that roughly only two dozen readings fit that category, less than
two-tenths of one percent of all his work.

As mentioned at the beginning of the chapter, Cayce's visions
about change evolved over time. The following reading, 1152-11,
is one of the last he gave on the subject. Delivered several months
prior to the bombing of Pearl Harbor, he predicts that it will
take until 1944 or 1945 to achieve peace, and he even envisions
that specific Masonic Order principles will be part of the peace
plan.

Reading 1152-11 certainly contains some stark statements,
such as predicting the destruction of major cities in the United
States. But whereas earlier readings targeted 1998, here no time-
table is proffered. What's more, Cayce suggests developments will
be more gradual in nature ("changes here are gradually coming
about"), and even identifies parts of the country that will be *safety
lands* once changes begin. We should be careful, however, about
how to interpret such a statement because throughout his work
safety is achieved mentally in our thoughts, feelings, and purposes, and is not a place we go to physically to escape harm.

THIS PSYCHIC READING, 1152-11,
WAS GIVEN BY EDGAR CAYCE ON AUGUST 13, 1941.
The conductor was Gertrude Cayce.

GC: You will have before you the body and enquiring mind of
[1152], present in this room, who seeks information, advice and
guidance as to her health, her life and work. Feeling that a new
life of service to humanity is calling her, you will please give
the entity definite information as to just what this work is, and
where she should live in order to best carry out this work. The
entity submits herself to these sources for guidance, being perfectly willing to give up all personal belongings and to follow in
the way that HE leads. You will give the entity that needed in order to be in the right place and at her right work. Then you will
answer the questions she submits, as I ask them:

EC: Yes, we have the body, the enquiring mind, [1152], present
in this room. This in part and in various phases we have had
before.

As to counsel and advice, conditions that are existent and
that are to be might well be given at this time to the entity. However, the choice as to place and activity should be within self.
For, the individual entity is a free-willed individual. Circumstances, vibrations, individuals and varied activities alter those
things to which the body does respond. And as there are changing conditions, changing in the group and the universal thought
as in relation to those conditions to be met, all of these should
be taken into consideration.

It is evident that there are strenuous conditions imminent in the affairs of the land, owing to thought as respecting the relationships in varied portions of the world.

And, as has been and is indicated, unusual combinations are being made; and those individual groups or nations that have heretofore manifested friendly or brotherly relationships are now soon to be as enemies.

It is self-evident that there will be the attempt to use a great deal of propaganda as regarding conditions in France, Italy, Germany, Russia, Spain, Norway, Turkey, the Holy Land and India.

A great number of individuals formulated into groups who have declared specific or definite policies will be questioned as to purpose and as to the ideal. Some of such will be drawn into coalition with questionable groups.

Hence this is not, in the immediate, the time for the joining definitely with any individual group's activity other than that which stands alone on Christ and Christ's principles.

For, with those changes that will be wrought, Americanism—the ism—with the universal thought that is expressed and manifested in the brotherhood of man into group thought, as expressed by the Masonic Order, will be the eventual rule in the settlement of affairs in the world.

Not that the world is to become a Masonic order, but the principles that are embraced in same will be the basis upon which the new order of peace is to be established in '44 and '45.

When these things are considered, then, it is self-evident that individuals should be up and doing. Especially the entity, with its abilities, has definite work to do in the present.

The entity has the ability to work with or through individual groups,—not as a propagandist, but—as has been so oft indicated—do not magnify the differences of various groups, but rather UNIFY the sameness as expressed in many of them that hold to the principles as given in Him.

For, the time is at hand when individuals who have—as this entity—seen and given so much, and experienced so much as to the meaning of the advent of the Son of man, the Prince of Peace, the Lord of Lords, the King of Kings, must now more than ever magnify and glorify Him in the relationships of individuals one to another.

There are so many groups that have such as a background, yet their working hypothesis, their working labels are under influences that belie that principle in its APPLICATION to individuals.

All of these should be taken into consideration by this entity; and its abilities as a speaker, its abilities as a writer should be directed in those conditions and affairs that will more and more unite seekers in every phase of life, in every position, in every portion of the country, to that standard set by Him. Not as in a church, not as in an ism or cult, but in that every soul does the best he can where he is—and all with one ideal: "I am my brother's keeper—Christ the Lord is my brother!"

As to conditions in the geography of the world, of the country,—changes here are gradually coming about.

No wonder, then, that the entity feels the need, the necessity for change of central location. For, many portions of the east coast will be disturbed, as well as many portions of the west coast, as well as the central portion of the U.S.

In the next few years lands will appear in the Atlantic as well as in the Pacific. And what is the coast line now of many a land will be the bed of the ocean. Even many of the battlefields of the present will be ocean, will be the seas, the bays, the lands over which the NEW order will carry on their trade as one with another.

Portions of the now east coast of New York, or New York City itself, will in the main disappear. This will be another generation, though, here; while the southern portions of Carolina, Georgia—these will disappear. This will be much sooner.

The waters of the lakes will empty into the Gulf, rather than the waterway over which such discussions have been recently made. It would be well if the waterway were prepared, but not for that purpose for which it is at present being considered.

Then the area where the entity is now located [Virginia Beach for reading] will be among the safety lands, as will be portions of what is now Ohio, Indiana and Illinois, and much of the southern portion of Canada and the eastern portion of Canada; while the western land—much of that is to be disturbed—in this land—as, of course, much in other lands.

Then, with the knowledge of these,—first the principles, then the material changes.

The choice should be made by the entity itself as to location, and especially as to the active work.

To be SURE there is work to be done by the entity, DEFI-NITE work.

Join with all of those who declare that the Lord has come and that His day is again at hand.

Ready for questions.

Q Should this work start by early fall?
A Start today!
Q I have for many months felt that I should move away from New York City.
A This is well, as indicated. There is too much unrest; there will continue to be the character of vibrations that to the body will be disturbing, and eventually those destructive forces there—though these will be in the next generation.
Q Will Los Angeles be safe?
A Los Angeles, San Francisco, most all of these will be among those that will be destroyed before New York even.

Q Should California or Virginia Beach be considered at all, or where is the right place that God has already provided for me to live?

A As indicated, these choices should be made rather in self. Virginia Beach or the area is much safer as a definite place. But the work of the entity should embrace most all of the areas from the east to the west coast, in its persuading—not as a preacher, nor as one bringing a message of doom, but as a loving warning to all groups, clubs, women's clubs, writers' clubs, art groups, those of every form of club, that there needs be—in their activities—definite work towards the knowledge of the power of the Son of God's activity in the affairs of men.

✦

A NEW ORDER IN WORLD AFFAIRS

History moves in cycles. In the late 1930s, when reading 3976-18 was given, the level of change nationally and internationally was as high as it is now. Unexpected, swift, dramatic change leaves us wondering where the world is headed.

Look carefully at this short but powerful statement that Edgar Cayce made a little more than a year before World War II began. Its themes and message are just as potent today as then. A "new order of conditions" is arising, he announced. The positive potential in times of change depends on the attitudes and ideals of the individual. A very specific ethical code and outlook is prescribed: to be each other's loving guardians or *keepers; leveling* is another way it's described. It boils down to simply this: *oneness.* In a world of extraordinary diversity, the human family must find ways to stay in touch with its underlying oneness.

Many students of Cayce see reading 3976-18 as his most important visionary statement about world politics and the prospects for global harmony. Pace University political science professor Dr. Linda Quest offered an eloquent interpretation of it in an address at Atlantic University's graduation ceremonies in 1993. In part, she said:

Since 1989 there has been a "pole shift" in world affairs. There's also been a pole shift in your backyard, in your city streets, and in your hometown. This remarkable transition can best be seen as it plays out in the current events of the world and of nations.

The issue can be seen as the tension between two sides of a paradox. We must have both freedom and the sense of community. How will we achieve it? We are at a historic moment—the like of which has never been before in all of human experience. The rise of freedom has brought difficulty. We can see the problem this way: There were 186 sovereign states in the world at the start of 1993, and a number of additional affiliated territories bringing the total number of "places" to 252. The number might seem large, but it isn't when you realize that there are at least 5,000 "nations" in the world! By the word nations, I'm referring to entities which have language, culture, history, government, territories, or territorial claims. These 5,000 are somehow squeezed into 252 places.

We can notice that many of these national entities are tribal or ancestral in character. They are not recognizably modern in many, many instances, but the rise in freedom has encouraged them to cut loose. Many are engaged in acts of succession, and some are engaged in a movement for annexation. The people involved may call their efforts the struggle for freedom, but not *all of those who are strug-gling for freedom are also struggling toward the twenty-first century.* Some, whether they know it or not, are beating a path toward extinction. Those who insist upon the schisms, the divisions, and the separations, block themselves, and they heave stumbling blocks in the path of others as well. This is the road of the reckoning and what Cayce called "leveling." What will come out in the end for these people is probably the loss of their language, culture, history, gov-ernment, and property, *if any of those elements is used in op-position to the principle of one humanity or the value of the individual.* Those entities—those "nations"—can't endure.

As author of two books about Edgar Cayce's perspective on world affairs, Dr. Quest is an insightful interpreter of his political and social vision. Her analysis of Cayce's concept of leveling is sobering, especially as we look at world events in the opening years of the twenty-first century. In the midst of international tur-moil today, his vision is invaluable: the fundamental oneness of all life and our Creator's promise to guide us through the fog and diversions of our own making.

THE READING
❖

THIS PSYCHIC READING, 3976-18,
WAS GIVEN BY EDGAR CAYCE ON JUNE 20, 1938.
The conductor was Gertrude Cayce.

GC: You will have before you the work of the Association for Research and Enlightenment, Inc., in studying and presenting the psychic work of Edgar Cayce. It is desired to present on Monday evening, June 27th, material presented through this channel, for the Seventh Annual Congress, on national and international affairs which will be in keeping with the ideal and purposes of the work being undertaken by the Association. You will consider the type of audience which will be present, the need for informative information which will not be spectacular or sensational, yet that will be constructive. Advise us also as to the manner of presentation. You will give the first discourse on this subject.

EC: Yes, we have the work of the Association for Research and Enlightenment, Inc., and the policies and ideals and purposes of same; as related to national and international affairs that would not be spectacular but constructive—and in keeping with the ideals.

As has been and is being understood by many, there are changes being wrought in the nation, as well as in the interrelationships with other nations.

All of these may be considered from the one angle.

It is also understood, comprehended by some, that a new order of conditions is to arise; that there must be many a purging in high places as well as low; that there must be the greater consideration of each individual, each soul being his brother's keeper.

There will then come about those circumstances in the political, the economic and the whole relationships where there will be a leveling—or a greater comprehension of this need.

For as the time or the period draws near for these changes that come with the new order, it behooves all of those who have an ideal—as individuals, as well as groups or societies or organizations, to be practicing, applying same in their experience—and their relationships as one to another.

For unless these are up and doing, then there must indeed be a new order in *their* relationships and their activities.

For His ways will carry through. For as He gave, "Though the heavens and the earth may pass away, my word will *not* pass away."

All too often has this message been forgotten in the pulpits and in the organizations, not only in the national relationships but in the international relationships.

And as the dealings are as one to another, unless these are in keeping with those tenets they must fail; for all power in heaven and in earth hath been given into His hands.

Then as we approach all phases of human relationships, these must be taken into consideration.

And there *cannot* be one measuring stick for the laborer in the field and the man behind the counter, and another for the man behind the money-changers. *All* are equal—not only under the material law but under the *spiritual*.

And *His* laws, *His* will, will not come to naught!

Though there may come those periods when there will be great stress, as brother rises against brother, as group or sect or race rises against race—yet the leveling must come.

And *only* those who have set their ideal in Him and practiced it in their dealings with their fellow man may expect to survive the wrath of the Lord.

In thy dealings, then—whether at home, in thy dealings with state or the national situations, or the international affairs—there must come *all* under that purpose, that desire.

And then there should be, there *will* be those rising to power that are able to meet the needs. For none are in power but that have been given the opportunity by the will of the Father—from which all power emanates.

Hence those will be leveled with the purpose, "My word shall *not* fail!"

In presenting such—well that it be given as extract, or as that from such sources to be used or taken as those present see fit.

We are through for the present.

❖

SUMMARY
of Edgar Cayce's Social Vision

• •

Edgar Cayce sees the world essentially as a meaningful place. The social and political dimensions of life are where spiritual principles can be applied. Echoing the words of the Bible, Cayce often reminded people that "we are our brother's [and sister's] keeper." We *do* have social responsibilities to each other. What's more, he warns us that unless society awakens to a deeper sense of the unity of all life, there are very difficult times ahead for us; whether social unrest or catastrophic changes in the earth, humanity will not continue to be as selfish or disrespectful of nature as it has been. But his warnings are *prophecy,* not *prediction.* The future is not predetermined, and someone like Cayce reminds us of the positive potential for the future. Collectively, we will shape what happens.

EPILOGUE

❖

A LEGACY SUCH AS THAT LEFT TO US BY EDGAR CAYCE IS
actually a *living* entity. It grows with our capacity to understand it. Some of Cayce's readings will always be part of the *essential* legacy, if only because they address core issues. And while other readings may seem obscure or confusing to us today, they may become clear to future generations. The broadening frontiers of archaeology, psychology, and medicine may allow for Cayce to be appreciated in new ways, and tomorrow there may be a whole new version of what is considered essential.

Cayce's own dream, in 1936, described in chapter 8, is his prophecy, his hope, that his teachings would benefit humanity in the long run, living well into the mid-twenty-second century. One can only wonder which readings will be considered essential 150 years from now, and what type of evidence will be cited to back them up.

In the decades, even centuries, to come, Edgar Cayce's work as a prophet may be appreciated more fully. His real legacy, in fact, may be a whole new way of *being* for humanity. We tend to consider Cayce the prophet in light of some two dozen readings, with their overt statements about the possible future; someday, *all* 14,306 of them may be considered prophetic. Collectively, their insights about the human condition and ideas about how to live on this earth could be a blueprint for society in the future.

The Cayce health readings on the body and healing—including information about "energy" medicine, and their novel view of how the systems in the body interrelate—might one day be the framework for mainstream medicine, whether Cayce is remembered or not. Similarly, his tolerant, inclusive view of the religions of the world may have foreshadowed a worldwide acceptance of the value of all religions.

Likewise, Cayce's invitation to see how research and enlightenment can be married may have foretold a convergence of science and religion in the years ahead. And his transpersonal psychology, with its personal spirituality (dreams, meditation, prayer, ideals) and personal accountability, may have pioneered a new approach to mental health and well-being.

What is defined as *essential* in Edgar Cayce's work ultimately depends on his impact on *individual* lives. Over ninety percent of his readings were tailored to the individual, even though he hoped to see his work reach "groups, and classes, and masses." So, fascinated as you, the reader, may be in Cayce's ideas, only by *testing* them in your own life can you find what is truly essential about him for you.

APPENDIX 1

HOW TO READ AND STUDY
A CAYCE READING

❖

Virtually everyone who has worked with the readings of Edgar Cayce has initially felt challenged. Not only was his method of producing the readings unorthodox, so, too, was the information that came out of them. Their unusual format and style of language can take some getting used to.

When people contacted Cayce with their questions, a specific appointment was made. He generally gave two readings a day, one in the morning, the other in the afternoon. He would lie on a couch and induce an altered state of awareness in himself, although it looked a lot like sleeping to the casual observer. While in this state, he responded to any suggestions or questions asked of him. It's the stenographic records of these discourses that came to be called *readings*.

Each reading is a richly informative collection of principles about health, life purpose, or spiritual advice. The vast majority of them were given to individuals who requested advice. Each was assigned a two-part case number to ensure privacy; the first set of digits replaces the person's name, the second set, following a hyphen, referred to which reading it was in the series of readings for that person. For example, reading 900-13 was the thirteenth reading Cayce gave for a man known as number 900.

A small percentage of the readings were for groups of people (series 281 was a prayer group; 262 was the original "A Search for God" study group), or about a topic of interest (series 364 was on Atlantis; 3744 was on psychic phenomena).

Cayce always had other people in the room with him when he was in a trance giving a reading. A *conductor,* often his wife, Gertrude, would supervise by giving him a suggestion to induce an altered state and asking the questions once he was in that state. The suggestion was a carefully worded command telling Cayce what type of information was being requested. A stenographer, usually his secretary Gladys Davis, recorded his answers verbatim, and many times there were also observers present.

Typically, what followed was a general discourse from Cayce:

- If the reading was for someone who was ill, Cayce would give a *physical reading* in which he analyzed the various systems of the body—digestive, circulatory, nervous—then recommend various natural remedies.
- If the reading was for someone who was requesting guidance in understanding his or her purpose in life, Cayce would give a *life reading* in which he analyzed the strengths and weaknesses of the soul. Often, he first would speak in astrological terms about traits and tendencies, then he would relate details of past lives whose influence might be being experienced in the present.
- If the reading was for someone who was requesting spiritual advice, Cayce gave a *mental-spiritual reading,* which opened with a lesson about spiritual law and principles for living.

While questions were generally posed to the entranced Cayce following an opening discourse, on occasion there were no questions submitted so the entire reading consisted of the opening discourse followed by some additional remarks. The transcription of the reading included the discourse, questions exactly as stated, if submitted, and Cayce's exact responses.

When excerpts from the readings appear in books or magazines, they are almost always limited to the text itself. However, more in-depth research into the readings requires knowing the background of the person who requested the reading and a follow-up report on what was done with the information obtained from the reading. For almost all of those people who received advice from Cayce, that kind of supplemental information was made available as an appendix, or *report,* to the reading.

A frequently asked question is, What was the *source* of the information that came through Edgar Cayce? When Cayce himself was asked, he replied that his own higher self—his superconscious mind—was the source. In other words, he didn't claim it was a noncorporeal being speaking through him, but it was his own inner wisdom. The information it obtained came either from the unconscious mind of the individual getting the reading, or from what Cayce called the *Akashic Records,* an ancient Indian Sanskrit term referring to a record of the subtle energy of all events of history, including all thoughts and feelings.

Edgar Cayce's superconscious mind often expressed information in a style quite different from our conversational style today. Although the language and sentence structure are sometimes difficult to decipher, with a few guidelines you'll become more proficient in understanding what was meant.

- Slow down your reading pace. In many readings, the sentences are exceedingly long, and it may help to insert punctuation mentally for pauses or to make the sentences shorter. You may even wish to read passages aloud.
- Be patient when doing research. Something in a reading may make no sense to you, even after several attempts. Rather than getting bogged down, keep reading. Further clarification may

appear later in the reading. Or maybe it will become clear after a few days or even weeks. Even the most experienced student of Cayce encounters problems sometimes.

- Develop an understanding of the language style of the readings, which were often biblical in both tone and content. In a waking state, Edgar Cayce was a devoted student of the Bible, and it is only natural that some biblical material would find its way into his readings. More than anything else, this tendency shows the reverence Cayce had for the readings themselves. He took each reading very seriously, and he felt that each was a sacred trust given to him.

It's only fair to ask: If Edgar Cayce was so insightful when he was in a trance, why couldn't he have found a way of speaking that would be easier to understand? One explanation offered by Cayce scholars is that this difficulty with communication was because his mind was operating on another level of consciousness in which words are often an inadequate means of expression. He was trying to communicate in three-dimensional, logical terms the information that he could perceive with far greater depth and understanding.

Perhaps, too, we have to *work* with this information to really find value and meaning in it. If everything was obvious immediately, we might read only superficially and never roll up our sleeves to understand what it's all about. Sometimes, Cayce even seems like a poet, composing with words whose rich, deep meaning require conscious effort and patience to understand. But just like a wonderful passage of poetry that takes a little extra work, the results are well worth the effort. We begin understanding ourselves in a new way as his images, metaphors, aphorisms, and biblical references find resonance within ourselves.

APPENDIX 2

. .

EDGAR CAYCE AND ASTROLOGY

✛

Edgar Cayce supported the fundamental premise of astrology that the planets and stars have a relationship to human temperament and behavior. In fact, he encouraged the study of astrology.

Q Would it be well for me to make a study of astrology?
A Well for everyone to make a study of astrology!   311-10

Cayce differs from many astrologers, however, in the area of causation. The fact that Mars was on the ascendant, near the horizon, at the moment of birth does not cause one to behave in a certain way as an adult. In Cayce's view, it's the other way around: Because of past life experiences in the material world, and noncorporeal experiences the soul has had before birth (so-called *interplanetary sojourns*), the soul *chooses* to be born when the planets depict best its own innate patterns—when the planets "bear witness to" it, as Cayce puts it.

Most schools of psychology categorize people according to temperament or disposition. Carl Jung, for example, judged temperament according to an individual's innate tendency to favor one polar extreme over another: thinking versus feeling, sensation versus intuition, introversion versus extroversion. In a similar fashion, Cayce felt astrology could help pinpoint individual temperament.

But Edgar Cayce rarely referred to astrology as being predictive. The planets and stars do not shape our future. Astrology, he said, was suggestive of happiness and success in one arena, the choice of one's career, going so far as to say in one reading that "eighty percent of the individuals may have their abilities indicated from the astrological aspects in the direction of vocational guidance" (5753-3). In the life readings, Cayce usually identified two or three planets with the greatest influence on the individual, but even then *influence* had more to do with the impact of one's own tendencies and memories than any exterior force.

For Edgar Cayce, there were eight planets, other than the earth itself, that defined the fundamental elements of temperament. The characteristics he assigned to these planets can be pieced together from the hundreds of readings in which he employed astrology.

Mercury: Tendency to intellectualize and analyze; a quick mind; likes to get the facts.

Venus: Prefers to do things in partnership; appreciates the beauty of people and places; vulnerable.

Mars: Likes competition, challenge, and activities that demand physical energy; tendency toward anger.

Jupiter: Relates to large endeavors; likes philosophy and getting the "big picture"; comfortable with power and money; expansive and liberal.

Saturn: Conservative, cautious, and reluctant to change (which, ironically, often causes sudden changes in life); disciplined and persistent.

Uranus: Swings in mood or emotion from one extreme to another; high-strung; scientific and inventive; highly intuitive or psychic.

Neptune: Attracted to the mysterious; mystical, idealistic, otherworldly, and devotional; attracted to the sea and other forces of nature.

Pluto: Combustive, explosive, passionate, and self-oriented.

It remains a mystery how Cayce identified the two or three essential planets that corresponded to a given individual's temperament type, and it's that confusion that has kept his approach to astrology from gaining wider acceptance. Students of astrology can't figure out how he determined which of all the planets on the birth chart were the most influential. For example, the exact time and place of birth was known for many who received readings, but there seems to be no consistent method that Cayce used to select two or three planets from the birth horoscope configuration. It may well be that astrology was primarily a language tool that Edgar Cayce used to describe his clairvoyant insights into personality patterns and temperament.

• •

❖

"There is no soul but what the sex life becomes the greater influence in life"   911-2

We are all challenged to find meaning in our sexuality. Its powerful influence affects our health, our sense of well-being, our creativity, even our spirituality. It is a direct way that we engage the spiritual life-force. And sometimes, in the midst of a loving, intimate relationship, it's where we discover the most important opportunities for *spiritual* development.

If we were to list the roles played by Edgar Cayce in his readings—psychic diagnostician, holistic physician, dream interpreter—most of us wouldn't think to add *sex therapist*. Yet that's exactly what he was for dozens of people. And what makes Cayce an extraordinary therapist is how he skillfully wove issues involving sex into a broader vision of life. He saw sexuality in terms of dimensions of consciousness and the seven spiritual centers, and its impact on our values and ideals.

These points are made dramatically in the story of a forty-one-year-old woman who sought advice from Cayce about her sex life. It had been troubled throughout her adult years, and she turned to him for both a life and a physical reading hoping to get answers about her difficult marriage, her unfulfilled sexual needs, and her quest to connect with the spiritual side of life.

Hers is one of the best-documented case histories in which Edgar Cayce helped a person understand sexuality in terms of growth of the soul. The records include many long, candid letters written between the woman and Cayce, and there is a definite air of secrecy about her requests because she worried her husband would find out that she felt strongly compelled to resume an affair with a longtime admirer.

By the time the woman contacted Cayce, confusion and tension had begun to wear on her and distressing physical symptoms began to surface. A physician recommended estrogen hormone therapy, but she worried that it would only enhance her sexual urges. In her letter requesting the first reading, she described the tremendous tension throughout her eighteen years of marriage. She and her husband had *never* had intimate relations; he had always been impotent, through no fault of his own. "There is simply not the physical development necessary," as she put it.

The woman nonetheless recognized her own passionate nature and strong sexual urges. In the early years of her marriage, she dealt with her disappointment by having a series of affairs. One was especially noteworthy: For many years, she had been idolized and pursued by a man whose infatuation went all the way back to when they knew each other as children, but she didn't learn of his love until after becoming engaged to her husband.

Some years after she married, they encountered one another again. He was married now—unhappily so, apparently—and she was in the throes of frustration over her husband's impotence. She initiated intimacy with her admirer, then broke it off, as she wrote in a letter to Cayce, because she "did not wish to 'two-time' his wife."

But after years of not seeing her, the lover suddenly reappeared. Although he was still married, their reunion was passionate, according to the woman. "From the minute we met again, the flame came back to him in its full intensity, *and* I responded. I am trying to release us, but I find my health going down." It was at this point that she consulted Edgar Cayce, asking:

1. What are my obligations to my husband and to this man who has recently returned to my life?
2. Would a liaison with some trusted friend help me so I could function positively and rhythmically in carrying on the normal business of home life and work? A bachelor, perhaps— i.e., someone other than this former romantic interest?

Life reading 2329-1 was largely an analysis of the woman's sexuality and the opportunities it presented to her now to foster growth of the soul. The reading was in no way judgmental, in no way did it compare her physical and emotional impulses with anyone else's. We are measured against our own spiritual values and ideals only, according to Cayce.

The reading pinpointed a pivotal tendency in her soul to allow emotions and sex to get her into fixes. The natural ease with which she moved into sexual relations was related in large part to past life experiences. How could she break the pattern? By examining how she set ideals and values in her life. In so doing, she had to confront a strong inclination to let physical gratification and the emotions involved shape her life—what Cayce called "that universal urge arising from Venus," something he linked to memories in the soul from previous incarnations. She had been a mail-order bride of sorts in the pioneer days of the American West; in this lifetime, she didn't have the chance to let the desires of her heart lead her to a marriage partner and bartered herself instead to a man with whom she was not a very good fit. Yet she learned to make the best of it and experienced significant soul growth because of it.

In another lifetime, she was the victim of an abusive medieval custom—one of the most powerfully shaping memories she had to face. When her then husband went off to the Crusades, he locked her in a chastity belt. She was deeply distressed and vengefully angry. "This brought periods of disturbing forces of many natures; the determining to sometime, somewhere, be free, and to 'get even.'" And who was this Crusader? He was none other than her current husband, now impotent, now potentially very vulnerable to her affairs.

The woman's past life effect on the current situation vividly makes a point: Sexuality is the one thing in life that brings to bear all the key ingredients that make up the human soul. But it's not only the place we readily get into trouble; it's also where we can just as readily make great strides. The woman had to deal with the frustration of being married to a man who was impotent; she also had to wrestle with her own urges to act on her emotional and sexual needs. These needs were the challenges about which she was starting to make important choices.

The woman had resisted any temptation to "get back" at her husband. She was very discreet and made sure that she didn't flaunt her extramarital experiences hurtfully. On the other hand, she wasn't sure that she could live without sex. But she knew that she didn't want to hurt her husband while working out her own needs. She even explored alternatives: Just before turning to Cayce, she spent an intense period trying to raise the kundalini energy inside her up another level through daily meditation, but the results had been only partially satisfying.

So should the woman resume the affair with her married lover? Edgar Cayce was rather direct in his advice: "Keep self unspotted from the world." He may have been so direct because she herself had said she felt strongly against having sex with a married man. Cayce added a further bit of cryptic advice: "As to what the conduct should be, let it never be for the only emotional satisfaction— but creative in its nature." Perhaps the woman could find a way to be involved with this man in a way that primarily engaged her creativity—for example, attending the symphony or taking a painting class together. But no doubt that would have been difficult.

In response to the woman's question about finding a bachelor to fulfill her desires, Cayce left her considerably more room to make choices. "Such questions as these can only be answered in what is thy ideal. . . . There is no condemnation in those who DO such for helpful forces, but if for personal, selfish gratification, it is sin." In essence, he was encouraging her to make sure that the motive of love ("helpful forces") was the directing influence.

The story further continued to unfold. The woman requested two more readings, and she kept up a correspondence with Edgar Cayce for several years, apparently heeding his advice about avoiding further entanglement with her former lover. She did stay with her husband, but whether she pursued an affair with a bachelor isn't revealed.

What can we learn from a story like this? Few of us have ever faced a situation personally quite like hers. But if Cayce's philosophy is sound, we all *do* face *some* type of soul-engaging challenge when it comes to our sexuality. It's a universal condition: "There is no soul but what the sex life becomes the greater influence in life."

What must be remembered, however, is that sexuality leaves us with a wide array of free choices. Reading 911-2 goes on to say that this sexual influence *doesn't* always mean "gratification in the physical act." Whenever we're *creative,* we engage the forces that are closely related to sexuality.

Edgar Cayce encouraged people to always remember that there is a force behind the creative polarity of masculine-feminine. Sexuality enhances growth of the soul *if* our deepest motive is to find the *oneness* of all life. We miss the mark if we make the other person into the object of our longing only.

While sexuality is where we're most likely to encounter selfishness, dominance, fear, or just plain self-doubt, it's also where we feel the creative forces most intensely. Cayce saw sexuality as the arena where we have the best chance to make the greatest strides in growth. This is where we can uncover the fundamental oneness of all energy. This is where we can create new life.

Sexuality is where the immediacy of spiritual energies is revealed in our physical bodies. Sexual expression is so powerful because it's the movement of the creative force, the kundalini, through the spiritual centers. All seven centers are involved, but, as discussed earlier, the effects are especially felt in the intense awakening of the reproductive glands, which relate to personal security and physical survival, just as they ensure the survival of the species; and in the cells of Leydig, located in the reproductive and adrenal glands, and linked to the masculine-feminine balance.

The altered state of consciousness accompanying sexual ecstasy is similar to what may be experienced as the kundalini moves up through the other spiritual centers. If we keep in mind that *ecstasy* means "to be taken outside of ourselves," then we recognize how the experience of sexual ecstasy is truly a spiritual one. That's why Cayce said sex involves exercising the highest emotions a physical body can experience; he referred to sex as "the highest vibrations that are experienced in the material world" (911-5).

Edgar Cayce's advice about sexuality has a universal quality. It's natural for us to desire and need to experience the highest emotions possible physically. Sexuality is bound to be a profound influence in our lives one way or another. And because the creative polarity of the masculine-feminine is so strong, sexuality intensely challenges our mind and free will.

Whether or not we can recall any of our own past lives, Cayce reasons that sexual experiences are recorded in our souls and have a bearing on our current outlook and behavior. So do the values and ideals we've chosen in this lifetime. The message from the readings is simply this: Our sexuality is basic to who we are, and it is unavoidably involved in the challenges and growth potential of our spiritual lives.

APPENDIX 4

•   •

RECOMMENDED RESOURCES

❖

BIOGRAPHIES

A. Robert Smith, ed., *Edgar Cayce, My Life as a Seer: The Lost Memoirs* (New York: St. Martin's Press, 1997). Edgar Cayce wrote very little himself, although his diary and journals have been edited into this autobiographical volume.

Charles Thomas Cayce and Jeanette Thomas, eds., *The Work of Edgar Cayce as Seen Through His Letters* (Virginia Beach, Va.: ARE Press, 2000). A selection of his letters was edited by his grandson and the administrator of the Edgar Cayce Foundation, the organization that serves as the legal custodian of the Edgar Cayce readings. These letters give the flavor of how difficult Cayce's personal life often grew, especially during the Depression years. The letters also demonstrate how Cayce sometimes continued to counsel and help people, even after they had received their readings from him.

Sidney Kirkpatrick, *Edgar Cayce: An American Prophet* (New York: Riverhead Books, 2000). This extremely well-researched and -documented book is also the most recent biography and now stands as the most authoritative.

Thomas Sugrue, *There Is a River* (New York: Holt, 1943). Published while Edgar Cayce was still alive, the book was authored by a well-known newspaper writer and friend of the Cayce family. For decades, it stood as the definitive biography, but perhaps it suffers from not dealing adequately with some of the darker sides of the Cayce story, especially the difficulties surrounding organizations that tried to grow around Cayce's work. One noteworthy aspect of this book is the lengthy appendix, a comprehensive chapter-length statement of the philosophy found in Cayce's teachings.

Harmon Bro, *A Seer Out of Season* (New York: St. Martin's Press, 1989). This noteworthy biography was written by a scholar, minister, and psychotherapist who knew Cayce personally and who was very skilled in describing the context in which Cayce's work can be seen for modern life.

Jess Stearn, *Edgar Cayce: The Sleeping Prophet* (Garden City, N.Y.: Doubleday, 1967). A best-selling overview of Edgar Cayce's life story and the prominent topics in his readings, it was Stearn's book that helped launch widespread interest in Cayce's work. Although dated in some respects, it is still worth reading as a classic among Cayce biographies.

THE TEACHINGS

Harold Reilly and Ruth Hagy Brod, *The Edgar Cayce Handbook for Health Through Drugless Therapy* (New York: Macmillan, 1975). This is the most comprehensive and usable book about Cayce's health maintenance ideas. Dr. Reilly is widely respected as the one who played the pivotal role in systematizing the health maintenance recommendations of Edgar Cayce.

K. Paul Johnson, *Edgar Cayce in Context* (Albany, N.Y.: State University of New York Press, 1998). A scholarly analysis of Edgar Cayce's teachings arranged according to the four roles that he played in his work: holistic health adviser, Christian theosopher, clairvoyant time traveler, and esoteric psychologist. It is among the most significant books written about Cayce in recent years.

Bruce McArthur, *Your Life: Why It Is the Way It Is and What You Can Do About It* (Virginia Beach, Va.: ARE Press, 1993). Edgar Cayce emphasized how certain universal laws govern life, and this book covers the fundamentals of how they work.

Mark Thurston and Christopher Fazel, *The Edgar Cayce Handbook for Creating Your Future* (New York: Ballantine, 1992). An effective primer that describes the twenty-four most important ideas in Edgar Cayce's philosophy and psychology of the soul.

OTHER RESOURCES

The Association for Research and Enlightenment (ARE) is a membership and research organization found by Edgar Cayce in 1931, and it continues to offer educational programs, books and magazines through the ARE Press, and Cayce-oriented health services. Learn more about ARE by visiting www.edgarcayce.org.

Atlantic University, the school cofounded by Edgar Cayce, offers an extensive array of classes, most of which can be taken through distance learning. Visit their online catalog at www.atlanticuniv.edu.

BIBLIOGRAPHY

❖

A Search for God. Bks. 1 and 2. Virginia Beach, Va.: ARE Press, 1942.

Beyerstein, Dale. "Edgar Cayce: The 'Prophet' Who 'Slept' His Way to the Top." *Skeptical Inquirer* 20 (1) (January 1996): 32–37.

Bro, Harmon. *A Seer Out of Season.* New York: St. Martin's Press, 1989.

Callan, J. P. "Holistic Health or Holistic Hoax?" *Journal of the American Medical Association* 241 (11) (1979): 1156.

Frankl, Viktor. *Man's Search for Meaning.* Boston: Beacon Press, 1959.

Johnson, K. Paul. *Edgar Cayce in Context.* Albany: State University of New York Press, 1998.

Jung, C. G. *The Collected Works of C. G. Jung.* Vol. 6, *Psychological Types.* Princeton, N.J.: Princeton University Press, 1971.

May, Gerald. *Will and Spirit.* New York: Harper and Row, 1983.

Mein, Eric. *Keys to Health.* New York: St. Martin's Press, 1989.

Puryear, Herbert. *The Edgar Cayce Primer.* New York: Bantam, 1982.

Quest, Linda. *The Politics of Hope.* Virginia Beach, Va.: ARE Press, 1971.

———. *Peace by Choice.* Virginia Beach, Va.: ARE Press, 1974.

Reed, Henry. *Your Mind.* Virginia Beach, Va.: ARE Press, 1989.

Reilly, Harold, and Ruth Hagy Brod. *The Edgar Cayce Handbook for Health Through Drugless Therapy.* New York: Macmillan, 1975.

Smith, A. Robert, ed. *Edgar Cayce, My Life as a Seer: The Lost Memoirs.* New York: St. Martin's Press, 1997.

Schoch, Robert M. *Voyages of the Pyramid Builders.* New York: Tarcher/Penguin, 2003.

Stearn, Jess. *Edgar Cayce: The Sleeping Prophet.* Garden City, N.Y.: Doubleday, 1967.

Sugrue, Thomas. *There Is a River.* New York: Holt, 1943.

INDEX

✣

Mark Thurston, Ph.D., is an educator, psychologist, and author of eighteen books about practical spirituality. His previous publications include *Soul-Purpose: Discovering and Fulfilling Your Destiny, Dreams: Tonight's Answers for Tomorrow's Questions,* and *Synchronicity as Spiritual Guidance.* He is also coauthor of two highly practical guidebooks to the Cayce material: *The Edgar Cayce Handbook for Creating Your Future* (with Christopher Fazel) and *Twelve Positive Habits of Spiritually Centered People* (with his daughter, Sarah Thurston).

Dr. Thurston currently serves as a faculty member in transpersonal psychology and director of academic affairs at Atlantic University in Virginia Beach, Virginia. His courses include a training program designed to equip people to serve as spiritual mentors.

In 1998, Dr. Thurston was executive producer and on-air host of *The New Millennium,* a series of twenty-six television programs produced at WHRO, a PBS affiliate. Those programs, which aired for two years on the Wisdom Channel, focused on the most important topics in the Edgar Cayce material.

Dr. Thurston is also the cofounder of the Personal Transformation and Courage Institute, a nonprofit educational organization offering intensive courses in life purpose and transformational healing.

He can be contacted at www.soul-purpose.com/courage.